Warren F. Dicharry, C.M.

GREEK WITHOUT GRIEF *An Outline Guide to New Testament Greek*

Loyola University Press

CHICAGO 60657

To my Greek teachers and students over the years,
from all of whom I have learned so much,
this labor of love is gratefully dedicated.

Contents

Preface

What Is New Testament Greek?

The New Testament was written in that form of the Greek language known as Koine or "Common" Greek; namely the popular, everyday, international Greek spoken and written throughout the area of Graeco-Roman culture for centuries before, during, and after the time of Jesus Christ. Historically, Koine (pronounced coy-nay) was a development of Attic Greek, the Greek dialect which was perfected at Athens in the Golden Age of Pericles and was later spread far and wide by Alexander the Great. As confirmed by many recently discovered papyri, Koine Greek was so flexible that it served as the vehicle for literary compositions of varying quality, as well as for commercial transactions, personal letters, and private conversations. This same flexibility is also richly exemplified in the New Testament.

Why Learn New Testament Greek?

Every book of the New Testament, certain books of the Old Testament (according to the wider Alexandrian canon in general use at the time of Jesus), the Septuagint translation of the Old Testament (to which the New Testament generally refers), very many ancient writers (especially historians and philosophers), and almost all the early Christian literature were written in Koine Greek. A knowledge of this language, then, opens up vast areas of primary source material, especially for the study of Sacred Scripture, Patrology (the Church Fathers), Sacred Theology, Ecclesial and Secular History, and Philosophy. "Everything suffers in translation," however good that translation may be. Hence the advantage of reading and studying the sources, particularly the Word of God, in the original language. Sainte Therese, the "Little Flower" of Lisieux, echoed the unfulfilled desire of many Christians when she declared in her autobiography, "If I had been a priest I should have made a thorough study of Hebrew and Greek so as to understand the thought of God as he has vouchsafed to express it in our human language."

Besides the advantage already mentioned, there are many other benefits derived from the study of New Testament Greek. For example: the orderly training of the mind (especially in the ability to analyze, reason, and memorize); assistance in mastering other languages such as Latin (with its derived Romance Languages) and even English, by frequent comparison of forms and syntax; and especially the acquisition of a rich vocabulary for both everyday and scientific use through the knowledge of so many English words derived from Greek.

But all these advantages, real as they are, tend to be overshadowed in the minds of many people by the actual or imagined difficulty involved in learning Greek, which has become nothing short of proverbial. It was the great William Shakespeare who first voiced, in substance, the popular expression, "It's all Greek to me!" in a remark of Casca to Cassius about Cicero in the first act of *Julius Caesar.*

And, in a statement almost equally famous, at least in Hellenic circles, the great sage and lexicographer Dr. Samuel Johnson is quoted by Boswell as declaring, "Greek, Sir, is like lace; every man gets as much of it as he can." Finally, in modern times, Sir Winston Churchill has made the characteristically whimsical observation, "Naturally I am biased in favor of boys learning English; and then I would let the clever ones learn Latin as an honour, and Greek as a treat."

It is my fond hope that *Greek Without Grief* may be instrumental in enabling not only "the clever ones" but all interested students of at least average acumen and above-average dedication to study, especially those called to a special ministry of preaching and/or teaching in the Church, and to read with comparative ease and success the New Testament of the Bible in the language that was providentially chosen by its Divine and human authors for the expression, propagation, and preservation of the Word of God. If this fond hope should be realized to some significant degree, I shall consider myself richly rewarded indeed!

As a matter of fact, this fond hope has already been realized to some extent. In its initial mimeographed form, personally published and marketed in 1980 and revised or reprinted every year since then, *Greek Without Grief* has been sold all over the United States, including Alaska and Hawaii. Such a positive development, however, has been tempered by the apparent lack of interest on the part of my fellow Catholics, including seminarians and priests, not just in my book but in New Testament Greek generally. This of course saddens me, because it is so clear from all the pertinent documents that the first duty of priests is to preach the Word of God, and how can one do that effectively without some knowledge of the biblical languages, especially that of the New or Christian Testament? It is my hope that, with the enthusiasm of Loyola University Press, and especially its Director, Father Daniel Flaherty, S.J., not only in publishing this new and more formal edition of *Greek Without Grief,* but also in using it to promote New Testament Greek, the situation will be greatly improved.

How Study New Testament Greek?

Many approaches to the study of Greek have been attempted, with varying degrees of success. Inductive methods are more interesting; deductive methods more orderly. But both generally fail in either or both of two ways. First, they tend to discourage the average student with a bewildering multiplicity of forms, syntax, vocabulary, and exercises presented in such a scattershot fashion that it is easy to "miss the forest for the trees." Secondly, they do not equip the student with some practical method for continuing and developing his knowledge of Greek after the completion of the formal course. Of all those who have learned the language to some degree, many if not most have sooner or later abandoned it for lack of an effective aid in recalling or referring to its forms and vocabulary. *Greek Without Grief,* as the title indicates, is a practical attempt to correct these deficiencies for the benefit of the student, containing as it does these special features:

1. Everything is presented in outline form for the sake of greater clarity and coherence.

2. Emphasis is placed on learning in an orderly, even scientific way (which can also be very exciting), the basic forms, usage, and vocabulary—the building blocks of Greek—so essential for lasting knowledge and development. For example, the different parts of speech (nouns, verbs, etc.) based on the same root or stem are treated together for more systematic understanding and remembrance.

3. Some exercises are included as necessary for building familiarity with the essential forms, syntax, and vocabulary, but only from Greek into English and entirely from the New Testament, so that the student is immediately introduced to the Sacred Text itself.

4. Vocabulary is kept to a minimum and chosen according to two criteria; namely, frequency of usage in the New Testament, and the existence of English derivatives for easier learning and vocabulary building in both Greek and English.

5. An extensive subject index in English is provided, plus a complete index of all the Greek words presented in the vocabulary lists. In addition, there is a brief appendix called "Teaching Aids" intended

for those who are either teaching others or teaching themselves in private study. It consists of two sections: one, a further explanation of matters not fully treated in the text for lack of space; and two, a complete list of all the New Testament texts used in the exercises, with the caution that this list should be used not so much to find the "correct" translation of the exercises but simply to compare possible translations and to enable one more easily to research the grammar, vocabulary, and morphology involved in these particular New Testament texts.

This outline course, which provides a concise but very complete skeleton of New Testament Greek, should enable the student to concentrate on reading the New Testament itself as quickly as possible and continue reading it indefinitely, especially with the aid of an invaluable tool such as *A Grammatical Analysis of the Greek New Testament* by Max Zerwick and Mary Grosvenor, published in 1981 by the Biblical Institute Press of Rome, Italy, and available in the United States through Loyola University Press of Chicago. The great advantage of this admirable work is that it explains everything in the Greek New Testament as it occurs, from the beginning of Matthew to the end of Revelation, thus eliminating the tedious necessity of searching for words, forms, and usage in dictionaries and grammars. Such a help, in my opinion, is a virtual necessity in enabling the student to derive not only profit but enjoyment from reading the Greek New Testament.

In addition to the above-mentioned work, the following are selectively recommended for the particular reasons indicated:

1. Aland, Kurt, et al., editors, *The Greek New Testament* (*with Dictionary*), New York, NY: United Bible Societies, 3rd. ed., 1983. (All things considered, this is the clearest text.)

2. Zerwick-Smith, *Biblical Greek*, Rome, Italy: Biblical Institute Press, 1977, distributed in the U.S. by Loyola University Press, Chicago, IL. (This is especially helpful for intermediate and advanced students in refining their knowledge of the nuances of NT Greek. Also, Zerwick-Grosvenor's *Analysis* makes particular references to this useful work.)

3. Gromacki, Robert, *Biblical Greek Vocabulary Cards*, Springfield, OH: Visual Education Association, 1979. (This is an excellent aid in building a NT Greek vocabulary.)

Greek Without Grief was written for use by a competent teacher and some interested students, with complete and lively classroom participation. But it also allows, I think, for self-teaching with tutorial supervision according to the needs and abilities of the individual student. In either case, it is most desirable that students who attempt this course have some prior knowledge of forms and syntax from the study of English in an orderly fashion (unfortunately, not something that can always be presumed these days), and especially from the study of Latin, German, or one of the Romance Languages. Any attempt to teach elementary forms and syntax "from scratch" (a Greek athletic idiom) would probably double the size of this work and defeat one of its primary purposes—viz., that of being comparatively brief, simple, and inexpensive.

It is my personal experience and observation that *Greek Without Grief* can be extremely helpful not only to beginners in New Testament Greek but also and especially to those many students who have taken a year or two of Greek studies, perhaps a few years ago, and feel a crying need to "pull it all together." In other words, it can serve to rescue from oblivion or at least from "mothballs" that initial knowledge of Greek which many have acquired with great labor but no longer find useful because of the "law of diminishing returns." Once "pulled together" in the orderly fashion provided by this course, the knowledge of NT Greek can be useful and actually used the rest of one's life, thanks especially to that marvelous tool mentioned above, Zerwick-Grosvenor's compact *Grammatical Analysis of New Testament Greek* or similar work, to which my book serves to introduce the student.

Whatever the student's situation or schedule, it is strongly recommended that some time (at least a half hour) be devoted to homework each day because a language like Greek (or any language for that matter) is best learned through frequent exposure and practice. Also, it is imperative that the student reject one of the fallacies of our age, namely the fear of memorization. In rejecting an earlier system of education which featured rote memory without full understanding, much of modern education has unfortunately gone to the opposite extreme and emphasized understanding to the virtual exclusion of any attempt at memorization. The simple fact is, however, that both are absolutely essential, especially in a language like NT Greek. In fact, both our understanding and memory are capable of almost limitless development if properly exercised. We have all come to learn the value of regular physical exercise; it remains but to apply the same theories to the development of both our mental and spiritual powers.

Some Final Points of Importance

1) Each of the twenty lessons in this work is somewhat lengthy, for two reasons: first, to avoid a piecemeal treatment characteristic of so many introductions; and secondly, to make it possible to cover the material in large blocks in a more intensive course or when classes are limited to once a week.

2) It should be quite easy, however, for teachers and students to divide the lessons into smaller units according to the length and frequency of classes and study opportunities.

3) Insofar as possible, the material in each lesson should be thoroughly learned before the exercises pertaining to that lesson are tackled. This will avoid the seemingly practical but really self-defeating student habit of doing the exercises first and later attempting, if there is time, to learn the content of the lesson.

My most sincere thanks are due to my family, relatives, friends, colleagues, and students for their encouragement, support, and often invaluable assistance. I especially wish to thank by name Mr. Dante Valori, Mrs. Linda Thomas, Mrs. Elodie Emig, and Fr. Daniel Flaherty, S.J., without all of whom this "labor of love" would never have reached publication.

Any corrections, suggestions, or comments from teachers or students using this work will be greatly appreciated by its author,

Warren F. Dicharry, C.M.
Vincentian Evangelization
Timon House, 1302 Kipling
Houston, Texas, 77006.

I Basic Elements of NT Greek

I. The Alphabet:

Derived from Phoenician (Canaanite, Hebrew), the Greek alphabet (so named from its first two letters) contains 24 letters, best learned in groups of four.

No.	Name	Small Letters	Capital Letters	Pronounced as in:	Remarks and References	Examples
1.	**Alpha**	α	A	father	unchanging	κατά
2.	**Beta**	β	B	boy	unchanging	βιός
3.	**Gamma**	γ	Γ	girl	see next page	γε
4.	**Delta**	δ	Δ	dear	unchanging	διά
5.	**Epsilon**	ε	E	debt	cf. Eta	δέκα
6.	**Zeta**	ζ	Z	adze (or zoo)	double: δ + ς	γάζα
7.	**Eta**	η	H	they	cf. Epsilon	γῆ
8.	**Theta**	θ	Θ	thin	*not* like they	θεός
9.	**Iota**	ι	I	idiom	changing	ἴδιος
10.	**Kappa**	κ	K	kind	unchanging	κακός
11.	**Lambda**	λ	Λ	line	unchanging	καλός
12.	**Mu**	μ	M	mind	unchanging	μετά
13.	**Nu**	ν	N	nine	unchanging	νῦν
14.	**Xi**	ξ	Ξ	index	double: κ + ς	δόξα
15.	**Omicron**	o	O	soft	cf. Omega	λόγος
16.	**Pi**	π	Π	pain	unchanging	πέντε
17.	**Rho**	ρ	P	rain	trilled or not	παρά
18.	**Sigma**	σ, ς	Σ (C)	sigh	*not* like rose (see next page)	σός
19.	**Tau**	τ	T	tie	unchanging	τέλος
20.	**Upsilon**	υ	Υ	tune	or French u	γυνή
21.	**Phi**	ϕ	Φ	Philip	unchanging	φίλος
22.	**Chi**	χ	X	Christ	or German ch	χάρις
23.	**Psi**	ψ	Ψ	apse	double: π + ς	ψυχή
24.	**Omega**	ω	Ω	sofa	cf. Omicron	δῶρον

II. **Remarks on the NT Greek alphabet:**

A. GENERAL REMARKS:

1. *The Capital Letters,* while important, are not used as frequently as in English, being employed only with *proper names* and, in some editions of the Greek NT, at the *beginning of paragraphs* and direct *quotations.*

2. *In learning the alphabet,* it is important not to confuse certain Greek letters with English letters which they resemble, e.g. Greek *Gamma* (γ) and *Upsilon* (Y) with English "y" and "Y," Greek *Eta* (η, H) with English "n" and "H," Greek *Nu* (ν) with English "v," Greek *Rho* (ρ, P) with English "p" and "P," Greek *Chi* (χ, X) with English "x" and "X."

B. SPECIAL REMARKS (according to *alphabet number* on previous page):

1. Note, under No. 3, that when a *Gamma* (γ) precedes what is called a "palatal or guttural mute" (κ, γ, χ, ξ), it is called a *Gamma nasal* and pronounced like <u>ng</u> in si<u>ng</u>, e.g.: σύ<u>γγ</u>ενις, τυ<u>γχ</u>άνω, σάλπι<u>γξ</u>.

2. Also, under No. 18, not only are there *variant forms of the small Sigma*—σ being used within a word and ς only at the end of a word—but also *variant forms of the capital Sigma,* Σ sometimes being replaced by C, especially in early writings and inscriptions, e.g. "Jesus Christ" can be written ΙΗΣΟΥΣ ΧΡΙΣΤΟΣ or ΙΗCΟΥC ΧΡΙCΤΟC, abbreviated to I̅C̅ X̅C̅.

III. **Division of Greek letters of the alphabet:**

A. IMPORTANCE: As in any language, it is important in NT Greek to be able to recognize and identify particular types of letters because they function in particular ways, as will become more evident during the course.

B. SINGLE LETTERS:

1. **Vowels** ("sound carriers"), divided into:
a. *short* (ε, o), *long* (η, ω), and *either short* or *long* (α, ι, υ).
b. *strong* or *open* (α, ε, o, η, ω), and *weak* or *closed* (ι, υ).

2. **Consonants** ("sounding with"), the remaining letters, especially:
a. *mutes* or *stops: labial* (π, β, φ), *palatal* (κ, γ, χ), *lingual* (τ, δ, θ). (*Note:* π, κ, τ are called *smooth;* β, γ, δ, *middle;* φ, χ, θ, *rough.*)

b. *liquids* or *semi-vowels:* λ, μ, ν, ρ. (And, by affinity, *Gamma nasal.*)

c. *sibilant(s):* σ, ς (also the *Sigma* included in ζ, ξ, ψ).

C. DOUBLE LETTERS:

1. **Double consonants,** as already indicated: ζ, ξ, ψ.

2. **Double vowels,** called *diphthongs* or *digraphs,* are combinations of *two vowels in a single syllable,* normally formed from a union of a strong vowel and a weak vowel in that order, and are divided into:

a. *proper diphthongs* (and their pronunciations):

αι like ai in aisle (ψυχαί)   αυ like au in kraut (ταύτας)
ει like ei in eight (λύεις)   ευ like eu in feud (γονεύς)
οι like oi in oil (λόγοι)   ου like ou in soup (δοῦλος)
υι like ui in quit or suite (εἰδυῖα)

b. *improper diphthongs:* 1) rare ην, ων (two sounds); 2) vowels with an *Iota subscript,* silent but important for *inflection* and *meaning,* e.g. νέᾳ, γῇ, θεῷ (omissible when not thus important, e.g. σῴζω/σώζω).

IV. Other Basic Elements of NT Greek:

A. INTRODUCTION: In addition to the alphabet, whose importance is obvious, there are several other elements of NT Greek which require very special attention because of their *importance for pronunciation and reading* as well as for *translation and interpretation* of the Greek text.

1. **Proper pronunciation and reading** of words, phrases, and sentences contribute greatly to correct translation and interpretation as well as to personal confidence, hence the need of *regular practice in reading aloud,* both in private study and as part of classroom learning.

2. The **basic elements** which follow not only aid in proper pronunciation and reading, with the benefits just mentioned, but are even sometimes essential in *distinguishing one word from another,* thus facilitating correct translation and interpretation.

B. SYLLABIFICATION: division of Greek words into syllables—

1. **Importance:** Students tend to panic when required to pronounce Greek words, especially long ones, but the task is greatly simplified if they remember to *divide the words—* particularly the longest ones—*into syllables,* and then calmly pronounce each syllable as it occurs.

2. **Guidelines:**

a. *In General:*

1) A Greek word has *as many syllables* as it has *vowels and diphthongs*, e.g.: βα-σι-λεί-α, δι-και-ο-σύ-νη.

2) *Most* (but not all) *syllables end in a vowel or diphthong*, e.g.: ἀ-λή-θει-α, γραμ-μα-τεύς, ἐ-θαμ-βοῦν-το.

b. *In Particular*, especially regarding consonants:

1) There is *no hard and fast rule* about consonants, the tendency being to pronounce them with the following vowel or diphthong if they are pronounceable that way; otherwise, to divide them, e.g.: ἀ-πο-θνή-σκω, σφρα-γί-ζω, σάλ-πιγ-γος.

2) *In dividing consonants*, certain principles seem to be operative:

a) **Prefixes** of various kinds usually *remain intact*, divided from the rest, e.g.: πρό-δρο-μος, προσ-φέ-ρω, ἄν-υ-δρος.

b) **Consonants** which are *repeated* are usually *divided* in the middle, e.g.: γλῶσ-σα, σάβ-βατον, κρά-βατ-τος.

c) **Combinations of consonants** tend to follow certain patterns:

A *mute* plus a *liquid* remain *intact*: ἀρ-χι-τρι-κλί-νος.
A *liquid* plus a *mute* are *divided*: ἀν-έρ-χον-ται.
Two mutes or *two liquids* are *divided*, except ππ, φθ; κτ, χθ; and μν: πτέ-ρυξ, φθό-νος, μνῆ-μα.

C. BREATHING MARKS:

1. **Importance:** Proper attention to breathing marks is essential both for correct *pronunciation and reading*, and often for *distinguishing words*, e.g.: ἤ (or) ἥ (who, fem.); ἔξω (outside), ἕξω (I will have).

2. **Guidelines:**

a. *In General:*
Initial vowels, diphthongs, and **Rho** always have a breathing mark, placed *over* single vowels and Rho and over the second vowel of a diphthong, but *before* initial capitals, except in inscriptions, when they are omitted, e.g.: ἄγω, εἰς, Ἰησοῦς, ΙΗΣΟΥΣ.

b. *In Particular:*
There are **two breathing marks—smooth** and **rough:**

1) *The smooth breathing mark* (᾿) indicates that there is no change in pronunciation, e.g.: αἰών, εἴκοσι, οὖν.

2) *The rough breathing mark* (ʽ), usually a substitute for a Sigma or the "Lost Digamma" (written "F" but pronounced "W"), indicates that a *rough or "h" sound* is added to the initial vowel, diphthong, or Rho, e.g.: ἵστημι, αὕτη, ἕξ, ῥῆμα.

D. ACCENTUATION:

1. **Importance:** Proper attention to Greek accents is important, not only for correct *pronunciation and reading* as well as *distinguishing among words*, but also for *distinguishing among forms of the same word*, e.g.: τις, τίς - εἰμί, εἶμι - λαλεῖ, λάλει - πλήρου, πληροῦ.

2. **Guidelines:**

a. *In General:*
With rare exceptions, *every NT Greek word* carries one of *three accents:* the acute (´), grave (`), or circumflex (ˆ, ˜).

1) *Originally*, these accents represented *tones or pitches*, much like those in Chinese:
   a) The **acute** (´) indicated a *rising* or sharp tone: ἀγαθός.
   b) The **grave** (`) indicated a *falling* or heavy tone: ἀγαθὸς θεός.
   c) The **circumflex** (ˆ) indicated a *combination* of both: ἀγαθῶν.

2) *Today*, the accents are used primarily to indicate the syllable to be *stressed* and to help in *distinguishing* words and forms, but any attention paid to the quality of accents will be repaid in the form of a smoother, more meaningful reading of the text.

b. *In Particular:*
Attention will be called to important points of accentuation relating to each lesson in NT Greek as it occurs, but for now certain more general points will suffice:

1) Accents can stand only on *one of the final three syllables*, in this manner:
   a) The **acute** (´) can stand on *any of the final three:* ἄνθρωπος.
   b) The **circumflex** (ˆ), on *either of the final two:* γνῶσις.
   c) The **grave** (`) can stand *only on the final syllable:* καὶ . . .

2) In sentences, an *acute accent on the final syllable* normally *changes to the grave* when another word follows immediately, that is, without any punctuation in between,

thus providing a smooth flow of words, e.g.: Ἀγαπητοί, μὴ παντὶ πνεύματι πιστεύετε (1 Jn. 4:1).

3) **Proclitics** are small words which have *no accent* of their own, but rather *"lean forward"* on the following word, with which they are pronounced, e.g.: Ἐν ἀρχῇ ἦν ὁ λόγος . . .

4) **Enclitics** are also small words which either *have no accent or lose their accent* to the preceding word, on which they "lean backward" and with which they are pronounced, e.g.: Ἐγώ εἰμι.

E.   PUNCTUATION:

1. **Importance:** As in any language, proper attention to punctuation is very necessary for both *intelligent reading* and *effective interpretation*.

2. **Guidelines:**

a. Early NT manuscripts generally had no punctuation at all nor any division between words, sentences, paragraphs, and chapters, a fact which must be borne in mind in reading the New Testament, because of the real possibility of differences in translation and interpretation stemming from different punctuations and divisions, e.g. Jn. 1:3–4, 9.

b. However, punctuation *was* known and used in the ancient world and, in the Greek NT, this system of punctuation became standard:

1) The Greek **comma** (,) and **period** (.) are *like those in English* in both appearance and usage.

2) But the Greek **question mark** (;) is *like our semicolon,* while the Greek **colon and semicolon** (·) are a *single dot above the line.*

F.   COLLOCATION (word order): Often *subject-verb-object(s)* as in English, but Greek (unlike Latin) likes to "lead with its verb" in sentences, clauses, and (infinitive/participial) phrases, followed by subject and object(s).

G.   CHANGES BETWEEN ADJACENT VOWELS for smooth pronunciation occur:

1. **In the same word,** by *contraction:* adjacent vowels *uniting* into a long vowel or diphthong, e.g. in contract verbs (Ch. 17), λάλει (λάλε+ε).

2. **In adjacent words,** by one of three ways, namely:

a. **Crasis,** when two words *unite* into one, sometimes retaining the second word's breathing mark: ἐάν (εἰ+ἄν), κἀγώ (καί+ἐγώ), ταὐτά (τα+αὐτά).

   b. **Elision,** when a preposition or conjunction *drops* its final
     vowel, an *apostrophe* marking the elision and a *preceding mute*
     becoming rough (p. 5) *before* a rough breathing: ἐπ' αὐτῷ, ἐφ' ᾧ.
   c. **Liaison,** when a *final Epsilon* (ε) or *Sigma Iota* (σι) adds *Nu* (ν),
     called **Nu-Movable** (or Movable Nu), before an *initial vowel* or
     sometimes even an initial consonant: ἔλεγεν, λέγουσιν, πᾶσιν.

V. **Exercises:** In addition to learning the salient material presented
   above, practice *dividing, pronouncing, reading,* and soon *learning*
   what follows:

A. USEFUL EXPRESSIONS:

Χαῖρε, Χαίρετε = $\begin{cases} \text{Hello!} \\ \text{Goodbye!} \end{cases}$

Πάρειμι = Present!

Καλημέρα, Καλησπέρα = Good Morning, Good Afternoon!

Εὖγε, Καλῶς = Good!

B. SIGN OF THE CROSS: Ἐν τῷ ὀνόματι τοῦ πατρὸς καὶ τοῦ υἱοῦ καὶ τοῦ
   (From Mt. 28:20) ἁγίου πνεύματος. Ἀμήν.

C. THE LORD'S PRAYER:
   (Mt. 6:9–13)
   Πάτερ ἡμῶν ὁ ἐν τοῖς οὐρανοῖς,
   ἁγιασθήτω τὸ ὄνομά σου, ἐλθέτω ἡ βασιλεία σου,
   γενηθήτω τὸ θέλημά σου, ὡς ἐν οὐρανῷ καὶ ἐπὶ γῆς.

   τὸν ἄρτον ἡμῶν τὸν ἐπιούσιον δὸς ἡμῖν σήμερον
   καὶ ἄφες ἡμῖν τὰ ὀφειλήματα ἡμῶν,
   ὡς καὶ ἡμεῖς ἀφήκαμεν τοῖς ὀφελέταις ἡμῶν.
   καὶ μὴ εἰσενέγκῃς ἡμᾶς εἰς πειρασμόν,
   ἀλλὰ ῥῦσαι ἡμᾶς ἀπὸ τοῦ πονηροῦ. (Ἀμήν.)

   (ὅτι σοῦ ἐστιν* ἡ βασιλεία καὶ ἡ δύναμις καὶ ἡ δόξα εἰς
   τοὺς αἰῶνας. Ἀμήν.) (From I Chr. 29:11–13, some MSS.,
   the Didache, Diatesseron, Apostolic Constitutions, Chrysostom.)

   *ἐστί (εἰμί = I am) takes Nu-Movable by analogy with σι.

2 The First Two Declensions

The Article and Nouns

I. Introduction to NT Greek Declensions:

A. IMPORTANCE: To English-speaking students, declensions (and conjugations) may seem foreign and burdensome, but it is actually such inflection, common in many languages both ancient and modern, that gives NT Greek its admirable precision, so helpful in understanding the New Testament.

B. In NT Greek, there are THREE DECLENSIONS, divided into two groups:

    1. The *strong vowel declensions,* comprising:
    a. The **A-Declension,** predominantly *feminine.*   (FIRST)
    b. The **O-Declension,** predominantly *masculine and neuter.*

                                              (SECOND)

    2. The *consonant and weak vowel declension,* of *mixed genders.*
                                              (THIRD)

C. IN GENERAL, NT Greek declensions include:

    1. *Two numbers,* singular and plural. (Classical Greek also has a dual.)

    2. *Three genders,* masculine, feminine, and neuter.

    3. *Five cases:* which indicate the following:
    a. **Nominative:** the *subject* and what agrees with it (except the subject of the infinitive).
    b. **Genitive:** *possession, agency,* etc. (of, by, from, than, during).
    c. **Dative:** *indirect object, means, manner,* etc. (to, with, at, in, for).
    d. **Accusative:** *direct object* or what agrees with it, plus the subject of the infinitive.
    e. **Vocative:** *person(s) directly addressed* (The vocative is omitted as rare and usually obvious.)
    (N.B. More case usage will be explained later in this chapter.)

II. **The Endings of the strong vowel declensions and of the definite article:**

A. These endings are ADDED TO THE STEM of each word to provide all numbers, genders, and cases of *all nouns, pronouns, adjectives, and participles* of the strong vowel declensions (i.e. the first and second declensions).

B. They are easily observed in the DEFINITE ARTICLE (English "the"), the only article in Greek, which *agrees* with its noun in *gender, number,* and *case.*

C. LONG AND SHORT SIGNS (¯/˘) indicate the *quantity* of *ambiguous* endings, but do not appear in the Greek text.

	THE ARTICLE Singular				THE ENDINGS Singular		
	Masc.	*Fem.*	*Neut.*		*Masc.*	*Fem.*	*Neut.*
Nom.	ὁ	ἡ	τό	*Nom.*	ος	ᾱ - η - ᾰ	ον
Gen.	τοῦ	τῆς	τοῦ	*Gen.*	ου	ᾱς - ης - ης	ου
Dat.	τῷ	τῇ	τῷ	*Dat.*	ῳ	ᾳ - ῃ - ῃ	ῳ
Acc.	τόν	τήν	τό	*Acc.*	ον	ᾱν - ην - ᾰν	ον
	Plural				Plural		
Nom.	οἱ	αἱ	τά	*Nom.*	οἴ	αἴ	ᾰ
Gen.	τῶν	τῶν	τῶν	*Gen.*	ων	ων	ων
Dat.	τοῖς	ταῖς	τοῖς	*Dat.*	οις	αις	οις
Acc.	τούς	τάς	τά	*Acc.*	ους	ᾱς	ᾰ

III. **Nouns of the O-declension:** Commonly called the "second declension" but here treated first because it is the *simplest* of all three declensions.

A. EXAMPLES OF THE O-DECLENSION, *masculine* and *neuter:*

1. **λόγος, ου, ὁ:** *word,* from λέγω = I say, speak (logic, dialogue).

2. **ἔργον, ου, τό:** *work,* verb ἐργάζομαι = I (do a) work (erg, energy).

B. NOTATION: In dictionaries and grammars, as well as in this course, Greek nouns are given in the *nominative,* the *genitive ending* to indicate the declension, and the (definite) *article* to indicate the gender.

C. DECLENSION OF MASCULINE AND NEUTER
   O-DECLENSION NOUNS:

	MASCULINE			NEUTER	
	Sing.	Plur.		Sing.	Plur.
Nom.	λόγος	λόγοι	*Nom.*	ἔργον	ἔργα
Gen.	λόγου	λόγων	*Gen.*	ἔργου	ἔργων
Dat.	λόγῳ	λόγοις	*Dat.*	ἔργῳ	ἔργοις
Acc.	λόγον	λόγους	*Acc.*	ἔργον	ἔργα

D. VOCABULARY OF MASCULINE AND NEUTER
   O-DECLENSION NOUNS (*alphabetical order*):

MASCULINE

ἄγγελος: messenger (angel)
ἀδελφός: brother (Philadelphia)
ἄνθρωπος: man (anthropology)
ἀπόστολος: apostle (apostolic)
δοῦλος: slave (hierodule)
θάνατος: death (euthanasia)
θεός: god (theology, theophany)
κόσμος: world (cosmos, cosmic)
κύριος: lord (church, "Kyrie")
λαός: people (laity, lay, laic)
νόμος: law (autonomy, economy)
οἶκος: house (economy, ecology)
οὐρανός: heaven (Uranus, uranium)

MASC. (cont'd)

πρεσβύτερος: elder (presbyter, priest)
τόπος: place (topic, topography)
υἱός: son (Lat. *filius*, hence filial)
φίλος: friend (philanthropy)

NEUTER

δαιμόνιον: demon (demonic, demoniac)
δῶρον: gift (Theodore, Dorothy)
εὐαγγέλιον: gospel (evangelist)
ἱερόν: temple (hierarchy, hieratic)
μυστήριον: mystery (mystify, mystic)
σημεῖον: sign (semantic, semaphore)

E. EXCEPTIONS:

1. *A few O-declension nouns are feminine*, e.g.:

   βίβλος, ου, ἡ: book (Bible)
   διάλεκτος, ου, ἡ: language (dialect)
   ἔρημος, ου, ἡ: desert (hermit)
   ὁδός, οῦ, ἡ: way, road (exodus, method)

2. *A few are either masculine or feminine*, e.g.:

   διάκονος, ου, ὁ, ἡ: servant (deacon)
   θεός, οῦ, ὁ, ἡ: god-dess (theist)
   κάμηλος, ου, ὁ, ἡ: camel (camelopard)
   παρθένος, ου, ὁ, ἡ: virgin (Parthenon)

IV. **Nouns of the A-declension,** commonly called the "first declension":

A. SIMPLE RULES FOR THE A-DECLENSION:

 1. *The plural is completely uniform,* always using the *Alpha* endings.

 2. *The singular,* however, *admits of variations:*
 a. **A nominative in Eta** (η) *retains the Eta* throughout the singular.
 b. **A nominative in Alpha** (α), *preceded by Epsilon, Iota, or Rho* (ε, ι, ρ) (think of Eire, Ireland), keeps *Alpha* (usually long) in the singular.
 c. **A nominative in Alpha** (α), *not preceded by Epsilon, Iota, or Rho,* changes its *short Alpha to Eta* in the *genitive* and *dative* singular.

B. EXAMPLES OF THE FEMININE NOUNS
 OF THE A-DECLENSION:

 1. **φωνή, ῆς, ἡ:** sound, voice; verb φωνέω = I sound (phonics, telephone)

 2. **οἰκία, ας, ἡ:** house, dwelling; verb οἰκέω = I dwell (ecumenical)

 3. **δόξα, ης, ἡ:** glory, opinion; from δοκέω = I think (doxology, -doxy)

C. DECLENSION OF FEMININE NOUNS OF THE
 A-DECLENSION:

	Singular				Plural		
Nom.	φωνή	οἰκία	δόξα	Nom.	φωναί	οἰκίαι	δόξαι
Gen.	φωνῆς	οἰκίας	δόξης	Gen.	φωνῶν	οἰκιῶν	δοξῶν
Dat.	φωνῇ	οἰκίᾳ	δόξῃ	Dat.	φωναῖς	οἰκίαις	δόξαις
Acc.	φωνήν	οἰκίαν	δόξαν	Acc.	φωνάς	οἰκίας	δόξας

D. VOCABULARY OF FEMININE NOUNS OF THE
 A-DECLENSION:

ἀγάπη, ης: (spiritual) love (agape)

ἀρχή, ῆς: beginning, rule (monarchy)

βασιλεία, ας: kingdom (basilica)

γῆ, ῆς: earth, land (apogee, geography)

γλῶσσα, ης: tongue, language (gloss)

γραφή, ῆς: writing (telegraph)

εἰρήνη, ης: peace (irenic, Irene, Irenaeus)

ἐκκλησία, ας: church (ecclesial)

ζωή, ῆς: (spiritual) life (Zoe, mesozoic)

ἡμέρα, ας: day (ephemeral)

καρδία, ας: heart (cardiac, cardiovascular)

κεφαλή, ῆς: head (acephalous, electroencephalogram)

παραβολή, ῆς: parable (parabola)

σκηνή, ῆς: tent, tabernacle (scene)

σοφία, ας: wisdom (philosophy, sophist)

συναγωγή, ῆς: synagogue, congregation

σωτηρία, ας: salvation (soteriology)

τιμή, ῆς: honor, price (Timothy)

ψυχή, ῆς: soul (natural) life (psyche)

ὥρα, ας: hour (horologe, horoscope)

E. EXCEPTIONS:

1. Among nouns of the A-declension are *several masculines*, especially indicating vocations, professions, or occupations.

2. Of these, the *only ones commonly used in the New Testament* are the following:

a. **μαθητής, οῦ, ὁ**: disciple; from μανθάνω = I learn (mathematics)

b. **προφήτης, ου, ὁ**: prophet; from πρό + φημί = I speak for (prophecy)

3. These masculines are *declined exactly like feminines* of the A-declension excepting the *nominative* and *genitive singular* in ης and ου.

V. Use of the cases in NT Greek:

A. INTRODUCTION: While the brief remarks about case uses on page 8 form an accurate summary, the importance of properly translating and interpreting the New Testament requires a fuller knowledge of case usage, especially *independent* case usage, i.e. *without prepositions*, which will be treated later.

B. THE NOMINATIVE CASE has two principal uses, namely to indicate:

1. *The subject* of a sentence or clause, and *all other words* which either modify or are in apposition with the subject: Ἀνδρέας ὁ ἀδελφὸς Σίμωνος Πέτρου = <u>Andrew, the brother</u> of Simon Peter.

(Jn. 1:40)

2. *The predicate* (predicate nominative), which is identified with the subject through a *connecting verb*, expressed or implied: Καὶ ὁ λόγος σὰρξ ἐγένετο = And the word became <u>flesh</u>.

(Jn. 1:14)

C.   THE GENITIVE CASE is used to express *many relationships,*
especially:

1. *Possession* and *relationship:* αὐτῶν ἐστιν ἡ βασιλεία τῶν
   οὐρανῶν = Theirs is the kingdom of heaven (the heavens)
   (Mt. 5:3, 10). Μαρία ἡ τοῦ Κλωπᾶ = Mary (the wife) of Clopus.
   (Jn. 19:25)

2. *Time during which* something occurs: ἦλθεν πρὸς αὐτὸν νυκτὸς
   = He (Nicodemus) came to him (Jesus) during the night.
   (Jn. 3:2)

3. *Value* and *comparison:* ἐδύνατο γὰρ τοῦτο πραθῆναι πολλοῦ =
   for this could have been sold for much (Mt. 26:9). μείζονα
   ταύτης ἀγάπην οὐδεὶς ἔχει = greater love than this no one has.
   (Jn. 15:13)

4. *The subject and/or object* of a non-verbal action or situation
   (subjective or objective genitive): ἡ γὰρ ἀγάπη τοῦ Χριστοῦ
   συνέχει ἡμᾶς = For the love of Christ constrains us.
   (II Cor. 5:14)

5. *Apposition* (epexegetical genitive): λήμψεσθε τὴν δωρεὰν τοῦ
   ἁγίου πνεύματος = you will receive the gift of the Holy Spirit.
   (Acts 2:38)

6. *Part of the whole* (partitive genitive), sometimes *even after*
   verbs, especially of *perception:* ἀκούοντες μὲν τῆς φωνῆς
   μηδένα δὲ θεωροῦντες = hearing indeed the sound but seeing
   no one. (Acts 9:7)

D.   THE DATIVE CASE is also used to express *many relationships,*
especially:

1. *The indirect object* of a verb, with or without a direct object:
   δώσω σοι τὰς κλεῖδας τῆς βασιλείας τῶν οὐρανῶν = I will give
   to you the keys of the kingdom of heaven (the heavens).
   (Mt. 16:19)

2. *Time at which* something occurs: καὶ τῇ τρίτῃ ἡμέρᾳ
   ἐγερθήσεται = and on the third day he will rise (be raised).
   (Mt. 17:22)

3. *Possession,* with a verb expressed or implied: ὄνομα αὐτῷ
   Ἰωάννης = his name (was) John [the name to him (was) John].
   (Jn. 1:6)

4. *Means or instrument:* ἀνεῖλεν δὲ Ἰάκωβον . . . μαχαίρῃ = but
   he (Herod) killed James . . . with the sword (Acts 12:2)

5. *Manner* and *respect:* Ἡρῴδης λάθρᾳ καλέσας τοὺς μάγους = Herod, having called the Magi <u>secretly</u> (Mt. 2:7); μακάριοι οἱ καθαροὶ <u>τῇ καρδίᾳ</u> = blessed (are) the clean <u>of heart</u>. (Mt. 5:8)

6. *Interest:* ἐμοὶ γὰρ τὸ ζῆν Χριστὸς καὶ τὸ ἀποθανεῖν κέρδος = For <u>to me</u> to live (is) Christ and to die (is) gain. (Phil. 1:21)

E. THE ACCUSATIVE CASE is used to express:

1. *The direct object* of a verb and all other words which modify or are in apposition with the direct object: εἰρήνην τὴν ἐμὴν δίδωμι ὑμῖν = <u>my peace</u> I give (to) you. (Jn. 14:27)

2. *The subject of an infinitive:* Ῥαββί, καλόν ἐστιν ἡμᾶς ὧδε εἶναι = Rabbi, it is good <u>for us</u> to be here (that <u>we</u> are here).

(Mk. 9:5)

3. *Duration of time:* καὶ ἰδοὺ ἐγὼ μεθ' ὑμῶν εἰμι πάσας τὰς ἡμέρας = and behold I am with you <u>all days</u>. (Mt. 28:20)

VI. Helpful Hints on Accents:

A. INTRODUCTION:

1. Since this course naturally stresses *reading instead of writing*, accents and their proper placement on words are not of the highest importance.

2. However, since they do have a *definite value,* as previously indicated, some additional guidelines on accentuation will be helpful at this time.

3. Also as indicated, the *three Greek accents* can stand only on the final three syllables, called the *antepenult* (ima), *penult* (ima), and *ultima.*

B. GUIDELINES:

1. *In general, all declinable words except participles* (namely nouns, pronouns, adjectives, and the article) *accent,* throughout their declension, the *same syllable as the nominative,* if the *ultima* permits:

a. **A short ultima** permits an *acute* accent on any of the last three syllables or a *circumflex* accent on the penult, if that is long, e.g.: ἄνθρωπος, κόσμος, θεός, δῶρον, ἔργον, ἱερόν, γλῶσσα.

b. **A long ultima** permits only an *acute* accent on the penult or an *acute* or *circumflex* accent on the ultima, e.g.: ἀνθρώπου, δώρῳ, ζωή, γῆ.

2. *In the first and second declensions:*

a. All syllables containing **long vowels or diphthongs** are *long*, except **final** οι and αι, e.g. the nom. plur. endings: ἄνθρωποι, γλῶσσαι.

b. An **acute accent on the ultima** in the nominative becomes a *circumflex* in the genitive and dative, sing. and plur., e.g.: θεοῦ, ἱερῷ, ὁδῶν, γραφαῖς.

3. *Specifically, in the first declension:*

a. While there is **no regularity about nominative accents** generally, *first declension nouns in Eta* tend to accent the ultima: ἀρχή, ζωή.

b. **All nouns of the first declension** take a *circumflex accent on the ultima* in the genitive plural: ἡμερῶν, ὡρῶν, γλωσσῶν, μαθητῶν.

4. *Enclitics* normally transfer their accents to the *ultima of the preceding word* (if accented on the antepenult or with a circumflex on the penult), causing it to have *two accents:* ἄγγελός ἐστι, δῶρόν σου.

VII. Exercises:

A. THE PRINCIPAL EXERCISE of this lesson is that of *learning the declensions* contained in it, not just passively but *actively,* for speedy recognition.

B. As an indication of ACTIVE LEARNING of the declensions (and bearing in mind that the *article agrees* with its noun *in gender, number, and case*) please *translate* and *decline* the following underlined expressions:

1. ἡ ἡμέρα τοῦ κυρίου.
2. τὸ δῶρον τοῦ θεοῦ.
3. ἡ βίβλος τῶν προφητῶν.
4. τὸ μυστήριον τῆς βασιλείας.

C. As an indication of PASSIVE LEARNING, *read aloud* and *translate:*

1. Ἀρχὴ τοῦ εὐαγγελίου Ἰησοῦ Χριστοῦ υἱοῦ θεοῦ.
   of Jesus Christ

2. Φωνὴ βοῶντος ἐν τῇ ἐρήμῳ, Ἑτοιμάσατε τὴν ὁδὸν κυρίου.
   of one crying in   Prepare

3. Ἐν ἀρχῇ ἦν ὁ λόγος, καὶ ὁ λόγος ἦν πρὸς τὸν θεόν.
   was   and   "with"

4. Ἐγώ εἰμι ἡ ὁδὸς καὶ ἡ ἀλήθεια καὶ ἡ ζωή.
   I   am   truth

3 The First Two Declensions

Adjectives and Pronouns

I. Adjectives of the first and second declensions:

A. INTRODUCTION:

  1. *Adjectives*, which describe the quality or quantity of nouns, **agree** with the nouns to which they refer in **gender, number,** and **case.**

  2. NT Greek has *many first-and-second declension adjectives;* the first declension providing the feminine, the second the masculine and neuter.

B. EXAMPLES:

  1. **ἀγαθός, ή, όν**: good, upright, faithful, noble (Agatha)

  2. **ἅγιος, α, ον**: holy, clean, consecrated (hagiography, Hagiographa)

C. DECLENSION:

	MASC.	FEM.	NEUT.		MASC.	FEM.	NEUT.
		Singular				Singular	
N.	ἀγαθός	ἀγαθή	ἀγαθόν	N.	ἅγιος	ἁγία	ἅγιον
G.	ἀγαθοῦ	ἀγαθῆς	ἀγαθοῦ	G.	ἁγίου	ἁγίας	ἁγίου
D.	ἀγαθῷ	ἀγαθῇ	ἀγαθῷ	D.	ἁγίῳ	ἁγίᾳ	ἁγίῳ
A.	ἀγαθόν	ἀγαθήν	ἀγαθόν	A.	ἅγιον	ἁγίαν	ἅγιον
		Plural				Plural	
N.	ἀγαθοί	ἀγαθαί	ἀγαθά	N.	ἅγιοι*	ἅγιαι*	ἅγια
G.	ἀγαθῶν	ἀγαθῶν	ἀγαθῶν	G.	ἁγίων	ἁγίων	ἁγίων
D.	ἀγαθοῖς	ἀγαθαῖς	ἀγαθοῖς	D.	ἁγίοις	ἁγίαις	ἁγίοις
A.	ἀγαθούς	ἀγαθάς	ἀγαθά	A.	ἁγίους	ἁγίας	ἅγια

*N.B.: Final αι and οι are normally *short* throughout NT Greek.

D. VOCABULARY:

ἄξιος, α, ον: worthy (axiom, axiology)

ἔσχατος, η, ον: last (eschatology)

καινός, ή, όν: new, recent (Cenozoic)

κακός, ή, όν: bad, evil (cacophony)

καλός, ή, όν: good, noble (calligraphy)

λοιπός, ή, όν: left, rest (eclipse)

μέσος, η, ον: middle (Mesopotamia)

νέος, α, ον: new, young (neon, neopaganism)

μικρός, ά, όν: small (microbe)

ὀλίγος, η, ον: few (oligarchy)

μόνος, η, ον: sole (monk, monopoly)

ὅλος, η, ον: whole (holocaust)

σοφός, ή, όν: wise (sophomore)

νεκρός, ά, όν: dead (necropolis)

E. USAGE: There are *three principal uses* of adjectives in NT Greek:

1. The **attributive** (or modifying) adjective always *follows the article* (if one is used) either before or after the noun, e.g.: "the good man" can be expressed by: ὁ ἀγαθὸς ἄνθρωπος or ὁ ἄνθρωπος ὁ ἀγαθός.

2. The **predicative** adjective, which predicates something of the subject through a connecting verb expressed or implied, *does not follow an article*, before or after the subject, e.g.: "*the man is good*" can be expressed by: ὁ ἄνθρωπός (ἐστιν) ἀγαθός or ἀγαθὸς (ἐστιν) ὁ ἄνθρωπος.

3. The **substantival** adjective is one which is *used as a noun*, when the noun itself is omitted as obvious, e.g.: οἱ ἀγαθοί = the good men. Also note the *important*: καὶ τὰ λοιπά = and the rest (κτλ. = etc.)

II. Pronouns of the first and second declensions:

A. INTRODUCTION:

1. Like many nouns and adjectives, *the most commonly used pronouns* also follow the pattern of the first and second declensions:

a. This includes the **relative, intensive, demonstrative, reflexive,** and **reciprocal** pronouns, all of which will be treated in this chapter.

b. Also treated here will be the **personal pronoun** of the **first and second persons,** which follows the pattern sometimes of the first and second declensions, sometimes of the third, sometimes of neither.

c. The **interrogative** and **indefinite** pronouns τίς, τί and τις, τι follow the pattern of the third declension and will be studied later.

2. Unlike nouns and adjectives, *pronouns of the first and second declension use **o** instead of **ov** in the *neuter nominative and accusative singular.*

B. THE RELATIVE PRONOUN: **who, which, what—**

1. *Declension:* the simplest pronoun to decline, the *relative pronoun* comprises the first and second declension *endings*, plus *rough breathings* and *accents*, thus:

	MASC.	FEM.	NEUT.		MASC.	FEM.	NEUT.
		Singular				Plural	
Nom.	ὅς	ἥ	ὅ	*Nom.*	οἵ	αἵ	ἅ
Gen.	οὗ	ἧς	οὗ	*Gen.*	ὧν	ὧν	ὧν
Dat.	ᾧ	ᾗ	ᾧ	*Dat.*	οἷς	αἷς	οἷς
Acc.	ὅν	ἥν	ὅ	*Acc.*	οὕς	ἅς	ἅ

   (*Caution:* Carefully *distinguish* the *relative pronoun* from the *article!*)

2. *Usage:*

a. *In general:* The relative pronoun **agrees with its antecedent** in *gender* and *number*, its *case* depending on its **role in the relative clause,** e.g.: ῍Ιδε ἀληθῶς Ἰσραηλίτης ἐν ᾧ δόλος οὐκ ἔστιν = Behold truly an <u>Israelite in whom</u> there is no guile!
   (Jn. 1:47)

b. *Exceptions* of importance include the following:

   1) *The antecedent is sometimes omitted;* the relative pronoun, never, e.g.: ἐγώ εἰμι ὅν ζητεῖτε = I am (he) <u>whom</u> you seek.
   (Acts 10:21)

   2) *The relative pronoun is often assimilated* to the case of its antecedent, especially when the *antecedent* is in the *genitive or dative* and the *pronoun* would have been in the *accusative,* e.g.: δόξασόν με τῇ δόξῃ ᾗ εἶχον πρὸ τοῦ τὸν κόσμον εἶναι = Glorify me <u>with the glory which</u> I had before the world came to be. (Jn. 17:5)

   3) *The neuter relative pronoun* is regularly used:

      a) **To refer to a whole statement,** e.g.: ὅ καὶ ἐποίησαν ἀποστείλαντες, κτλ. = <u>Which</u> also they did, sending, etc.
   (Acts 11:30)

      b) **To introduce a translation,** e.g.: βασιλεὺς Σαλήμ ὅ ἐστιν βασιλεὺς εἰρήνης = King of Salem, <u>i.e.</u> King of Peace.
   (He. 7:2).

   4) *With the correlative expressions* **μὲν** *and* **δὲ,** which often defy translation, the relative pronoun can mean "one" . . . "(an)other," e.g.: ὅς μὲν πεινᾷ, ὅς δὲ μεθύει = <u>One</u> is hungry, <u>another</u> is drunk. (I Co. 11:21)

C. THE INTENSIVE PRONOUN: **self, same**—αὐτός, ἡ, ὁ (autonomy, autopsy, automobile)

1. *Declension:* The next simplest pronoun to decline, it just adds the stem αὐτ- to the first and second declension *endings for pronouns,* thus:

	MASC.	FEM.	NEUT.		MASC.	FEM.	NEUT.
		Singular				Plural	
N.	αὐτός	αὐτή	αὐτό	N.	αὐτοί	αὐταί	αὐτά
G	αὐτοῦ	αὐτῆς	αὐτοῦ	G.	αὐτῶν	αὐτῶν	αὐτῶν
D.	αὐτῷ	αὐτῇ	αὐτῷ	D.	αὐτοῖς	αὐταῖς	αὐτοῖς
A.	αὐτόν	αὐτήν	αὐτό	A.	αὐτούς	αὐτάς	αὐτά

(*Caution:* Carefully *distinguish* the intensive from the demonstrative pronoun for "this," which is similar and will be studied next.)

2. *Usage:* the intensive pronoun is *used as such* and as a *personal pronoun*—

a. *As an intensive pronoun,* it has *three principal constructions:*
   1) **Attributive** (between article and noun), meaning "same," e.g.: ὁ αὐτὸς ἄνθρωπος = the <u>same</u> man. (or: the <u>very</u> man)
   2) **Predicative** (before or after article and noun), meaning "self," e.g.: ὁ ἄνθρωπος <u>αὐτός</u> / <u>αὐτὸς</u> ὁ ἄνθρωπος = the man <u>himself</u>.
   3) **Substantive** (after article, without noun), e.g.: οἱ αὐτοί = the <u>same men</u>, or frequently: <u>ταῦτά</u> (τὰ + αὐτά) = the <u>same things</u>.

b. *As a personal pronoun,* it is used for the *third person* in *oblique cases,* i.e. the *genitive, dative,* and *accusative* (the nominative being supplied by the demonstrative pronoun), e.g.: ὅσοι ἔλαβον <u>αὐτόν</u> ἔδωκεν <u>αὐτοῖς</u>, κτλ. = Whoever received <u>him</u>, he gave <u>them</u>, etc. (Jn. 1:12)

D. THE DEMONSTRATIVE PRONOUNS: **this, that**—οὗτος, ἐκεῖνος.

1. *Declension:*

a. Both follow the pattern of first and second declension endings for pronouns, but only one is regular and simple: ἐκεῖνος.

b. οὗτος is confusing until one notes that the *diphthong sound in the stem always matches the vowel or diphthong sound in the ending,* e.g. an o-sound before an o-sound, a-sound before a-sound (Alpha or Eta).

	MASC.	FEM.	NEUT.		MASC.	FEM.	NEUT.
		Singular				Singular	
N.	οὗτος	αὕτη	τοῦτο	N.	ἐκεῖνος	ἐκείνη	ἐκεῖνο
G.	τούτου	ταύτης	τούτου	G.	ἐκείνου	ἐκείνης	ἐκείνου
D.	τούτῳ	ταύτῃ	τούτῳ	D.	ἐκείνῳ	ἐκείνῃ	ἐκείνῳ
A.	τοῦτον	ταύτην	τοῦτο	A.	ἐκεῖνον	ἐκείνην	ἐκεῖνο

(continued on next page)

	Plural				Plural	
N.	οὗτοι	αὗται	ταῦτα	N.	ἐκεῖνοι	ἐκεῖναι	ἐκεῖνα
G.	τούτων	τούτων	τούτων	G.	ἐκείνων	ἐκείνων	ἐκείνων
D.	τούτοις	ταύταις	τούτοις	D.	ἐκείνοις	ἐκείναις	ἐκείνοις
A.	τούτους	ταύτας	ταῦτα	A.	ἐκείνους	ἐκείνας	ἐκεῖνα

(*Reminder:* Carefully *distinguish* the demonstrative pronoun οὗτος (this) from the intensive pronoun αὐτός above. Check similarities and differences.)

2. *Usage:* Both of the demonstrative pronouns, but especially οὗτος, are used not only as *demonstratives*, but also as *personal pronouns:*

a. As demonstrative pronouns, they have *two principal constructions:*

   1) **Predicative,** in the *second position* (before article and noun), e.g.: οὗτος ὁ ἀγαθὸς φίλος = this good friend.
   (N.B. The Greek article is used but *not translated* into English.)

   2) **Substantive** (without article or noun), e.g.: οὗτοι = these men, ταῦτα = these things (distinguish from ταὐτά = the same things).

b. As personal pronouns, they are used for the *nominative* of the *third person* (the other cases being supplied by the intensive pronoun), e.g.: οὗτος ἔσται μέγας . . . He will be great . . .

(Lk. 1:32)

   1) NT Greek sometimes uses αὐτός instead of οὗτος in the *nominative*, especially for *emphasis* or in *reference* to a subject already mentioned, e.g.: μακάριοι οἱ καθαροὶ τῇ καρδίᾳ, ὅτι αὐτοὶ τὸν θεὸν ὄψονται = blessed (are) the clean of heart, for they will see God. (Mt. 5:8)

   2) While αὐτός is almost always a personal pronoun when used alone (without article or noun), οὗτος, used alone, can still mean "this," e.g.: τοῦτό ἐστιν τὸ σῶμά μου. = This is my body. (Mt. 26:26)

E. THE PERSONAL PRONOUN:

1. *Introduction:*

a. The **first and second persons** of the personal pronoun have their own forms which follow sometimes the first and second declensions, sometimes the third, and sometimes neither.

b. Perhaps students with a knowledge of Latin and/or one or more of the Romance Languages can best learn the personal pronoun by association with one or more of those languages.

2. *Declension* of: ἐγώ = I (egoism), σύ = you, ἡμεῖς = we, ὑμεῖς = you (plural).

	SINGULAR			PLURAL	
Nom.	ἐγώ	σύ	*Nom.*	ἡμεῖς	ὑμεῖς
Gen.	ἐμοῦ, μου	σοῦ, σου	*Gen.*	ἡμῶν	ὑμῶν
Dat.	ἐμοί, μοι*	σοί, σοι*	*Dat.*	ἡμῖν	ὑμῖν
Acc.	ἐμέ, με	σέ, σε	*Acc.*	ἡμᾶς	ὑμᾶς

3. *Usage:*
   a. **The nominatives,** singular and plural, are used only for *clarity* or *emphasis,* the subject being already contained in the inflected verb.
   b. **The accented singular forms** are used for *emphasis* and especially with *prepositions;* otherwise, the enclitic unaccented forms are employed.

F. PRONOMINAL ADJECTIVES: Some NT Greek words have characteristics both of pronouns and adjectives; hence, some are declined more like *pronouns,* some more like *adjectives,* of the first and second declensions, e.g:

ἄλλος, η, ο: (an)other (allergy)
ἕκαστος, η, ον: each, every
ἐμός, ή, όν: my, mine
ἕτερος, α, ον: other (heterodoxy)
ἡμέτερος, α, ον: our, ours

ἴδιος, α, ον: one's own (idiom, idiot)
σός, σή, σόν: your, yours [singular]
ὑμέτερος, α, ον: your, yours [plural]

G. THE REFLEXIVE PRONOUN (*personal* and *intensive* pronouns combined):

   1. *Introduction:* This pronoun, which "reflects back" to the subject, is declined according to the *regular* first and second declensions, *except* that (being exclusively reflexive) it *does not have a nominative case.*

   2. *Declension* of the *first and second person singular:* myself, yourself.

	FIRST PERSON SINGULAR			SECOND PERSON SINGULAR	
	Masculine	Feminine		Masculine	Feminine
G.	ἐμαυτοῦ	ἐμαυτῆς	G.	σεαυτοῦ	σεαυτῆς
D.	ἐμαυτῷ	ἐμαυτῇ	D.	σεαυτῷ	σεαυτῇ
A.	ἐμαυτόν	ἐμαυτήν	A.	σεαυτόν	σεαυτήν

*N.B.: Final αι and οι are normally *short* throughout NT Greek.

3. *Declension* of the *third person singular and plural:* himself, themselves.

	THIRD PERSON SINGULAR				THIRD PERSON PLURAL		
	Masc.	Fem.	Neut.		Masc.	Fem.	Neut.
G.	ἑαυτοῦ	ἑαυτῆς	ἑαυτοῦ	G.	ἑαυτῶν	ἑαυτῶν	ἑαυτῶν
D.	ἑαυτῷ	ἑαυτῇ	ἑαυτῷ	D.	ἑαυτοῖς	ἑαυταῖς	ἑαυτοῖς
A.	ἑαυτόν	ἑαυτήν	ἑαυτό	A.	ἑαυτούς	ἑαυτάς	ἑαυτά

4. *Usage:*
a. NT Greek uses the reflexive pronoun only when **needed for clarity.**
b. Also, NT Greek uses the **third person plural** for the first and second person plural, as well, e.g.: . . . ἵνα μὴ πεποιθότες ὦμεν ἐφ᾽ ἑαυτοῖς = so that we may not be full of trust in <u>ourselves</u>.
(II Co. 1:9)

H. THE RECIPROCAL PRONOUN:

1. *Introduction:* the reciprocal pronoun, formed from the pronominal adjective ἄλλος, η, o (an/other), expresses *relationship or interaction* between two or more people of the first, second, or third person.

2. *Declension* of ἀλλήλων: each other, one another (parallel).

	Masculine	Feminine	Neuter
Gen.	ἀλλήλων	ἀλλήλων	ἀλλήλων
Dat.	ἀλλήλοις	ἀλλήλαις	ἀλλήλοις
Acc.	ἀλλήλους	ἀλλήλας	ἄλληλα

3. *Usage:* NT Greek can express reciprocity by either the *reciprocal* or the *reflexive* pronoun, sometimes by both in the same sentence, e.g.: ἀνεχόμενοι <u>ἀλλήλων</u> καὶ χαριζόμενοι <u>ἑαυτοῖς</u> . . . = bearing with <u>one another</u> and forgiving <u>one another</u> . . . (Col. 3:13)

III. Exercises:

A. *The principal exercise,* of course, is to *learn thoroughly* the content of this chapter on adjectives and pronouns, especially the latter.

B. *Be able to decline* any and all first and second declension *adjectives* in this chapter, as well as all the *pronouns* and *pronominal adjectives,* particularly the *relative, intensive,* and *demonstrative pronouns.*

C. *Succeeding lessons and exercises* will provide plenty of practice in the adjectives and pronouns. For now, let us content ourselves with adding to our *Useful Expressions:* Παρακαλῶ = Please! Εὐχαριστῶ = Thanks!

4 Prepositions, Particles, Article

I. **General Introduction:**

A. So far, we have been concerned mainly with nouns, adjectives, pronouns, and (to some extent) the article or, in brief, with the *declinable words* and *groups of words* which form primary "building blocks" of NT Greek.

B. Now, it is time to expand our study to include *phrases,* for which purpose our principal concern in this chapter will be with *prepositions,* those *indeclinable* little words which play such an important role in NT Greek.

C. In addition to prepositions, it will also be appropriate to examine not only *adverbs used as prepositions,* but also the very important *adverbial particles,* and the principal uses of the *article* in NT Greek.

II. **The Regular or Proper Prepositions:**

A. USAGE IN GENERAL:

1. Though *originally adverbs,* these words came to be used *exclusively as prepositions* governing nouns, pronouns, infinitives, and substantival participles and, *as verbal prefixes,* adding meaning or emphasis to verbs.

2. *As prepositions,* they govern a *variety of cases,* sometimes with quite *divergent meanings* of the same preposition with different cases, as will be evident from our study of the individual prepositions.

3. Their *accentuation is regular:*
a. **Prepositions of one syllable** take an *acute accent* or *none at all.*
b. **Prepositions of two syllables** take an *acute accent on the ultima.*
c. **In both instances,** of course, the *acute accent changes to a grave* since a proper preposition cannot end a phrase, clause, or sentence.

B. USAGE IN PARTICULAR:

1. *Prepositions governing only one case:* genitive, dative, *or* accusative.

a. The **Genitive only:**

   1) **ἀντί**: over against, instead of, for (antidote, antithesis)
   2) **ἀπό**: from, away from, by, of (apostle, apostasy, apogee)
   3) **ἐκ, ἐξ**: out of, from within, from (ecstasy, exodus, exegesis)
   4) **πρό**: before, ahead of, for (prophet, prologue, prow)

b. The **Dative only:**

   1) **ἐν**: in, within, among (energy, enthusiasm, encyclopedia)
   2) **σύν**: with, together (syntax, syllable, symbol, synthesis)

c. The **Accusative only:**

   1) **ἀνά**: up, upwards; each, with numbers (analogy, analysis)
   2) **εἰς**: into, in; times, with numbers (episode, eisegesis)

2. *Prepositions governing two cases:* genitive *and* accusative.

a. **διά**: with **gen.** = through; with **acc.** = on account of (diagnosis)
b. **κατά**: with **gen.** = against; with **acc.** = down, acc. to (catalogue)
c. **μετά**: with **gen.** = with, among; with **acc.** = after (metaphorical)
d. **περί**: with **gen.** = concerning; with **acc.** = around (perimeter)
e. **ὑπέρ**: with **gen.** = on behalf of; with **acc.** = above (hyperbole)
f. **ὑπό**: with **gen.** = by (agency); with **acc.** = under (hypocrite)

3. *Prepositions governing three cases:* genitive, dative, *and* accusative.

a. **ἐπί**: w. **gen.** = on, upon; w. **dat.** = at, by; w. **acc.** = to (epilogue)
b. **παρά**: w. **gen.** = from; w. **dat.** = beside; w.**acc.** = along (parallel)
c. **πρός**: w. **gen.** = in the interest of; w. **dat.** = near; w. **acc.** = to, toward, in relationship with (prosody, proselyte)

(N.B. The New Testament uses πρός almost exclusively with the *accusative* case, but it is included here with all three cases for completeness' sake.)

III. Improper or adverbial prepositions:

A. INTRODUCTION:

1. These prepositions are called improper or adverbial because they retain their *adverbial quality* more fully and have *limited use as prepositions.*

2. Unlike the regular or proper prepositions, they are *never prefixed* to verbs, *govern the genitive* almost exclusively, are *rarely accented on the ultima,* and have *very few English derivatives.*

B.   Of 42 such prepositions in the New Testament, these are THE MOST COMMON, though not nearly so common as the regular or proper prepositions:

1. **ἄχρι(ς):** up to, until (acropolis)
2. **ἐγγύς:** near (rarely with the dative)
3. **ἔμπροσθεν:** in front of, before (ἐν + πρός + θεν)
4. **ἕνεκα(κεν):** on account of
5. **ἐνώπιον:** in sight of, before (ὤψ = eye, face)
6. **ἔξω:** outside of (exoteric) (ἐκ, ἐξ = out of)
7. **ἕως:** until, as far as (also conjunction)
8. **μέχρι:** as far as, until (also conjunction)
9. **ὀπίσω:** behind, after
10. **πέραν:** beyond, across (fr. πέρας = end, boundary)
11. **πλήν:** besides, except (fr. πλέον = more)
12. **χωρίς:** without, apart (fr. χώρα = place, spot)

IV. Adverbial Particles:

A.   INTRODUCTION:

1. This classification includes a *wide variety of words*, some used as conjunctions, some used postpositively (normally the second word of a sentence or clause), but all *very common* and *very important*.

2. There are *not many English derivatives* from this group, but origins or relationships with Greek words already studied can be helpful.

3. Unlike the prepositions, these *adverbial particles* have *no regular accentuation*.

4. It will be helpful to the student to present these particles in *two groups*, based on their *frequency of use* in the Greek New Testament.

B.   THE MOST COMMON ADVERBIAL PARTICLES in the New Testament: (*150–500 times*):

1. **ἀλλά:** but, rather (cf. ἄλλος = other)
2. **γάρ:** for (postpositive conjunction)
3. **δέ:** but, however (postpositive)
4. **ἤ:** or, than (cf. rel. pron.)
5. **καί:** and, also (opp. of δέ)
6. **μέν:** on one hand (postpositive)
7. **οὐ(κ, χ):** not (κ, χ with vowels)
8. **οὖν:** then, therefore (transition)
9. **οὕτως:** thus (fr. οὗτος = this)
10. **τε:** and, also (enclitic; Lat. -*que*)
11. **τότε:** then, at that time
12. **ὡς:** as, as if (from ὅς?)

C. OTHER COMMON ADVERBIAL PARTICLES in the New Testament (*50–150 times*):

1. **διό:** therefore (διά + ὅ)
2. **ἐκεῖ:** there (cf. ἐκεῖνος)
3. **ἔτι:** still, yet
4. **εὐθύς:** immediately
5. **ἤδη:** already, now
6. **μᾶλλον:** more, rather
7. **νῦν:** now, at present (now)
8. **οὐδέ:** neither, not even (οὐ + δέ)
9. **οὔτε:** neither, nor (οὐ + τε)
10. **πάλιν:** back, again (palimpsest)
11. **πῶς:** how? (interrogative of ὡς)
12. **ὧδε:** thus, here, hither (ὅ + δέ)

V. Usage of the Article in NT Greek:

A. INTRODUCTION:

1. *Importance:* NT Greek being characterized by *precision*, the student should pay close attention to the *presence or absence of the article,* as it may directly affect the interpretation of a passage, e.g.: καὶ ὁ λόγος ἦν πρὸς τὸν θεόν, καὶ θεὸς ἦν ὁ λόγος = and the word was "with" God, and the word was God. (Jn. 1:1) (Person distinguished from Nature)

2. *Origin:* To grasp the use of the article in NT Greek, it is helpful to bear in mind that it was *originally a demonstrative pronoun,* a circumstance which tends to color and explain its use in the New Testament.

B. GENERAL USAGE: The NT Greek article is used, in general, *much like the English definite article,* especially to *designate, emphasize,* or *refer* to a determinate person, place, or thing, e.g.: Ὁ προφήτης εἶ σύ; = Are you the Prophet? Jn. 1:21.

C. PARTICULAR USAGE: However, NT Greek does not always use the article as we do in English, especially in the *following important instances:*

1. *Use of the article* where English would use a *pronoun:*
a. As a **demonstrative pronoun:** οἱ παρ᾽ αὐτοῦ ἐξῆλθον κρατῆσαι αὐτόν . . . = Those with him came out to take charge of him . . . (Mk. 3:21)
b. As a **personal pronoun:** ὁ δὲ οὐκ ἀπεκρίθη αὐτῇ λόγον. = But he did not answer her a word. (Mt. 15:23)
c. As a **relative pronoun:** Πάτερ ἡμῶν ὁ ἐν τοῖς οὐρανοῖς . . . = Our Father who (are) in the heavens . . . (Mt. 6:9)
d. As a **possessive pronoun:** ὁ ποιμὴν ὁ καλὸς τὴν ψυχὴν αὐτοῦ τίθησιν ὑπὲρ τῶν προβάτων = The good shepherd gives his life for his sheep. (Jn. 10:11)

2. *Addition of the article* where it would be *omitted in English:*

a. **Before proper names:** ὡς ἤκουσεν τὸν ἀσπασμὸν τῆς Μαρίας ἡ Ἐλιζάβετ . . . = as <u>Elizabeth</u> heard <u>Mary's</u> greeting . . . (Lk. 1:41)

b. **Before special titles:** ὑμεῖς φωνεῖτέ με Ὁ διδάσκαλος καὶ Ὁ κύριος . . . = you call me "<u>Teacher</u>" and "<u>Lord</u>" . . . (Jn. 13:13)

c. **Before God as a person:** Ἴδε ὁ ἀμνὸς τοῦ θεοῦ . . . = Behold the lamb of <u>God</u> . . . (Jn. 1:29)

d. **Before geographical names:** Διοδεύσαντες δὲ τὴν Ἀμφίπολιν καὶ τὴν Ἀπολλωνίαν . . . = Passing through Amphipolis and Apollonia . . . (Acts 17:1)

e. **Before abstract nouns:** ἡ χάρις * καὶ ἡ ἀλήθεια * διὰ Ἰησοῦ Χριστοῦ ἐγένετο. = <u>grace</u> and <u>truth</u> came through Jesus Christ.

(Jn. 1:17)

3. *Omission of the article* where it would be *added in English:*

a. **After prepositions:** Ἐν ἀρχῇ ἦν ὁ λόγος, καὶ ὁ λόγος ἦν πρὸς τὸν θεόν = <u>In the beginning</u> was the word, and the word was with God. (Jn. 1:1)

b. **Before nouns** and their **following genitive:** εἴπερ πνεῦμα θεοῦ οἰκεῖ ἐν ὑμῖν . . . = since <u>the Spirit of God</u> dwells in (among) you . . . (Rm. 8:9)

c. But, **contrariwise,** when the **following genitive does take an article,** so normally does the **noun which precedes it:** τὸ πνεῦμα τοῦ θεοῦ οἰκεῖ ἐν ὑμῖν . . . = <u>the Spirit of God</u> dwells in (among) you . . . (I Co. 3:16)

VI. Appendix I: Bone Rules for Prepositions—

[INTRODUCTION: This "silly ditty" did not seem worthy of inclusion in the body of this chapter, but for those who may find it useful for distinguishing and remembering the *proper prepositions* and their *general case uses,* I am providing it, on an optional basis, in this Appendix.]

1. **Ἀντί, ἀπό,** with **ἐξ** and **πρό,**
   All take the **Genitive,** you know.

2. To **ἐν** and **σύν** the **Dative** give;
   Ἀνά and **εἰς, Accusative.**

3. **Διά, κατά, μετά, περί,**
   Ὑπέρ, ὑπό, with **two** can be.

4. **Ἐπί, παρά,** along with **πρός,**
   Can each of these **three cases** boast.

(N.B. Multiple subjects and *neuter plurals* take a *singular verb.*)

VII. Exercise I: Recognition—Identify the following words *rearranged alphabetically:*

1. ἀλλά	12. ἐκεῖ	23. ἤδη	34. πάλιν
2. ἀνά	13. ἔμπροσθεν	24. μᾶλλον	35. παρά
3. ἀντί	14. ἐν	25. μέν	36. πέραν
4. ἀπό	15. ἕνεκα	26. μετά	37. περί
5. ἄχρι	16. ἐνώπιον	27. μέχρι	38. πλήν
6. δέ	17. ἔξω	28. ὀπίσω	39. πρό
7. διά	18. ἐπί	29. οὐδέ	40. πρός
8. διό	19. ἔτι	30. οὐκ	41. πῶς
9. ἐγγύς	20. εὐθύς	31. οὖν	42. τέ
10. εἰς	21. ἕως	32. οὔτε	43. τότε
11. ἐκ	22. ἤ	33. οὕτως	44. ὡς

(N.B. It is the ability to recognize "little words" such as these that can make the difference between a *confused* and a *clear understanding* of Greek.)

VIII. Appendix II. "To Be" or "To Come to Be": As an aid in appreciating the riches of *John's Prologue,* let us look briefly at **two important contrasting verbs:**

εἰμί: *I am,* of which the usual form in John 1 is ἦν: he, (she), it was.

γίνομαι: *I come to be, I become;* of which the usual form in John 1 is ἐγένετο: he (she, it) came to be, became, came.

IX. Exercise II: Please *read aloud, translate,* and *explain the underlined portions* of this selection from the beginning of John's Gospel—

Ἐν ἀρχῇ ἦν ὁ λόγος, καὶ ὁ λόγος ἦν πρὸς τὸν θεόν, καὶ θεὸς ἦν

ὁ λόγος. οὗτος ἦν ἐν ἀρχῇ πρὸς τὸν θεόν. πάντα δι᾽ αὐτοῦ ἐγένετο*,

all things

καὶ χωρὶς αὐτοῦ ἐγένετο οὐδὲ ἓν ὃ γέγονεν. ἐν αὐτῷ ζωὴ ἦν, καὶ ἡ

one (thing) came to be

ζωὴ ἦν τὸ φῶς τῶν ἀνθρώπων· καὶ τὸ φῶς ἐν τῇ σκοτίᾳ φαίνει, καὶ

light ・ light ・ darkness ・ shines

ἡ σκοτία αὐτὸ οὐ κατέλαβεν. ἐγένετο ἄνθρωπος ἀπεσταλμένος

extinguished ・ sent forth

παρὰ θεοῦ, ὄνομα αὐτῷ Ἰωάννης· οὗτος ἦλθεν εἰς μαρτυρίαν, ἵνα

name ・ John ・ came ・ witness ・ that

μαρτυρήσῃ περὶ τοῦ φωτός, ἵνα πάντες πιστεύσωσιν δι᾽ αὐτοῦ.

he might witness ・ light ・ that ・ all ・ might believe

*A Reminder: Neuter plural subjects and multiple subjects take a singular verb.

οὐκ ἦν ἐκεῖνος τὸ φῶς, ἀλλ**' ἵνα μαρτυρήσῃ περὶ τοῦ φωτός. ἦν
               light   that he might witness   light

τὸ φῶς τὸ ἀληθινόν, ὃ φωτίζει πάντα ἄνθρωπον, ἐρχόμενον εἰς τὸν
  light   true   enlightens   every   coming

κόσμον. ἐν τῷ κόσμῳ ἦν, καὶ ὁ κόσμος δι' αὐτοῦ ἐγένετο, καὶ ὁ

κόσμος αὐτὸν οὐκ ἔγνω. εἰς τὰ ἴδια ἦλθεν καὶ οἱ ἴδιοι αὐτὸν οὐ
                 knew

παρέλαβον. ὅσοι δὲ ἔλαβον αὐτόν, ἔδωκεν αὐτοῖς ἐξουσίαν τέκνα
accepted.   As many as   received   he gave   authority   children

θεοῦ γενέσθαι, τοῖς πιστεύουσιν εἰς τὸ ὄνομα αὐτοῦ, οἳ οὐκ ἐξ
    to become   believing

αἱμάτων οὐδὲ ἐκ θελήματος σαρκὸς οὐδὲ ἐκ θελήματος ἀνδρὸς
bloods   will   of flesh   of man

ἀλλ**' ἐκ θεοῦ ἐγεννήθησαν. καὶ ὁ λόγος σὰρξ ἐγένετο καὶ
         were begotten   flesh

ἐσκήνωσεν ἐν ἡμῖν, καὶ ἐθεασάμεθα τὴν δόξαν αὐτοῦ, δόξαν ὡς
pitched tent   we beheld

μονογενοῦς παρὰ πατρός, πλήρης χάριτος καὶ ἀληθείας. Ἰωάννης
of only begotten   full   grace   truth   John

μαρτυρεῖ περὶ αὐτοῦ καὶ κέκραγεν λέγων, Οὗτος ἦν ὃν εἶπον,
witnesses   has cried out saying   I said

Ὁ ὀπίσω μου ἐρχόμενος ἔμπροσθέν μου γέγονεν, ὅτι πρῶτός μου
         coming   has come to be for   before

ἦν. ὅτι ἐκ τοῦ πληρώματος αὐτοῦ ἡμεῖς πάντες ἐλάβομεν, καὶ
because   fullness   all   received

χάριν ἀντὶ χάριτος· ὅτι ὁ νόμος διὰ Μωϋσέως ἐδόθη, ἡ χάρις καὶ
grace   grace   because   Moses   was given   grace

ἡ ἀλήθεια διὰ Ἰησοῦ Χριστοῦ ἐγένετο*. θεὸν οὐδεὶς ἑώρακεν
truth   no one   has seen

πώποτε· μονογενὴς θεὸς (υἱὸς) ὁ ὢν εἰς τὸν κόλπον τοῦ πατρὸς
(n)ever   only begotten   being   bosom   of father

ἐκεῖνος ἐξηγήσατο. (John 1:1−18)
      revealed (him)

**ἀλλά follows a *negative* expression.

5 Review and Development

I. **Introduction:**

A. We have now studied the *basic elements* of NT Greek, the *first and second declensions* of nouns, adjectives, pronouns, and the article, plus the *indeclinable little words—prepositions* and *adverbial particles.*

B. We have also had a "Taste of Honey" in *reading and translating* the simple yet profound language of *John's Prologue,* which has heartened and excited us to read more, even so soon in our study of NT Greek.

C. Our next study will plunge us into the fascinating world of *the Greek Verb* which is THE WORD of a sentence (from Latin *verbum,* meaning simply "word"), expressing as it does the *action or situation* of the subject.

D. But before taking this next great step, it is wise to *pause, review, and consolidate* the material studied so far, while also developing our knowledge further with additional vocabulary and continued reading from John.

II. **Review and Development according to chapters:**

A. CHAPTER 1: *Basic Elements of NT Greek—*

   1. *Review:*
   a. **Check and perfect knowledge** of the *alphabet, syllabification,* the *breathing marks,* and *punctuation.*
   b. **Re-study the entire chapter,** especially the *examples,* which should now be much more recognizable and understandable.

   2. *Development:* To improve reading ability, *practice reading aloud:*
   a. **The Lord's Prayer** on page 7 (try memorizing individual lines).
   b. **The Prologue of John's Gospel** on pages 29 and 30.

B.   CHAPTER 2: *Nouns of the first two declensions, and the article—*

1. *Review:*

   a. **Test remembrance** of all *declensions, vocabularies,* and *case usage.*

   b. **Translate** this sentence and *decline* the underlined words:
      ἡ ἀγάπη τοῦ μαθητοῦ (ἐστι) τὸ σημεῖον τῆς βασιλείας τοῦ θεοῦ.
      (is)

2. *Development:* Complete your basic knowledge of first and second declension nouns by learning the following, chosen for *importance and frequency.*

   a. **Second declension masculine nouns:**

   ἀγρός: field (agriculture)

   ἄνεμος: wind (anemometer)

   ἀριθμός: number (arithmetic)

   ἄρτος: bread, loaf of bread

   διδάσκαλος: teacher (didactic)

   ἥλιος: sun (helium)

   θρόνος: seat, chair (throne)

   καιρός: (appointed) time, event

   καρπός: fruit (carpology, harvest)

   λίθος: stone (lithium, neolithic)

   ναός: temple, sanctuary (nave)

   οἶνος: wine (enology, Lat. *vinum*)

   ὀφθαλμός: eye (ophthalmology)

   ὄχλος: crowd, mob (ochlocracy)

   πλοῦτος: wealth (plutocrat)

   πόλεμος: war (polemic)

   σταυρός: cross (to steer)

   στέφανος: crown (Stephen)

   φόβος: fear, terror (phobia)

   χρόνος: time (chronology, chronic)

   b. **Second declension neuter nouns:**

   βιβλίον: book (Bible, bibliography)

   δένδρον: tree (rhododendron)

   ζῷον: animal (zoo, zoology)

   θηρίον: wild beast (theriomorphic)

   ἱμάτιον: coat, cloak (himation)

   μαρτύριον: testimony (martyrdom)

   μνημεῖον: memorial (mnemonics)

   ξύλον: wood (xylophone, xylography)

   παιδίον*: young child (pediatrics)

   πλοῖον: boat, ship (πλέω = I sail)

   ποτήριον: cup (potion, symposium)

   πρόσωπον: face (prosopography)

   σάββατον: day of rest (Sabbath)

   συνέδριον: Sanhedrin (ἕδρα = seat)

   τέκνον*: offspring, child (τίκτω = I bear, give birth)

   * *Words for children are neuter.*

c. **First declension feminine nouns:**

ἀλήθεια: truth (ἀ = not + λανθάνω = I hide)

ἁμαρτία: sin, error (ἁμαρτάνω = I sin, go astray)

γενεά: birth, race (generation)

διακονία: service (diaconate)

διδαχή: teaching (Didache, didactic)

δικαιοσύνη: justice, righteousness

ἐντολή: commandment

ἐξουσιά: power, authority

ἐπιστολή: letter (epistle)

θάλασσα: sea (thalassic)

θύρα: entrance (door, thyroid)

θυσία: sacrifice (thurifer)

κοινωνία: communion, community

μαρτυρία: testimony (martyrdom)

μετάνοια: conversion (metanoia)

παρουσία: presence (parousia)

πληγή: blow, wound (plague)

προφητεία: prophecy (prophetic)

φυλακή: guard, watch (phylactery)

χρεία: need, use (catachresis)

d. **First declension masculine nouns:**

κρίτης: judge (critic, criterion)

στρατιώτης: soldier (stratagem)

τελώνης: tax-collector (toll)

ὑποκριτής: actor (hypocrite)

C. CHAPTER 3: *Adjectives and pronouns of the first two declensions—*

1. *Review:*

a. **Test remembrance of all declensions,** especially those of the *adjective,* and the *intensive, demonstrative,* and *personal pronouns.*

b. **Test remembrance of all usage or syntax,** especially of *adjectives,* and *relative, intensive,* and *demonstrative pronouns.*

2. *Development:* Complete your basic knowledge of first and second declension adjectives and pronouns by adding the following to your vocabulary:

a. **First and second declension adjectives:**

ἀγαπητός: beloved (agape)

ἀληθινός: true, truthful

δέξιος: right (dexiotropic)

δίκαιος: just, worthy (theodicy)

δυνατός: powerful, possible (dynamic)

ἐκλεκτός: chosen (eclectic)

καθαρός: clean (Catherine)

κρυπτός: hidden (crypt, cryptic)

λευκός: white (leukemia)

μακάριος: blessed (macarism)

ὅμοιος: like, similar
(homeopathy)
παλαιός: old, ancient
(paleontology)
πιστός: believing, faithful

πονηρός: evil, painful (n. Evil)
τέλειος: finished, perfect
(teleology)
τυφλός: blind (typhlology,
typhiosis)

b. **First and second declension pronominal adjectives:**
  1) *Of quantity* (demonstrative, interrogative, relative):
     τοσοῦτος: so great, so much; **ποσος:** how great, how much?
     ὅσος: as great as, much as
  2) *Of quality* (demonstrative, interrogative, relative):
     τοιοῦτος: of such a kind, such; **ποῖος:** of what sort?;
     οἷος: such as
c. **First and second declension numerical adjectives** (ordinal
  numbers):
  1) **πρῶτος:** first (proton, protein, prototype, protocol,
     protagonist)
  2) **δεύτερος:** second (deuteron, deuterium, Deuteronomy,
     deuterocanonical)
  3) **τρίτος:** third (triton, Triton, tritium, third, triangle)

D. CHAPTER 4: *Prepositions, adverbial particles, and the article—*

  1. *Review:*
  a. **Test knowledge of the meaning,** in general and in particular, of
     the proper and improper *prepositions* and *adverbial particles.*
  b. **Test knowledge of the usage,** in general and in particular, of the
     proper and improper *prepositions* and *the article.*

  2. *Development:* Complete your basic knowledge of first and
     second declension *adverbs* by adding the following to your
     vocabulary—
  a. **In General:**
     1) As adjectives relate to nouns, so *adverbs relate to verbs*
        (Ad-Verbs), *often crucially modifying the action or situation*
        of the subject as expressed in the verb.
     2) While easier than adjectives because they are **indeclinable**
        and **do not agree** with any other word, adverbs' importance
        to the meaning of the sentence requires their *recognition*
        and *understanding.*
  b. **In Particular:** It is most helpful to know something about the
     origin and *formation* of adverbs, in order to recognize them as
     adverbs and perhaps know something of their "thrust" even
     if never seen before.

1) **Adverbs classified according to origin:**
   a) From *adjectives* (the most common), by changing the masculine nominative singular from ος to ως, e.g.: **ἀξίως, δικαίως, κακῶς, καλῶς, ὁμοίως, κτλ.** (**καλῶς** = well)
   b) From *nouns* and *pronouns*, e.g.: **δωρεάν** = freely, gratuitously; **σήμερον** = today, this day; **αὐτοῦ** = here, there; **οὕτως** = thus.

2) **Adverbs classified according to ending:**
   a) *Adverbs of manner* ending in -ως: **καθώς** = just as; **οὕτως** = thus, so; **πῶς** = how?; **πώς** = somehow; **ὡς** = as, just as.
   b) *Adverbs of time* ending in -οτε: **ὅτε** = when; **πότε** = when?; **ποτέ** = sometime, once, ever; **τότε** = then.
   c) *Adverbs of place* ending in -ου: **αὐτοῦ** = here, there; **οὗ** = where; **ὅπου** = where, whither; **ποῦ** = where?; **πού** = somewhere.
   d) *Adverbs of direction* ending in -ω: **ἄνω** = up, above; **ἔξω** = outside; **ἔσω** = inside; **κάτω** = down; **ὑποκάτω** = underneath.
   e) *Adverbs of direction from,* ending in -θεν: **ἄνωθεν** = from above, again ("from the top"); **ἐκεῖθεν** = thence; **ἐντεύθεν** = thence, from there; **ἔσωθεν** = from within; **ὅθεν** = whence, from where; **πόθεν** = whence? from where?

3) **Some important adverbs which defy classification:**

   ἄρα: therefore, then, and so

   ἄρτι: now, just now

   γέ: indeed, even, truly (enclitic)

   οὐκέτι: no longer (οὐκ + ἔτι)

III. **Exercise:** Please *read aloud, translate,* and *explain the underlined portions* of this selection from the continuation of the Gospel of St. John—

Καὶ <u>αὕτη</u> ἐστὶν ἡ μαρτυρία <u>τοῦ</u> Ἰωάννου, ὅτε <u>ἀπέστειλαν</u> <u>πρὸς</u>
          is   sent out

<u>αὐτὸν</u> οἱ <u>Ἰουδαῖοι</u> <u>ἐξ</u> <u>Ἱεροσολύμων</u> ἱερεῖς καὶ Λευίτας ἵνα
            Jews   Jerusalem   priests   Levites   to

ἐρωτήσωσιν <u>αὐτόν</u>, Σὺ τίς εἶ; καὶ ὡμολόγησεν καὶ <u>οὐκ</u> ἠρνήσατο,
   ask   who are   he admitted   denied

καὶ ὡμολόγησεν ὅτι Ἐγὼ <u>οὐκ</u> εἰμὶ ὁ Χριστός. καὶ ἠρώτησαν <u>αὐτόν</u>,
               that   am   they asked

Τί <u>οὖν</u>; Σὺ Ἡλίας εἶ; καὶ λέγει, Οὐκ εἰμί. Ὁ προφήτης εἶ <u>σύ</u>; καὶ
What   Elias   are   he says   I am   are

ἀπεκρίθη, Οὔ. <u>εἶπαν</u> <u>οὖν</u> <u>αὐτῷ</u>, Τίς εἶ; ἵνα ἀπόκρισιν δῶμεν <u>τοῖς</u>
he answered   No! they said   Who are you?   that   answer   we may give

πέμψασιν ἡμᾶς· τί λέγεις περὶ σεαυτοῦ; ἔφη, Ἐγὼ φωνὴ βοῶντος
who sent   *What do you say*   *he said*   *of one crying*

ἐν τῇ ἐρήμῳ, Εὐθύνατε τὴν ὁδὸν κυρίου, καθὼς εἶπεν Ἡσαΐας
Make straight   *said*   *Isaiah*

ὁ προφήτης. Καὶ ἀπεσταλμένοι ἦσαν ἐκ τῶν Φαρισαίων. καὶ
those sent   *were*   *Pharisees*

ἠρώτησαν αὐτὸν καὶ εἶπαν αὐτῷ, Τί οὖν βαπτίζεις εἰ σὺ οὐκ εἶ ὁ
they asked   *said*   *Why*   *do you baptize*   *if*   *are*

Χριστὸς οὐδὲ Ἡλίας οὐδὲ ὁ προφήτης; ἀπεκρίθη αὐτοῖς ὁ Ἰωάννης
answered

λέγων, Ἐγὼ βαπτίζω ἐν ὕδατι· μέσος ὑμῶν ἔστηκεν ὃν ὑμεῖς οὐκ
saying   *baptize*   *water*   *has stood*

οἴδατε, ὁ ὀπίσω μου ἐρχόμενος, οὗ οὐκ εἰμὶ ἐγὼ ἄξιος ἵνα λύσω
know   *coming*   *am*   *to loose*

αὐτοῦ τὸν ἱμάντα τοῦ ὑποδήματος. Ταῦτα ἐν Βηθανίᾳ ἐγένετο
strap   *sandal*   *Bethany*   *happened*

πέραν τοῦ Ἰορδάνου, ὅπου ἦν ὁ Ἰωάννης βαπτίζων.
Jordan   *was*   *baptizing*

Τῇ ἐπαύριον βλέπει τὸν Ἰησοῦν ἐρχόμενον πρὸς αὐτόν, καὶ λέγει,
next day   *he sees*   *coming*   *he says*

Ἴδε ὁ ἀμνὸς τοῦ θεοῦ ὁ αἴρων τὴν ἁμαρτίαν τοῦ κόσμου. οὗτός
Behold   *lamb*   *takes away*

ἐστιν ὑπὲρ οὗ ἐγὼ εἶπον, Ὀπίσω μου ἔρχεται ἀνὴρ ὃς ἔμπροσθέν
is   *said*   *comes*   *a man*

μου γέγονεν, ὅτι πρῶτός μου ἦν. κἀγὼ οὐκ ᾔδειν αὐτόν, ἀλλ' ἵνα
has come to be because   *he was*   *And I*   *knew*   *that*

φανερωθῇ τῷ Ἰσραὴλ διὰ τοῦτο ἦλθον ἐγὼ ἐν ὕδατι βαπτίζων. Καὶ
he might be shown   *to Israel*   *came*   *baptizing*

ἐμαρτύρησεν Ἰωάννης λέγων ὅτι Τεθέαμαι τὸ πνεῦμα καταβαῖνον
witnessed   *saying*   :   *I have seen*   *spirit*   *descending*

ὡς περιστερὰν ἐξ οὐρανοῦ, καὶ ἔμεινεν ἐπ' αὐτόν· κἀγὼ οὐκ ᾔδειν
dove   *remained*   *And I*   *knew*

αὐτόν, ἀλλ' ὁ πέμψας με βαπτίζειν ἐν ὕδατι ἐκεῖνός μοι εἶπεν,
sent   *to baptize*   *water*   *said*

Ἐφ' ὃν ἂν ἴδῃς τὸ πνεῦμα καταβαῖνον καὶ μένον ἐπ' αὐτόν,
(may) see   *spirit*   *descending*   *remaining*

οὗτός ἐστιν ὁ βαπτίζων ἐν πνεύματι ἁγίῳ. κἀγὼ ἑώρακα, καὶ
is   *baptizing*   *spirit*   *And I*   *have seen*

μεμαρτύρηκα ὅτι οὗτός ἐστιν ὁ υἱὸς τοῦ θεοῦ. (Jn. 1 : 19–34)
have witnessed   *that*   *is*

6 The Regular Verb—Part I

Formation of the Indicative

I. **Introduction:**

A. As in all languages, *the key to NT Greek* is an effective knowledge of the *forms and usage of the verb,* that all-important part of speech which supplies *relationship, movement,* even *life itself,* to every sentence.

B. Admittedly, the study of the NT Greek verb, with its many forms and variations, can discourage the student, unless *two very important considerations* are kept clearly in mind:

   1. That this course aims, not at an active knowledge of Greek to be used in speaking and/or writing, but rather a *passive knowledge,* especially the *ability to recognize forms,* for the purpose of *reading* NT Greek.

      (**Note,** however, that, even for a passive knowledge, an ability to conjugate forms is not only *very helpful* but perhaps even *indispensable.*)

   2. That Greek lends itself to a scientific and systematic study which can transform apparent confusion into admirable *order, symmetry,* and *beauty.*

C. We will now study the REGULAR VERB, so-called because its *stem* (root) ends in an *unchanging letter,* namely a *weak vowel* (ι or υ) or *diphthong:*

   1. *In general,* we will consider in order:
   a. The **structure** of the Greek verb, including **voices, moods, tenses.**
   b. The **systems** to which **all the forms** of the Greek verb are **reducible.**
   c. The **features** of the verb forms, which **need to be recognized** in order to identify those forms and understand their meaning.

   2. *In particular,* we will confine our detailed study in this chapter to the *indicative mood of the regular verb,* in comparison with which all other moods and all other verbs can then be more

easily examined. Our study of the indicative mood of the regular verb will feature:

   a. A **synopsis** of the most regular Greek verb in the indicative mood, incorporating the various considerations indicated above.

   b. A brief **vocabulary** of regular or mostly regular NT Greek verbs.

   c. **Exercises of conjugation and recognition,** designed to insure a basic working knowledge of the indicative mood of the regular verb.

D.   For the study of the Greek verb, we need an attitude of healthy curiosity, careful observation, clue-detection, and puzzle-solving, which will enable us to unlock the "mystery" of the Greek verb and understand the Greek New Testament.

II.   **The structure of the NT Greek verb** comprises the following:

A.   THREE VOICES: active, middle, and passive—

   1. The *active* and *passive* are as in English, e.g. *I love, I am loved.*

   2. The *middle* is used *reflexively,* i.e. the subject acting on itself or on something pertaining to itself, e.g. *I love myself, I love my work.*

B.   FIVE MOODS: indicative, subjunctive, imperative, infinitive, participle—

   1. The *indicative* is the *principal and most direct mood;* the others are all called subordinate or oblique moods.

   2. The *infinitive* and *participle,* which are *verbal nouns* and *adjectives* respectively, are here treated as subordinate moods in a broad sense.

   3. Another mood, the *optative* ("should-would"), not uncommon in classical Greek, is so rare in NT Greek that it is *omitted* from this course.

   4. *In general,* NT Greek moods follow the *same usage as in English,* but with some important differences which will be explained very shortly.

C.   SIX TENSES: 1) present,   2) imperfect,
   3) future,   4) aorist,
   5) perfect,   6) pluperfect.

   1. *The odd-numbered tenses* (1, 3, 5: present, future, perfect) are called *primary tenses.* The *even-numbered* (2, 4, 6: imperfect, aorist, pluperfect) are called *secondary tenses*—an **important distinction** to learn.

2. *In the indicative mood,* with which we are now concerned:
a. **The general meaning of the primary tenses** is as follows:
   1) *Present:* single or continued present action: *I love, I am loving.*
   2) *Future:* single or continued future action: *I will love, I will be loving.*
   3) *Perfect:* past action continuing in the present: *I have loved.*
b. **The general meaning of the secondary tenses** is as follows:
   1) *Imperfect:* continued or repeated past action: *I was loving.*
   2) *Aorist** (preterit): single past action*: *I loved, I once loved*.*
   3) *Pluperfect:* action before a past time: *I had loved.*

(Note that the designation primary and secondary does *not* indicate importance or frequency, for the most important and most frequently used tenses by far are the *present* and the *aorist*.)

3. *In the subordinate or oblique moods,* tense meanings are different, as will be explained when these moods are studied in detail.

III. **The systems of the NT Greek verb,** because of their importance in the study of Greek verbs, require very careful analysis ("systems analysis"), thus:

A. NATURE OR MEANING: The systems are *groupings* to which all voices, moods, tenses, and forms belong, and which are indicated in dictionaries, grammars, etc. by "principal parts," roughly corresponding to the three principal parts in English (e.g., *swim, swam, swum*) or the four in Latin.

B. THESE SYSTEMS, WITH THEIR PRINCIPAL PARTS, comprise the following SIX:

1. *The present system:*
a. **First principal part:** the *present indicative active—I love.*
b. Includes the *present tense* in all moods and voices, and the *imperfect indicative* in all voices: *I love, I am loved; I was loving, I was being loved.*

2. *The future system:*
a. **Second principal part:** the *future indicative active—I will love.*
b. Includes the *future indicative active and middle: I will love, I will love myself, my own.*

*The aorist, under single past action, may emphasize the *beginning* (inceptive or ingressive aorist), *completion* (perfective or culminative aorist), or *totality* (global or constative aorist).

3. *The aorist system:* resembling the *preterit* of Modern Languages—

a. **Third principal part:** the *aorist indicative active—I loved.*

b. Includes the *aorist active and middle* in all moods: *I loved, I loved myself, my own.*

4. *The perfect system:*

a. **Fourth principal part:** the *perfect indicative active—I have loved.*

b. Includes the *perfect active indicative, infinitive, and participle;* and the *pluperfect active indicative: I have loved, I had loved.*

5. *The perfect middle system:*

a. **Fifth principal part:** the *perfect indicative middle/passive: I have loved myself, my own; I have been loved.*

b. Includes the *perfect indicative, infinitive, and participle middle and passive: I have loved myself, my own; I have been loved.*

6. *The passive system* (also called the *aorist passive system*):

a. **Sixth principal part:** the *aorist indicative passive—I was loved.*

b. Includes the *aorist passive in all moods,* and the *future indicative passive: I was loved, I will be loved.*

(Note that several forms used in Classical Greek have been omitted here because they are *rare or nonexistent in the New Testament,* e.g.: the *future perfect indicative,* the *pluperfect indicative middle and passive,* the *future infinitive and participle* and *perfect subjunctive and imperative* in all voices.)

IV. The characteristic features of the NT Greek verb:

A. INTRODUCTION: *One of the principal keys* used to unlock the "mysteries" of the Greek verb is the ability to "dissect" any verb and identify its characteristic features, which are so many *clues* to its form and meaning.

B. THE BASIC FEATURE: the verb stem or root:

1. Characteristic of a *regular verb* is the *unchanging nature of its stem,* as seen in our basic regular verb λύω (stem λυ-): I loose, destroy (loose, lose, loss, less; ana-, cata-, dia-, paralysis), whose *principal parts* are: λύω, λύσω, ἔλυσα, λέλυκα, λέλυμαι, ἐλύθην.

2. Other verbs, *irregular* in various ways, either *modify the same stem* or actually *use different stems* for different systems, e.g.: βάλλω (βαλ), βαλῶ, ἔβαλον, βέβληκα, βέβλημαι, ἐβλήθην = throw (ballistics).

(Note that *verb forms* are characterized by *recessive accentuation,* that is, the accent recedes as far from the end of the verb as possible, with few exceptions, which will be noted later, e.g., in participles.)

C. FEATURES PRECEDING THE STEM: *augment* and/or *reduplication*—

1. *Augment* (increase) is a feature of *secondary tenses of the indicative* mood only, and exists in *two forms:*

a. **Syllabic augment:** which adds a syllable by prefixing an Epsilon to verbs beginning with a consonant, e.g. ἔλυον, ἔλυσα, ἐλύθην.

b. **Temporal augment:** which increases the time or length of the first syllable by lengthening an initial vowel: α, ε to η, o to ω, e.g. ἤκουσα (ἀκούω), ἤγειρα (ἐγείρω), ὤφειλον (ὀφείλω).

(Note that when a verb begins with a *diphthong*, the first vowel is normally lengthened, an Iota being *subscribed*, e.g. ηὔξησα (αὐξάνω), ηὐδόκησα (εὐδοκέω), ᾔτησα (αἰτέω).)

2. *Reduplication* (doubling) is a feature of the *perfect system(s)* in all moods, voices, and forms; and it is *also twofold:*

a. **Syllabic reduplication:** which adds a syllable to verbs beginning with a consonant, in *one of two ways*—

1) By prefixing the *initial consonant plus Epsilon* to verbs beginning with a single consonant or a mute and liquid, e.g. λέλυκα, γέγραφα (γράφω), κέκρικα (κρίνω).

(Note that an initial rough mute is changed to a smooth mute πέφευγα.)

2) By prefixing *Epsilon only* (like the syllabic augment) to verbs beginning with two consonants (except a mute and liquid), e.g. ἔσπαρμαι (σπείρω), ἐσταύρωμαι (σταυρόω).

b. **Temporal reduplication:** which increases the time or length of the first syllable by *lengthening an initial vowel or diphthong* (like the temporal augment), e.g. ἠγάπηκα (ἀγαπάω), ἤλπικα (ἐλπίζω), ὥρισμαι (ὁρίζω), ᾔτηκα (αἰτέω), ᾠκοδόμημαι (οἰκοδομέω).

(Note that the *pluperfect*, as a secondary tense of the perfect system, adds *augment to reduplication*, at least where augment is possible, e.g. ἐλελύκειν (λύω), ᾐτήκειν (αἰτέω).)

3. In the case of *composite verbs* (verbs with a prepositional or adverbial prefix), *augment* and/or *reduplication* take place as follows:

a. Augment and/or reduplication **follow a prepositional prefix,** e.g. ἀπέλυσα (ἀπολύω), καταβέβηκα (καταβαίνω).

b. They are **applied to an adverbial prefix** or are omitted, e.g.: ἠδίκησα (ἀδικέω), ηὐ(εὐ)λόγηκα (εὐλογέω), but εὐηγγέλισα (p. 96).

C. FEATURES FOLLOWING THE STEM: system signs, variable vowels, endings—

 1. *System signs:* Helpful clues for recognizing certain systems of the verb, especially the regular verb, e.g.:
 a. **Future system:** adds Sigma (σ) after the stem—λύσω, λύσομαι. (Note that this is also true of the future passive: λυθήσομαι.)
 b. **Aorist system:** adds Sigma Alpha (σα) after the stem—ἔλυσα, ἐλυσαμην, ἤκουσα (ἀκούω), ἐποίησα (ποιέω).
 c. **Perfect system:** adds Kappa Alpha (κα) after the stem in the *perfect,* Kappa Epsilon Iota (κει) in the *pluperfect*—λέλυκα, ἐλελύκειν, ἠγάπηκα (ἀγαπάω), ἐβεβλήκειν (βάλλω).
 d. **Passive system:** adds Theta Eta (θη) after the stem—ἐλύθην, λυθήσομαι; ἠγέρθην, ἐγερθήσομαι (ἐγείρω).

 2. *Variable vowels:* Omicron/Epsilon (o/ε) between stem/sign & endings:
 a. **In the indicative of the regular verb,** the variable vowels (o/ε) occur in the *present system* (present and imperfect), the *future system,* and the *future passive tense*—λύομεν, λύετε, ἔλυον; λύσομεν, λύσετε, λύσομαι; λυθήσομαι, λυθήσεσθε.
 b. **These same vowels** (o/ε) are added *between the stem or the system sign* and the *original endings,* and are often united with these endings to form the *developed endings* found in NT Greek—λύ+o+μι = λύω, λύ+ε+σι = λύεις, λύ+ε+τι = λύει, κτλ.
 c. **The vowel omicron** (o) is added *before endings beginning in Mu or Nu* (μ, ν)—λύομεν, λύομαι; ἔλυον, ἐλυόμην, κτλ.
 d. **The vowel Epsilon** (ε) is added *before all other endings*—λύετε, λύεσθε; ἔλυε, ἐλύετε, ἐλύετο; λύσεσθε, λυθήσεται.

 3. *Endings:* Primary and secondary, indicating person and number—
 a. **Importance:** As necessary as it is to know the declension endings of nouns, pronouns, and adjectives, it is *still more necessary* to know the verbal endings which are used, with few exceptions, all through the inflection or conjugation of the verb.
 b. **History:** The endings of the regular verb in NT Greek *evolved* in some instances *from earlier endings* (still used in "Mi-Verbs"), largely through interaction with the variable vowels.
 c. In the following list, we will **emphasize NT endings** but indicate the primitive endings in parentheses, leaving the explanation of their evolution to the teacher. (Cf. *Teaching Aids* at the end of book.)

PRIMARY ENDINGS		SECONDARY ENDINGS	
Active	**Mid-Pass.**	**Active**	**Mid-Pass.**
Singular		Singular	
1. ω (μι)	μαι	1. ν	μην
2. εις (σι)	η (σαι)	2. ς	ου/ω (σο)
3. ει (τι)	ται	3. —	το
Plural		Plural	
1. μεν	μεθα	1. μεν	μεθα
2. τε	σθε	2. τε	σθε
3. ουσι (νσι)	νται	3. ν/σαν	ντο

V. **Synopsis of the regular verb** in the *indicative mood*, according to *systems:* (abbreviations: A = Augment, R = Reduplication, ST = Stem, S = System Sign, V = Variable Vowels, PE = Primary Endings, SE = Secondary Endings.)

A. THE PRESENT SYSTEM: present and imperfect tenses—

1. *The present tense:* ST + V + PE (λύ + ο/ε + μι = λύ + ω)

	Active			**Mid-Pass.**	
	Sing.	Plur.		Sing.	Plur.
1.	λύω	λύομεν	1.	λύομαι	λυόμεθα
2.	λύεις	λύετε	2.	λύῃ	λύεσθε
3.	λύει	λύουσι	3.	λύεται	λύονται

2. *The imperfect tense:* A + ST + V + SE (ἔ + λυ + ο/ε + ν)

	Active			**Mid-Pass.**	
	Sing.	Plur.		Sing.	Plur.
1.	ἔλυον	ἐλύομεν	1.	ἐλυόμην	ἐλυόμεθα
2.	ἔλυες	ἐλύετε	2.	ἐλύου	ἐλύεσθε
3.	ἔλυε	ἔλυον	3.	ἐλύετο	ἐλύοντο

B. THE FUTURE AND AORIST SYSTEMS: future and aorist tenses, active-middle:

1. *The future tense:* ST + S + V + PE (λύ + σ + ο/ε + μι = λύ + σ + ω)

	Active			**Middle**	
	Sing.	Plur.		Sing.	Plur.
1.	λύσω	λύσομεν	1.	λύσομαι	λυσόμεθα
2.	λύσεις	λύσετε	2.	λύσῃ	λύσεσθε
3.	λύσει	λύσουσι	3.	λύσεται	λύσονται

2. *The aorist tense:* A + ST + S + SE ($\check{\epsilon}$ + λυ + σα + ν = $\check{\epsilon}$ + λυ + σα)

	Active			**Middle**	
	Sing.	Plur.		Sing.	Plur.
1.	ἔλυσα	ἐλύσαμεν	1.	ἐλυσάμην	ἐλυσάμεθα
2.	ἔλυσας	ἐλύσατε	2.	ἐλύσω	ἐλύσασθε
3.	ἔλυσε	ἔλυσαν	3.	ἐλύσατο	ἐλύσαντο

C. THE PERFECT SYSTEMS: perfect and pluperfect active; perfect middle-passive.

1. *The perfect tense:* R + ST + S + PE (λε + λύ + κα + μι = λέ + λυ + κα)

	Sing. (cf. aorist sing.)		Plural
1.	λέλυκα	1.	λελύκαμεν
2.	λέλυκας	2.	λελύκατε
3.	λέλυκε	3.	λελύκασι

2. *The pluperfect tense:* A + R + ST + S + SE ($\grave{\epsilon}$ + λε + λύ + κει + ν)

	Sing.		Plural
1.	ἐλελύκειν	1.	ἐλελύκειμεν
2.	ἐλελύκεις	2.	ἐλελύκειτε
3.	ἐλελύκει	3.	ἐλελύκεισαν

3. *The perfect middle and passive:* R + ST + PE (λέ + λυ + μαι)

	Sing.		Plural
1.	λέλυμαι	1.	λελύμεθα
2.	λέλυσαι	2.	λέλυσθε
3.	λέλυται	3.	λέλυνται

D. THE PASSIVE SYSTEM: aorist and future passive tenses—

1. *The aorist passive tense:* A + ST + S + SE ($\grave{\epsilon}$ + λύ + θη + ν)

	Sing.		Plural
1.	ἐλύθην	1.	ἐλύθημεν
2.	ἐλύθης	2.	ἐλύθητε
3.	ἐλύθη	3.	ἐλύθησαν

(*Note* that the *aorist passive tense* always uses the *active endings.*)

2. *The future passive tense:* ST + S + S + V + PE (λυ + θή + σ + ο/ε + μαι)

	Sing.		Plural
1.	λυθήσομαι	1.	λυθησόμεθα
2.	λυθήσῃ	2.	λυθήσεσθε
3.	λυθήσεται	3.	λυθήσονται

VI. **Vocabulary:** Verbs of the "regular type" most frequently used in the New Testament.

A. INTRODUCTION:

   1. In comparison with other types of verbs, the so-called "regular type" (with *unchanging stem*) has *very few examples* of frequent New Testament usage.

   2. Even of these few examples, there are "irregularities" to be noted:

   a. Some are **defective,** i.e., lacking one or more principal parts, either *omitted* altogether or put in *parentheses* (if there is no NT usage).

   b. Some are **deponent,** i.e., lacking active forms in one, more, or all of the principal parts, but *middle and/or passive forms have active meaning, or middle forms have active meaning while passive forms retain their passive meaning,* e.g. ἀκούσῃ, ἀκούσθησῃ: you will hear, you will be heard.

   c. Some simply have an **individual irregular principal part:** ἀκήκοα = I have heard.

B. THE PRINCIPAL "REGULAR VERBS" (underlining indicates "irregularities"):

   1. **ἀκούω,** ἀκούσω/ἀκούσομαι, ἤκουσα, ἀκήκοα, (ἤκουσμαι), ἠκούσθην: I hear, listen (acoustic)—with genitive/ accusative = mere hearing/understanding.

   2. **θεραπεύω,** θεραπεύσω, ἐθεράπευσα, (τεθεράπευκα), τεθεράπευμαι, ἐθεραπεύθην: I heal, cure (therapeutic, therapy).

   3. **πιστεύω,** (πιστεύσω), ἐπίστευσα, πεπίστευκα, πεπίστευμαι, ἐπιστεύθην: I believe, trust—with dative or εἰς + acc.

   4. **πορεύομαι,** πορεύσομαι, ἐπορευσάμην, πεπόρευμαι, ἐπορεύθην: I proceed, go (pore, porous, emporium).

   5. Also, *composite verbs,* e.g.: **ἀπολύω** (I free, release, dismiss) **ὑπακούω** (I heed, obey—with the dative)

VII. Exercises:

A. To test knowledge of this chapter, try to conjugate *from memory* the *indicative forms* of these verbs: ἀπολύω, πιστεύω, ὑπακούω.

B. Note that verb accents can *recede* back to the *prepositional prefix,* but not beyond the augment or reduplication, e.g.: ὑπῆγον.

C.   Finally, for practice in recognition, identify *from memory* the following forms, according to this *model:*

λύουσι: from λύω (λυ)—present indicative active, third person plural = they loose, are loosing.

1. λύει:

2. λύσει:

3. ἔλυσε:

4. λέλυσθε:

5. λυθήσῃ:

6. ἐλύθη:

7. ἔλυε:

8. ἐλύσατε:

9. ἐλύσατο:

10. ἐλελύκειτε:

11. ἐλυσάμην:

12. ἐλύσαμεν:

(Note: Please use this same model in identifying verb forms in the future.)

7 The Regular Verb—Part II

Usage of the Indicative

I. Introduction:

A. As already indicated on p. 25, the indicative is the *principal and most direct mood,* all others being referred to as subordinate or oblique moods.

B. We need not treat simple sentences or principal (independent) clauses in the indicative, their syntax being rather obvious. Instead, we will concentrate on a variety of SUBORDINATE CLAUSES in the indicative, which can be conveniently divided into **substantive clauses** and **adverbial clauses.**

C. In addition, it is important to note that there is a BASIC DIFFERENCE between the indicative and the oblique moods in their **use of negatives,** the indicative employing οὐ (κ, χ), p. 26, while the others normally use μή.

II. Substantive clauses: These are *noun or pronoun clauses* which represent a *substantive* rather than an adverbial idea; that is, they constitute, agree with, or modify the *subject or object* of the sentence rather than the verb, e.g. compare: "I do not <u>know when</u> he will come" with "<u>When</u> he comes, I <u>will go</u>."

A. NOUN CLAUSES: These are *statements* or *questions* which are equivalent to a noun as the *object of verbs of thinking, knowing, saying* or of *asking, inquiring, wondering.* They are divided into:

1. *Direct and indirect statements:*
a. **Direct statements** follow verbs of *thinking, knowing,* or *saying,* with either nothing or some form of punctuation between, e.g. εἶπεν αὐτῇ ὁ Ἰησοῦς, Ἐγώ εἰμι ἡ ἀνάστασις καὶ ἡ ζωή = Jesus said to her (Martha): "I am the resurrection and the life." (Jn. 11:25)
b. **Indirect statements** follow *the same verbs,* but are *introduced by a conjunction* ὅτι (that), e.g. πεπιστεύκατε ὅτι ἐγὼ παρὰ τοῦ θεοῦ ἐξῆλθον = <u>you have believed</u> <u>that</u> I came forth from (the

side of) God. (Jn. 16:27) (Direct statement: I came forth from God.)

c. **In practice,** however, there is often little difference because:

1) The conjunction ὅτι can often be understood as equivalent to a colon, introducing a direct statement, e.g. λέγει αὐτοῖς ὅτι <u>ἦραν</u> τὸν κύριόν μου = She (Mary Magdalene) says to them<u>:</u> "<u>They have taken away</u> my lord." (Jn. 20:13)

2) Indirect statements use *exactly the same tense* as would the equivalent direct statement, e.g. οὐκ <u>ᾔδει</u> ὅτι Ἰησοῦς <u>ἐστιν</u> = she <u>did not know that</u> it <u>was</u> Jesus (Jn. 20:14). (Direct statement: "<u>It is</u> Jesus.") (See also direct and indirect use in Jn. 21:7.)

2. *Direct and indirect questions:*

a. **Direct questions** normally follow verbs of *asking or saying* and are usually *introduced* by one of the following *interrogative expressions:*

1) *The interrogative pronoun:* τίς, τί (who, which, what, why?), which will be declined later according to the third declension, e.g. Σαοὺλ Σαούλ, <u>τί</u> με διώκεις; εἶπεν δέ, Τίς εἶ, κύριε; = Saul, Saul, <u>why</u> are you pursuing (persecuting) me? But he said: "<u>Who</u> are you, lord (sir)?" (Acts 9:4)

2) *Interrogative adverbs,* among which the most important are:

a) **The negatives** οὐ and μή, the former expecting an affirmative, the latter a negative answer, e.g.: Οὐκ εἰπόν σοι . . . ; = Did I <u>not</u> say to you . . . ? (Jn. 11:40) Μὴ καὶ ὑμεῖς θέλετε ὑπάγειν; = Do even you wish to go away? (Jn. 6:67)

b) **The conjunctions** πότε (when?), ποῦ (where?), πῶς (how?), e.g. λέγει αὐτῷ Σίμων Πέτρος, Κύριε, <u>ποῦ</u> ὑπάγεις; = Simon Peter says to him: "Lord, <u>where</u> are you going (away)?" (Jn. 13:26)

b. **Indirect questions** normally follow verbs of *asking, wondering, knowing,* or *saying* and are usually introduced by one of the following interrogative expressions:

1) *The interrogative pronoun* τίς, τί (who, which, what, why?), e.g. Οὐκ οἶδα <u>τί</u> λέγεις = I do not know <u>what</u> you are saying! (The direct question would be: "What are you saying?") (Mt. 26:70)

2) *Interrogative conjunctions,* especially:

a) **The conjunction** εἰ (if, whether—much as in English), e.g. Πιλᾶτος . . . ἐπηρώτησεν <u>εἰ</u> ὁ ἄνθρωπος Γαλιλαῖός ἐστιν = Pilate . . . asked <u>if</u> the man were a Galilean.

(Lk. 23:6) The direct question would be: "Is the man a Galilean?"

b) **The conjunctions** πότε (when?), ποῦ (where?), πῶς (how?), e.g. Κύριε, οὐκ οἴδαμεν ποῦ ὑπάγεις = Lord, we do not know <u>where</u> you are going. (Jn. 14:4) Direct: Where are you going?

c. As with direct and indirect statements, but to a lesser extent, the **distinction between direct and indirect questions** is not always sharply drawn, especially since:
1) The same interrogative expressions are used for both.
2) The same tense is used in indirect as in direct questions.
3) Indirect questions are always reducible to direct questions, as exemplified in the samples given above.

B. PRONOUN CLAUSES: Commonly called "relative clauses" and *introduced by a relative pronoun,* these clauses refer or *relate back* to the subject or object of the principal clause as their *antecedent.*

1. As already explained on page 18, the relative pronoun *agrees* with its antecedent *in gender, number, and case,* but admits of some important exceptions, which should be reviewed at this time.

2. *Relative clauses are divided into:*
a. **Simple or definite relative clauses,** which employ the simple or definite relative pronoun ὅς, ἥ, ὅ (who, which, what, that), e.g. Ῥαββί, ὃς ἦν μετὰ σοῦ πέραν τοῦ Ἰορδάνου, ᾧ σὺ μεμαρτύρηκας, ἴδε οὗτος βαπτίζει = Rabbi, (the one) <u>who</u> was with you across the Jordan, <u>to whom</u> you have witnessed, look! he is baptizing!
(Jn. 3:26)
b. **Indefinite relative clauses,** which use the indefinite relative pronoun ὅστις, ἥτις, ὅ τι (whoever, whichever, whatever), formed from a combination of the simple relative and the indefinite pronoun τις, τι (someone, anyone; something, anything), e.g. Μακάριος ὅστις φάγεται ἄρτον ἐν τῇ βασιλείᾳ τοῦ θεοῦ = Blessed is <u>whoever</u> will eat bread in the kingdom of God! (Lk. 14:15)
c. **Conditional relative clauses,** which use either the simple or the indefinite relative pronoun, but which (since they follow the usage of conditional sentences) will be treated under adverbial clauses.

3. Before proceeding to adverbial clauses, it will be helpful to make some *important observations* about the pronouns just mentioned:

a. The interrogative τίς, τί and indefinite τις, τι pronouns are **declined exactly alike, except** for their **accents:**

   1) The *nominative of the interrogative pronoun* τίς, τί always has an *acute accent*, which never becomes grave before another word, e.g. Τί ποιεῖτε = <u>What</u> are you doing? (Mk. 11 : 5)

   2) The *nominative of the indefinite* pronoun τις, τι is always *enclitic*, never taking an accent of any kind, e.g. ἐὰν μή τις γεννηθῇ ἄνωθεν, οὐ δύναται ἰδεῖν τὴν βασιλείαν . . . = Unless <u>one</u> be born from above, he cannot see the kingdom.
   (Jn. 3 : 3)

b. The indefinite relative pronoun ὅστις, ἥτις, ὅ τι:

   1) Is often used instead of the simple relative pronoun ὅς, ἥ, ὅ, without any notable difference of meaning, e.g. μὴ σὺ μείζων εἶ τοῦ πατρὸς ἡμῶν Ἀβραάμ, ὅστις ἀπέθανεν; = Are you greater than our father Abraham, <u>who</u> died? (Jn. 8 : 53)

   2) The **neuter nominative and accusative singular** is sometimes written ὅ τι as here to distinguish it in meaning and usage from the conjunction ὅτι (<u>that</u>, already seen, or <u>because</u>, about to be studied), but actually it is *all the same form*, the neuter of ὅστις with *different meanings*.

c. The declension of interrogative, indefinite, and indefinite relative pronouns will be given in full when we take up the liquid stems of nouns, pronouns, and adjectives of the third declension.

III. **Adverbial clauses:** These are clauses which *refer to the verb* (rather than the subject or object) of the principal clause, express an *adverbial idea*, and are generally introduced by an *adverbial conjunction*. Those which use the *indicative mood* in NT Greek are principally the following:

A. CAUSAL CLAUSES:

   1. These express the *cause or reason* explaining the action, situation, or thought of the principal clause.

   2. They are *most often introduced* by one of the following conjunctions:

   a. ὅτι (because), by far the most common and, as already seen, the same word as ὅτι meaning "that" and ὅτι or ὅ τι (whatever), e.g. Μακάριοι, οἱ πτωχοὶ τῷ πνεύματι, ὅτι αὐτῶν ἐστιν ἡ βασιλεία τῶν οὐρανῶν = Blessed (are) the poor in spirit, <u>because</u> (for) theirs is the kingdom of heaven (the heavens). (Mt. 5 : 3)

b. Other conjunctions, such as: ὡς (as), διότι (διά + ὅτι = on account of this that . . . , because), or ἐπεί, ἐπειδή (since), e.g. Πῶς ἔσται τοῦτο, ἐπεὶ ἄνδρα οὐ γινώσκω; = How will this be, since I do not "know" man? (Lk. 1:34) . . . διότι οὐκ ἦν αὐτοῖς τόπος = . . . because there was no place for them (Lk. 2:7).

B. COMPARATIVE CLAUSES:

1. Closely allied to causal clauses, but *emphasizing a comparison* between two actions or situations.

2. They are normally introduced by such comparative conjunctions as ὡς (as) or some variation of the same such as καθώς, ὥσπερ (as, just as), e.g. καθὼς ἀπέστειλέν με ὁ ζῶν πατὴρ κἀγὼ ζῶ διὰ τὸν πατέρα = Just as the living Father sent me and I live on account of the Father . . . (Jn. 6:57)

C. CONDITIONAL SENTENCES:

1. *Importance:* The special importance of these sentences in NT Greek derives from the fact that:
 a. There are at least **four different types** of conditional sentences, only two of which concern us at this time.
 b. Also, both **conditional relative** sentences and **temporal clauses** follow the pattern of conditional sentences.

2. *General usage of moods* in conditional sentences:
 a. The **indicative,** as might be expected, is used to express:
  1) What is *certain* in *past, present,* or (sometimes) *future.*
  2) What is *unreal* or *contrary-to-fact* in *past* or *present.*
 b. The **subjunctive,** as will be seen later, is used to express:
  1) What is *uncertain* or *undetermined* because still *future.*
  2) What is *undetermined* because *general* rather than particular.

3. *Use of the indicative* in conditional sentences:
 a. **Simple, real,** or **certain** conditions in *past, present,* or *future:*
  1) The *condition* takes εἰ (if) and a past, present, or future tense.
  2) The *conclusion* takes *any appropriate form* of the verb.
  3) *Example:* Εἰ ὁ κόσμος ὑμᾶς μισεῖ, γινώσκετε ὅτι ἐμὲ πρῶτον ὑμῶν μεμίσηκεν = If the world hates you, know (imperative) that it has hated me before you. (Jn. 15:18) (cf. p. 52: F,1,c.)
 b. Conditions **unreal** or **contrary-to-fact** in *past* or *present:*
  1) The *condition* takes εἰ (if) and a *secondary tense:* the Imperfect for present or continued past time; the Aorist for single past time.

2) The *conclusion* takes ἄν (untranslatable, but close to "would"), and a *secondary tense:* Imperfect or Aorist as above.

3) *Example:* εἰ ἐκ τοῦ κόσμου ἦτε, ὁ κόσμος ἄν τὸ ἴδιον ἐφίλει.
= If you <u>were</u> from the world, the world <u>would love</u> its own.
(Jn. 15:19) (Imperfect tense in both clauses.)

D. CONDITIONAL RELATIVE SENTENCES:

1. These are sentences with *relative clauses* which contain an *implied condition,* and hence they follow the pattern of conditional sentences.

2. They replace εἰ with: a) a *relative pronoun:* ὅς, ἥ, ὅ; b) an *indefinite relative:* ὅστις; or c) a *pronominal adjective.* (cf. pp. 18, 34, 49)

3. *Example:* ὅστις οὐ βαστάζει τὸν σταυρὸν ἑαυτοῦ καὶ ἔρχεται ὀπίσω μου οὐ δύναται εἶναί μου μαθητής. <u>Whoever</u> does not <u>carry</u> his (own) cross and <u>come</u> after me <u>cannot</u> be my disciple. (Lk. 14:27) (N.B. The implied condition is: if <u>anyone</u> does not . . . : <u>εἰ τις</u> . . .)

E. TEMPORAL CLAUSES:

1. These also contain, though not as clearly, *implied conditions* and so they also follow the pattern of conditional sentences.

2. Instead of εἰ (if), they use one of several temporal conjunctions, e.g. ὅτε, ὡς, ἐπεί (when), ἐν ᾧ (while), ἕως (while, until).

3. *Example:* Ὅτε οὖν ἤκουσεν ὁ Πιλᾶτος τοῦτον τὸν λόγον, μᾶλλον ἐφοβήθη = <u>When</u>, then, Pilate <u>heard</u> this word, he <u>feared</u> the more. (Jn. 19:8)

F. ADDITIONAL INDICATIVE USES: These are less frequent and important, but are included here for the sake of completeness and understanding:

1. *Concessive clauses:*
a. These are really conditional clauses, following **conditional usage.**
b. They are characterized by the addition of καί (and, even), usually placed after the conjunction εἰ (if), the combination taking on the meaning of: although, even though, though, even if.
c. **Example** Εἰ καὶ πάντες σκανδαλισθήσονται, ἀλλ᾽ οὐκ ἐγώ. = <u>Although</u> <u>(Even if)</u> all <u>will be scandalized</u>, yet not I! (Mk. 14:29)

2. *Result clauses:*
a. These are **exceptions** to the use of the **infinitive to express result.**
b. They are **introduced** by the conjunction ὥστε (ὡς + τέ = and so, so that) usually translated "so that" in dependent clauses and "Therefore," "And so," "Hence" in independent clauses.
c. **Example:** Οὕτως γὰρ ἠγάπησεν ὁ θεὸς τὸν κόσμον, ὥστε τὸν υἱὸν τὸν μονογενῆ ἔδωκεν . . . = For God so loved the world that he gave his only-begotten son . . . (Jn. 3 : 16)

IV. **Exercise:** These sentences are carefully chosen to exemplify both the *verbs* and *verb forms* already studied and the *usage of the indicative mood.* Teachers are encouraged to assign different sentences to different students, for the sake of greater sharing and learning without overburdening anyone.

1. Πᾶς οὖν ὅστις ἀκούει μου τοὺς λόγους τούτους καὶ ποιεῖ αὐτοὺς

Everyone   does

   ὁμοιωθήσεται ἀνδρὶ φρονίμῳ, ὅστις ᾠκοδόμησεν αὐτοῦ τὴν

will be likened   to a man   wise   built

   οἰκίαν ἐπὶ τὴν πέτραν.

rock

2. οὐδὲ ἀκούσει τις ἐν ταῖς πλατείαις τὴν φωνὴν αὐτοῦ.

nor   wide streets

3. καὶ ἐξῆλθεν ἀπ᾽ αὐτοῦ τὸ δαιμόνιον· καὶ ἐθεραπεύθη ὁ παῖς ἀπὸ

went out   boy

   τῆς ὥρας ἐκείνης.

4. σπλαγχνισθεὶς δὲ ὁ κύριος τοῦ δούλου ἐκείνου ἀπέλυσεν αὐτόν . . .

moved with pity

5. Καὶ ἠκολούθησαν αὐτῷ ὄχλοι πολλοί, καὶ ἐθεράπευσεν αὐτοὺς

followed   many

   ἐκεῖ.

6. λέγει αὐτῷ ὁ Πιλᾶτος, Οὐκ ἀκούεις πόσα σου καταμαρτυρουσιν;

says   Pilate   they witness against

7. Τίς ἄρα οὗτός ἐστιν ὅτι καὶ ὁ ἄνεμος καὶ ἡ θάλασσα ὑπακούει

   αὐτῷ;

8. ἤρξαντο τοὺς κακῶς ἔχοντας περιφέρειν ὅπου ἤκουον ὅτι ἐστίν.

they began   sick or ill   to carry about

9. Νῦν ἀπολύεις τὸν δοῦλόν σου . . . κατὰ τὸ ῥῆμά σου ἐν εἰρήνῃ.

word

10. ὅσα ἠκούσαμεν γενόμενα εἰς* τὴν Καφαρναοὺμ ποίησον καὶ

were done   Capernaum   do

    ὧδε ἐν τῇ πατρίδι.

hometown

*Note that the prepositions εἰς (into) and ἐν (in) are sometimes used interchangeably in NT Greek.

11. ἐπορεύθη εἰς πόλιν . . . καὶ συνεπορεύοντο αὐτῷ οἱ μαθηταὶ
    city

    αὐτοῦ καὶ ὄχλος πολυς.
    great

12. τίς δέ ἐστιν οὗτος περὶ οὗ ἀκούω τοιαῦτα;

13. ὅσα ἐν τῇ σκοτίᾳ εἴπατε ἐν τῷ φωτὶ ἀκουσθήσεται.
    darkness   you said   light

14. Εἰ Μωϋσέως καὶ τῶν προφητῶν οὐκ ἀκούουσιν, οὐδ' ἐάν* τις ἐκ
    Moses   not even if

    νεκρῶν ἀναστῇ πεισθήσονται.
    rises   will they be persuaded

15. Εἰ ἔχετε** πίστιν ὡς κόκκον σινάπεως, ἐλέγετε ἂν τῇ
    have   grain of mustard seed,   you would say

    συκαμίνῳ . . . Ἐκριζώθητι καὶ φυτεύθητι ἐν τῇ θαλάσσῃ· καὶ
    sycamore   Be uprooted   planted

    ὑπήκουσεν ἂν ὑμῖν.

16. ἐπίστευσεν ὁ ἄνθρωπος τῷ λόγῳ ὃν εἶπεν αὐτῷ ὁ Ἰησοῦς καὶ
    spoke

    ἐπορεύετο.

17. διὰ τοῦτο οὖν μᾶλλον ἐζήτουν αὐτὸν . . . ἀποκτεῖναι, ὅτι οὐ
    the more   they sought   to kill

    μόνον ἔλυεν τὸ σάββατον ἀλλὰ καὶ πατέρα ἴδιον ἔλεγεν τὸν
    only   father   was calling

    θεόν.

18. ἀμὴν ἀμὴν λέγω ὑμῖν ὅτι ἔρχεται ὥρα καὶ νῦν ἐστιν ὅτε οἱ
    I say   is coming   is

    νεκροὶ ἀκούσουσιν τῆς φωνῆς τοῦ υἱοῦ τοῦ θεοῦ . . .

19. εἰ γὰρ ἐπιστεύετε Μωϋσεῖ, ἐπιστεύετε ἂν ἐμοί . . .
    Moses

20. πεπιστεύκαμεν καὶ ἐγνώκαμεν ὅτι σὺ εἶ ὁ ἅγιος τοῦ θεοῦ.
    have known   are

21. μή τις ἐκ τῶν ἀρχόντων ἐπίστευσεν εἰς αὐτὸν . . . ;
    rulers

22. ἐγὼ δὲ ὅτι τὴν ἀλήθειαν λέγω, οὐ πιστεύετέ μοι . . . εἰ
    say

    ἀλήθειαν λέγω, διὰ τί ὑμεῖς οὐ πιστεύετέ μοι;

*The conjunction ἐάν (if) introduces another type of conditional
sentence, with the subjunctive, which will be studied in the
following chapter.
**This is an interesting example of a *mixed construction*,
combining a primary tense with two secondary tenses, all in the
indicative.

23. Ἤκουσεν Ἰησοῦς ὅτι ἐξέβαλον αὐτὸν ἔξω, καὶ εὑρὼν αὐτὸν
               they had cast out   finding

    εἶπεν, Σὺ πιστεύεις εἰς τὸν υἱὸν τοῦ ἀνθρώπου;
    said

24. ἔλεγον δὲ πολλοὶ ἐξ αὐτῶν, Δαιμόνιον ἔχει καὶ μαίνεται· τί
    said   many   he has   is mad

    αὐτοῦ ἀκούετε; ἄλλοι ἔλεγον, . . . μὴ δαιμόνιον δύναται τυφλῶν
                                       is able

    ὀφθαλμοὺς ἀνοῖξαι;
             to open

25. οὐκέτι λέγω ὑμᾶς δούλους, ὅτι ὁ δοῦλος οὐκ οἶδεν τί ποιεῖ
      I call   knows   does

    αὐτοῦ ὁ κύριος· ὑμᾶς δὲ εἴρηκα φίλους, ὅτι πάντα ἃ ἤκουσα
                     I have called   all things

    παρὰ τοῦ πατρός μου ἐγνώρισα ὑμῖν.
         father   I made known

8 The Regular Verb—Part III

Forms and Usage of the Subjunctive

I. Introduction:

A. Having studied the forms and usage of the indicative mood of the regular verb, we are now in a position to examine the *subordinate or oblique moods* by means of comparison and contrast with the indicative.

B. Of the OBLIQUE MOODS, we will study the most important, the *subjunctive,* in this chapter, reserving the imperative and infinitive for the following chapter and the participle until we study the third declension.

C. Our study in this chapter will comprise both the FORMATION and the USAGE of the *subjunctive,* together with carefully chosen examples and exercises designed to provide an effective knowledge of this important mood.

II. Formation of the subjunctive mood:

A. GENERAL UNDERSTANDING OF THE SUBJUNCTIVE:

  1. The subjunctive is rightly studied in comparison with the indicative, because it exists and functions *subordinate* and *auxiliary* to that mood.

  2. The subjunctive is a *primary mood* expressing *future or uncertain time,* a fact which will help us greatly to understand its characteristics.

B. VOICES AND TENSES IN THE SUBJUNCTIVE:

  1. *Like* the indicative, the subjunctive uses *all three voices.*

  2. *Unlike* the indicative, the subjunctive uses *only two tenses:*
  a. It **does not include:**
    1) The *imperfect* and *pluperfect,* which are secondary to the present and perfect respectively and confined to the indicative mood.

2) The *future,* unnecessary because the entire mood is future.

3) The *perfect,* which simply dropped out of usage in NT Greek.

b. It **does include** the present and aorist, which, however, **do not express time as such** but rather **aspect or duration** of future or uncertain time, as follows:

1) The *present* tense expresses *continued or repeated* action.

2) The *aorist* tense expresses *single or momentary* action.

(NB: This is a **distinction of great importance,** as will be seen.)

C. VERBAL FEATURES IN THE SUBJUNCTIVE:

1. The *basic feature,* of course, is the *root or stem,* which is the same in the present and aorist subjunctive as in those tenses of the indicative.

2. *Features before the stem:* None, neither augment nor reduplication—

a. There is **no augment** because the subjunctive is a primary mood, and also because augment is confined to the indicative mood anyway.

b. There is **no reduplication,** which is characteristic of the perfect systems, because the perfect has dropped out of the subjunctive.

3. *Features after the stem:* system signs, variable vowels, and endings—

a. **System signs:**

1) The *present* subjunctive, like the indicative, *has no system sign.*

2) The *aorist has system signs* resembling those in the indicative:

a) **Aorist active and middle:** Sigma (σ) instead of σα.

b) **Aorist passive:** Theta Epsilon (θε) instead of θη, the Epsilon (ε) being *absorbed* into the variable vowel and ending, the *contraction* being indicated by a *circumflex accent.*

b. **Variable vowels:**

1) Both the *present* and *aorist,* as tenses of a primary mood, have variable vowels as do the present and future indicative systems.

2) However, the *variable vowels are lengthened,* from o/ε as in the indicative to ω/η in the subjunctive.

c. **Endings:**

1) As a primary mood, the subjunctive uses the *primary*

endings, already studied on p. 43, the *developed endings* being seen *below.*

2) As in the indicative, the *aorist passive* uses the *active endings.*

III. Synopsis of the Regular Verb λύω (loose, destroy) **in the Subjunctive Mood:**

	PRESENT		AORIST		AOR. PASS.
	Act.	**M-P.**	**Act.**	**Mid.**	
	Sing.		Sing.		Sing.
1.	λύω	λύωμαι	λύσω	λύσωμαι	λυθῶ
2.	λύῃς	λύῃ	λύσῃς	λύσῃ	λυθῇς
3.	λύῃ	λύηται	λύσῃ	λύσηται	λυθῇ
	Plur.		Plur.		Plur.
1.	λύωμεν	λυώμεθα	λύσωμεν	λυσώμεθα	λυθῶμεν
2.	λύητε	λύησθε	λύσητε	λύσησθε	λυθῆτε
3.	λύωσι	λύωνται	λύσωσι	λύσωνται	λυθῶσι

(Note the great similarity among the three systems in the subjunctive, as well as the similarity between the aorist subjunctive and the future indicative.)

IV. Usage of the Subjunctive Mood:

A. INTRODUCTION:

1. *In general:* The subjunctive as a whole strongly implies the *future,* the *uncertain,* the *indeterminate,* the *tentative.*
a. Hence the **use of tenses to indicate,** not time, but **aspect.**
b. Hence also a tendency in NT Greek to **interchange** the *subjunctive* and the *future indicative,* even the forms contributing thereto.

2. *Negation:*
a. As already seen, the indicative normally uses οὐ as its negative.
b. The **subjunctive,** as an oblique mood, uses μή as its negative, e.g. Εἰς ὁδὸν ἐθνῶν μὴ ἀπέλθητε = Go <u>not</u> into the way of pagans (Mt. 10:5).
c. **For greater emphasis,** both negatives may be used, almost exclusively with the *subjunctive,* e.g. τὸ ποτήριον ὃ δέδωκέν μοι ὁ πατὴρ οὐ μὴ πίω αὐτό; = the cup which the (my) Father has given (to) me (to drink), shall I <u>not</u> drink it? (Jn. 18:11) (cf. p. 52:E, 2)

3. *Use of tenses in the subjunctive:*
a. As already indicated, tenses in the subjunctive do not express time past, present, or future **but rather aspect or duration of action.**

1) Thus, the *present* expresses *continued or repeated* action, e.g.: Ὅταν δὲ νηστεύητε, μὴ γίνεσθε ὡς οἱ ὑποκριταὶ . . . = But when(ever) you pray, do not be(come) like the hypocrites . . . (Mt. 6:16)

2) On the other hand, the *aorist* indicates *single or momentary* action, e.g. μὴ οὖν μεριμνήσητε εἰς τὴν αὔριον = do not be anxious (even once, at all) about tomorrow. (Mt. 6:34)

b. This is an **extremely important distinction,** which will have many applications in both the subjunctive and the other oblique moods.

4. *Major uses of the subjunctive:*

a. The subjunctive mood in NT Greek is used in **two principal ways:**

1) *Independent expressions,* which emphasize the *future and tentative* nature of the subjunctive.

2) *Dependent clauses,* which emphasize both the future or tentative nature of the subjunctive *and also its subordinate-oblique* role.

b. Both of these major uses will now be considered in turn, beginning with the first, which is **less common but also far simpler.**

B. INDEPENDENT USES OF THE SUBJUNCTIVE:

1. The subjunctive can be used *independently of any other clause,* particularly in expressions containing a future or tentative idea, e.g.:

a. **Deliberation:** Τί φάγωμεν; = What shall we eat? (Mt. 6:31)

b. **Tentative inquiry:** ἕτερον προσδοκῶμεν; = shall we expect another? (Mt. 11:3)

c. **Exhortation:** ἄγωμεν πρὸς αὐτόν = let us go to him. (Jn. 11:15)

2. In NT as in classical Greek, a favorite usage is that of the *aorist subjunctive with the negative μή in prohibitions* instead of the much harsher aorist imperative, e.g. καὶ μὴ εἰσενέγκῃς ἡμᾶς εἰς πειρασμόν = and lead us not into temptation. (Mt. 6:13)

C. DEPENDENT USES OF THE SUBJUNCTIVE: The subjunctive is commonly used in dependent or subordinate clauses, especially adverbial clauses containing a *future, tentative, uncertain,* or *indeterminate* idea, e.g.:

1. *Purpose (final) clauses:* which state the *purpose or end* of an action, whose fulfillment will, by implication, take place at some future time.

a. **Purpose clauses** in NT Greek are usually introduced by the conjunction ἵνα (that, so that, in order that), or by the negative ἵνα μή or simply μή (lest, so that . . . not), or less often by ὅπως or ὅπως μή, with the same meaning, e.g. Ἄγωμεν καὶ ἡμεῖς ἵνα ἀποθάνωμεν μετ᾽ αὐτοῦ = Let us also go <u>so that we may die</u> with him. (Jn. 11:16)

b. Because of the close **affinity between purpose and result,** ἵνα with the subjunctive sometimes expresses the latter, e.g. Ῥαββί, τίς ἥμαρτεν ἵνα τυφλὸς γεννηθῇ; = Rabbi, who (has) sinned, (with the result) <u>that he was born</u> blind? (Jn. 9:2)

c. Finally, by way of extension, ἵνα and the subjunctive may also express *content* (like a noun clause or infinitive), e.g. αὕτη ἐστὶν ἡ ἐντολὴ ἡ ἐμή, ἵνα ἀγαπᾶτε ἀλλήλους = this is my command, <u>that you love</u> one another. (Jn. 15:12)

2. *Conditional sentences:*

a. In our study of the subjunctive in conditional sentences, it will be helpful to review what has already been presented on pages 51–52.

b. The subjunctive is used in conditional sentences primarily to state **what is tentative or undetermined** because future or general, hence:

   1) *Future particular conditions* are structured as follows:
      a) The **condition** takes ἐάν (εἰ + ἄν) with the subjunctive.
      b) The **conclusion** takes *any form*, usually the future indicative.
      c) **Example:** ἐὰν γὰρ μὴ ἀπέλθω, ὁ παράκλητος οὐκ ἐλεύσεται πρὸς ὑμᾶς = for <u>if</u> I do <u>not</u> go away, the Paraclete <u>will not come</u> to you (Jn. 16:7).

   2) *General conditions* are structured as follows:
      a) The **condition** takes ἐάν with the *subjunctive*.
      b) The **conclusion** uses any *appropriate form* of the verb.
      c) **Example:** ἐὰν ἐμοί τις διακονῇ, ἐμοὶ ἀκολουθείτω = If anyone <u>ministers</u> to me, <u>let him follow</u> me (Jn. 12:26).

3. *Conditional relative sentences:*

a. As already seen, **these are implied conditions** couched in the form of relative clauses.

b. Hence, in **future particular conditions** and in **general conditions:**

   1) The εἰ of ἐάν is replaced by the simple relative pronoun ὅς or the indefinite relative pronoun ὅστις.

   2) The ἄν of ἐάν remains, thus indicating a future particular condition or a general condition and alerting the reader to expect the subjunctive. (But sometimes ἐάν remains intact.)

c. **Example:** ὃς ἂν θέλῃ ἐν ὑμῖν εἶναι πρῶτος, ἔσται πάντων δοῦλος
= (he) who <u>wishes</u> to be first among you <u>will be</u> the slave of all
(Mk. 10:44). (NB: Contrast with unreal conditions, p. 52.)

4. *Temporal clauses:*

a. These, too, are implied conditions, though less evidently so;
hence, they also **follow the pattern of conditional sentences.**

b. **When referring to future time** (or general time), then, the
subjunctive is used, and the *conjunction* can take any of
several forms:

  1) The εἰ of ἐάν is replaced by a *temporal particle,* usually ὅτε
  (when) or ἕως (until), the ἄν remaining, e.g.: ἀμὴν γὰρ λέγω
  ὑμῖν, ἕως ἂν παρέλθῃ ὁ οὐρανὸς καὶ ἡ γῆ, ἰῶτα ἓν ἢ μία
  κεραία οὐ μὴ παρέλθῃ* ἀπὸ τοῦ νόμου ἕως ἂν πάντα γένηται
  = for amen I say to you, <u>until</u> heaven and earth <u>pass away</u>,
  one "yod" or one "tittle" <u>shall not pass away</u>* from the law
  <u>until</u> all (things) <u>are done</u> (come to be) (Mt. 5:18).

  2) The entire conjunction ἐάν is replaced by a *temporal
  particle,* usually ἕως (until) *by itself* or *with the addition of:*

    a) οὗ, genitive of ὅς, e.g.: Μηδενὶ εἴπητε τὸ ὅραμα ἕως οὗ
    ὁ υἱὸς τοῦ ἀνθρώπου ἐκ νεκρῶν ἐγερθῇ = <u>tell</u> the vision to
    no one <u>until</u> the Son of Man <u>is raised</u> from the dead (Mt. 17:9).
    (*cf. 58:IV, A, 2, c above, b.1 for use of οὐ μή.)

    b) ὅτου, alternate genitive of ὅστις (along with οὗτινος), e.g.:
    οὐ μὴ φάγω αὐτὸ ἕως ὅτου πληρωθῇ ἐν τῇ βασιλείᾳ τοῦ
    θεοῦ = I will not eat it (the Passover) <u>until it is fulfilled</u>
    in the Kingdom of God. (Lk. 22:16)

5. *Concessive clauses* with καὶ ἐάν *and the subjunctive,* meaning
"even if, though, although," are omitted in this treatment
because examples of this construction can usually and more
naturally be translated: "and if."

V. **Exercises:**

A. Be able to *conjugate in the subjunctive* the regular verbs studied
so far.

B. Be able to *recognize subjunctive forms,* especially by comparison
or contrast with identical or similar forms in the indicative, e.g.:

  1. *Identical forms:* λύω (2), λύσω (2), λύῃ (3), λύσῃ (3)
  (NB: Numbers after the forms refer to the number of identical
  forms.)

  2. *Similar forms:* λύῃς + λύεις, λύῃ + λύει, λύωσι + λύουσι,
  λύσωμεν + λύσομεν, λύσητε + λύσετε, λυθῇ + ἐλύθη, κτλ.

C.   *Translate* these sentences and *explain* the underlined usages:

1. Καὶ εὐθέως ἠνάγκασεν τοὺς μαθητὰς ἐμβῆναι εἰς τὸ πλοῖον καὶ
   immediately   he compelled   to go into
   προάγειν αὐτὸν εἰς τὸ πέραν, ἕως οὗ ἀπολύσῃ τοὺς ὄχλους.
   to go before   other side

2. ὃ ἐὰν λύσῃς ἐπὶ τῆς γῆς ἔσται λελυμένον ἐν τοῖς οὐρανοῖς.
                          will be   loosed

3. ἐκείνοις δὲ τοῖς ἔξω ἐν παραβολαῖς τὰ πάντα γίνεται, ἵνα . . .
                                       all things   are (done)
   ἀκούωσιν καὶ μὴ συνιῶσιν . . . (NB: Mt. softens ἵνα to ὅτι.)
                  understand

4. καὶ ἐὰν ἀπολύσω αὐτοὺς νήστεις . . . , ἐκλυθήσονται ἐν τῇ ὁδῷ.
                            fasting   they will "give out"

5. Ὃς ἂν ἀπολύσῃ τὴν γυναῖκα αὐτοῦ καὶ γαμήσῃ ἄλλην
                        wife   marries
   μοιχᾶται . . .
   commits adultery

6. Ἐὰν ὑμῖν εἴπω οὐ μὴ πιστεύσητε . . . (ἢ ἀπολύσητε).
                tell

7. Ἐὰν μὴ σημεῖα καὶ τέρατα ἴδητε, οὐ μὴ πιστεύσητε.
                       wonders   see

8. περιτομὴν λαμβάνει ἄνθρωπος ἐν σαββάτῳ ἵνα μὴ λυθῇ
   circumcision receives
   ὁ νόμος.

9. καὶ ἐὰν τίς* μου ἀκούσῃ τῶν ῥημάτων καὶ μὴ φυλάξῃ, ἐγὼ οὐ
                            words   keeps
   κρίνω αὐτόν, οὐ γὰρ ἦλθον ἵνα κρίνω τὸν κόσμον ἀλλ’ ἵνα
   judge   I came
   σώσω τὸν κόσμον. (NB: κρίνω is used here in two different
   save
   moods.)

10. ἀπ’ ἄρτι λέγω ὑμῖν πρὸ τοῦ γενέσθαι, ἵνα πιστεύσητε ὅταν
          I tell   before it happens
    γένηται ὅτι ἐγώ εἰμι. (NB: ὅταν = ὅτε + ἄν)
    it happens   am

11. πῶς δὲ πιστεύσωσιν οὗ οὐκ ἤκουσαν; πῶς δὲ ἀκούσωσιν χωρὶς
    κηρύσσοντος; πῶς δὲ κηρύξωσιν ἐὰν μὴ ἀποσταλῶσιν;
    one who heralds   will they herald   they are sent

12. ἐφανερώθη ὁ υἱὸς τοῦ θεοῦ, ἵνα λύσῃ τὰ ἔργα τοῦ διαβόλου.
    was manifested   devil

*Not the interrogative but the indefinite, followed by an enclitic.

9 The Regular Verb—Part IV

The Imperative and Infinitive

I. Introduction:

A. Having seen the forms and usage of the indicative and subjunctive moods, we are now ready to continue our treatment of the regular verb with an examination of the FORMS AND USAGE OF THE IMPERATIVE AND INFINITIVE MOODS.

B. As already noted in our introduction to the subjunctive mood on page 56, the imperative and infinitive are *oblique or subordinate moods,* which are so named in comparison with the principal mood, the indicative.

C. It will be useful, however, to study the imperative and infinitive mostly *by comparison with the subjunctive,* the principal oblique mood, with which we are now familiar. Suitable examples and exercises will also be added.

II. Formation, synopsis, and usage of the imperative mood:

A. FORMATION:

   1. *Like the subjunctive,* the imperative:
   a. **Uses all three voices but only two tenses,** which do not express time (past, present, future) but **aspect** of action or situation: *present* for continued/repeated action, *aorist* for single/momentary action.
   b. Has **no features before the stem,** neither augment nor reduplication.
   c. **Employs system signs,** not in the present, but **only in the aorist.**

   2. *Unlike the subjunctive,* the imperative:
   a. **Uses the full system signs:** $\sigma\alpha$ in the aorist active and middle, and $\theta\eta$ in the aorist passive, as does the indicative mood.
   b. **Employs the variable vowel** o/ε only in the present tense and *does not lengthen it* as does the subjunctive.
   c. **Uses only second and third person endings** (obviously) which

resemble indicative endings but are *largely unique* to the imperative mood:

	ACTIVE		MID-PASS.	
	Sing.	Plur.	Sing.	Plur.
2.	τι-θι	τε	σο	σθε
3.	τω	τωσαν	σθω	σθωσαν

B.   SYNOPSIS of the regular verb λύω (loose, destroy) in the imperative mood:

	PRESENT		AORIST		AOR. PASS.
	Act.	**M-P.**	**Act.**	**Mid.**	
	Sing.		Sing.		Sing.
2.	λῦε	λύου	λῦσον	λῦσαι	λύθητι
3.	λυέτω	λυέσθω	λυσάτω	λυσάσθω	λυθήτω
	Plur.		Plur.		Plur.
2.	λύετε	λύεσθε	λύσατε	λύσασθε	λύθητε
3.	λυέτωσαν	λυέσθωσαν	λυσάτωσαν	λυσάσθωσαν	λυθήτωσαν

(Notes on the imperative endings:

1. The *second person singular is mostly irregular:* λῦε from λύεθ̷ι, λύου from λυεθ̷ο; λῦσον and λῦσαι deriving from popular usage.

2. The *aorist passive uses active endings* and τι or θι according to the stem.)

C.   USAGE of the imperative in NT Greek:

1. *In general:*
a. Of the oblique moods, **the imperative most closely parallels English usage,** expressing commands, prohibitions, and urgent requests in the second or third person, e.g. Ἄφετε τὰ παιδία ἔρχεσθαι πρός με = <u>Let</u> the little children (continue to) come to me. (Mk. 10:14)
b. As in other oblique moods generally, the **negative** (in prohibitions and negative requests) is normally μή, e.g. <u>μὴ κωλύετε</u> αὐτά = <u>Do not</u> (continue to) <u>hinder</u> them (Mk. 10:14).

2. *In particular:*
a. **Careful attention** to the use and meaning of the present and aorist tenses in the imperative **is absolutely essential** for understanding the text, as is evident in these examples:
   1) Mk. 10:14, quoted above, in which the *aorist* is used in the first part and the *present* in the second part.
   2) Jn. 20:17, an often misunderstood text: Μή μου ἅπτου, οὔπω γὰρ ἀναβέβηκα πρὸς τὸν πατέρα = <u>Do not hold</u> me, for I have not yet ascended to the (my) Father. (present tense = continued action; not aorist tense, which would mean "Do not touch me.")

b. As we have already noted on page 59, the **aorist imperative is never used in prohibitions** (or negative petitions) because it is considered too blunt; instead, the aorist subjunctive is substituted, e.g. Μὴ νομίσητε ὅτι ἦλθον καταλῦσαι τὸν νόμον . . . = Do not think that I came to destroy the law. (Mt. 5 : 17)

c. A "single or momentary action or situation" **requiring the aorist** may be one of *repetition* or *longer duration*, in which the emphasis is on the beginning, the completion, or (more often) the entire action or situation as a *single whole* (complexive or global aorist), e.g.: μάθετε ἀπ᾽ ἐμοῦ, ὅτι πραΰς εἰμι καὶ ταπεινὸς τῇ καρδίᾳ = learn from me, for (that) I am meek and humble of heart. (Mt. 11 : 29)

d. **NT prayers** ("urgent requests") are generally in the aorist, as exemplified in the Lord's Prayer (Mt. 6 : 9 – 13 and page 7), whose petitions are couched in the:

1) *Third person aorist imperative:* ἁγιασθήτω τὸ ὄνομά σου, ἐλθέτω ἡ βασιλεία σου, γενηθήτω τὸ θέλημά σου = Let your name be glorified, your kingdom come, your will be done . . .

2) *Second person aorist imperative:* τὸν ἄρτον ἡμῶν τὸν ἐπιούσιον δὸς ἡμῖν σήμερον· καὶ ἄφες ἡμῖν τὰ ὀφειλήματα ἡμῶν . . . ἀλλὰ ῥῦσαι ἡμᾶς ἀπὸ τοῦ πονηροῦ = give us today our daily (necessary, sufficient) bread; and forgive us (send away from us) our debts . . . but rather deliver us from evil (the evil one). (NB Lk. 11 : 3 – 4 has *"continue* to give" and "forgive us our *sins"*)

3) *Second person aorist subjunctive:* καὶ μὴ εἰσενέγκῃς ἡμᾶς εἰς πειρασμόν = and do not lead us into trial (test, temptation).

(NB: With this partial explanation of the Lord's Prayer, it would be helpful for the student to *translate the Our Father* as printed on page 7 in its entirety, even though we have not yet studied many of the words, especially the verbs, which are used. This will constitute one of the Exercises intended for this chapter.)

III. Formation, Synopsis, and Usage of the infinitive mood:

A. FORMATION: Viewed in comparison with the other moods studied so far—

1. *Like all* the other moods, the infinitive *has all three voices.*

2. *Like the subjunctive and imperative,* the infinitive *uses principally* the *present* and *aorist* tenses, generally to express *aspect*, not time; and, of course, it lacks augment, which is confined to the indicative.

3. *Like the indicative and imperative,* the infinitive *has the system sign* σα in the aorist active and middle, and θη in the aorist passive.

4. *Like the indicative,* the infinitive *includes a perfect tense,* which:
   a. **Expresses completeness,** perfection, sometimes past time.
   b. **Takes reduplication** according to the regular usage on page 41.
   c. **Uses the system sign** κε in the perfect active, none in the middle and passive. (κα in the indicative was influenced by aorist σα.)

5. *Like the imperative,* the infinitive:
   a. **Uses the variable vowel** ο/ε (unlengthened) **only** in the present.
   b. **Has its own unique endings,** which are not conjugated because it is related to the infinite.
      1) *Present endings:* active εν, middle and passive σθαι.
      2) *Aorist endings:* active ι, middle σθαι, passive ναι.
      3) *Perfect endings:* active ναι, middle and passive σθαι.

B. SYNOPSIS of the regular verb λύω (loose, destroy) in the infinitive:

   1. *Present:* active λύειν (λυ + ε + εν)
         mid-pass. λύεσθαι (λυ + ε + σθαι)

   2. *Aorist:* active λῦσαι (λυ + σα + ι)
         middle λύσασθαι (λυ + σα + σθαι)

   3. *Perfect active:* λελυκέναι (λε + λυ + κε + ναι)
         (Note accent on penult.)

   4. *Perfect middle and passive:* λέλυσθαι (λε + λυ + σθαι)

   5. *Aorist passive:* λυθῆναι (λυ + θη + ναι) (Note accent on penult.)

C. USAGE of the infinitive in NT Greek:

   1. *In general:* The infinitive in NT Greek is *far more common and varied* than in English, hence the importance of clearly knowing its usage.
   a. The infinitive, as a **verbal noun,** enjoys the properties of:
      1) *A noun:* Often being governed by a preposition and/or modified by an article as well as acting as the subject or object of a verb.
      2) *A verb:* Taking a subject/object (both *normally accusative*) and sometimes introduced by a conjunction or modified by an adverb.
   b. Sometimes a Greek infinitive can be translated by an English

infinitive, but **more often and more naturally by an English clause.**

c. Most often, **tenses in the infinitive** (especially present and aorist) refer to **aspect,** not time, but this is not true when the infinitive is used in indirect discourse or (sometimes) after a preposition.*

d. As with the other oblique moods, the infinitive in NT Greek uses the **negative** μή, even in indirect discourse (which comes closest to indicative usage), except when οὐ is used alone or together with μή for special emphasis or variety.

2. *In particular: The principal uses* of the infinitive in NT Greek can be arranged and summarized as follows:

a. **Complementary infinitive:** In this, its most natural use and the one closest to English usage, the infinitive simply *completes the sense* of a verb, noun, adjective, or even an entire statement:

   1) *Certain verbs* naturally take an infinitive, e.g.:

      a) **Impersonal verbs,** such as δεῖ (it is necessary), δοκεῖ (it seems good), ἔξεστι (it is lawful), e.g. <u>Δεῖ ὑμᾶς γεννηθῆναι ἄνωθεν</u> = <u>It is necessary</u> for you <u>to be begotten</u> from above (*or:* again, "from the top") Jn. 3 : 7.

      b) **Verbs of initiative, desire, power, duty, etc.,** such as:

ἄρχομαι: begin	**κελεύω:** command, order
βούλομαι: will, want	**μέλλω:** am about (to), am going (to)
δύναμαι: can, be able	
θέλω: wish, desire, want	**ὀφείλω:** ought, should

      e.g. <u>ἤρξατο</u> ὁ Ἰησοῦς <u>ποιεῖν</u> τε καὶ <u>διδάσκειν</u> = Jesus <u>began to do</u> and <u>to teach</u>. (Acts 1 : 1)

      c) **Verbs of motion or related ideas,** to express purpose, e.g. ὁ υἱὸς τοῦ ἀνθρώπου οὐκ ἦλθεν <u>διακονηθῆναι</u> ἀλλὰ <u>διακονῆσαι</u> καὶ <u>δοῦναι</u> τὴν ψυχὴν αὐτοῦ λύτρον ἀντὶ πολλῶν = the Son of Man <u>did not come to be served</u> but <u>to serve</u> and <u>to give</u> his life as ransom instead of (the) many. (Mt. 20 : 28)

   2) *Certain nouns,* especially those related to the above verbs, can also govern an infinitive, e.g. ἔδωκεν αὐτοῖς ἐξουσίαν τέκνα θεοῦ <u>γενέσθαι</u> = he gave them <u>power</u> (authority) <u>to become</u> children of God. (Jn. 1 : 12)

   3) *Certain adjectives,* normally in the neuter gender, can likewise govern an infinitive, e.g. Ῥαββί, <u>καλόν ἐστιν ἡμᾶς</u> ὧδε <u>εἶναι</u> = Rabbi, it is <u>good</u> for us <u>to be</u> here! (Mk. 9 : 5)

*This usage will be explained in section 2, d.

4) *A whole statement* or, as some prefer, a *demonstrative pronoun* may be completed or explained by an infinitive (often called epexegetical or explanatory), e.g. τοῦτο γάρ ἐστιν θέλημα τοῦ θεοῦ, ὁ ἁγιασμὸς ὑμῶν, ἀπέχεσθαι ὑμᾶς ἀπὸ τῆς πορνείας = for <u>this</u> is the will of God, your sanctification (consecration), <u>that you keep free</u> from immorality. (I Th. 4:3)

b. **Articular infinitive:** The infinitive *with an article** (which is always neuter and indeclinable) is used in various ways:

1) *As subject or predicate of a verb*, e.g. ἐμοὶ γὰρ τὸ ζῆν Χριστὸς καὶ τὸ ἀποθανεῖν κέρδος = for to me <u>to live</u> (is) Christ and <u>to die</u> (is) gain. (Phil. 1:21)

2) *As a modifying noun*, e.g. αἱ ἡμέραι <u>τοῦ τεκεῖν αὐτήν</u> = the days <u>of her delivery</u>. (Lk. 2:6)

3) *As object of a preposition**, in which usage the infinitive used sometimes indicates time before, during, or after that of the principal verb. Examples of these prepositions are:

ἀντί: instead of   **ἕως**: until, before
διά: because, on account of   **μετά**: after
εἰς: in order to, so that   **πρό**: before
ἐν: while   **πρός**: in order to, so that

e.g. ἐν τῷ ὑποστρέφειν αὐτοὺς ὑπέμεινεν Ἰησοῦς ὁ παῖς ἐν Ἰερουσαλήμ = <u>while they were returning</u>, the boy Jesus remained in Jerusalem. (Lk. 2:43)

4) *With τοῦ, the genitive of the article*, to express purpose, e.g. μέλλει γὰρ Ἡρῴδης ζητεῖν τὸ παιδίον τοῦ ἀπολέσαι αὐτό = for Herod is about to seek the child <u>in order to destroy</u> him.
(Mt. 2:13)

c. **Conjunctive infinitive:** The infinitive may also follow a conjunction as *the equivalent of an adverbial clause* expressing:

1) *Time* (temporal clause) with πρίν or πρὶν ἤ (before, until), e.g. <u>πρὶν Ἀβραὰμ γενέσθαι</u>, ἐγὼ εἰμί = <u>Before Abraham came to be</u>, I am. Jn. 8:58. (cf. Mt. 1:18 for use of πρὶν ἤ.)

2) *Result* (consecutive clause) with ὥστε (so that, with the result that), e.g. καὶ συνέρχεται πάλιν ὄχλος, ὥστε μὴ δύνασθαι αὐτοὺς μηδὲ ἄρτον φαγεῖν = and the crowd comes together again, <u>so that</u> (as a result) <u>they could not even eat bread</u>. (Mk. 3:20)

*NB: After prepositions, the article with the infinitive is in whatever case is governed by the preposition. Cf. page 25.

d. **Infinitive of indirect discourse:**

1) Besides the much more common use of ὅτι with the indicative, NT Greek also expresses indirect statements *after verbs of saying, believing, thinking, perceiving,* etc., by means of an infinitive.

2) *Tenses* (present, aorist, perfect) of the infinitive of indirect discourse *no longer refer to aspect but to time* (past or present) in relation to the time of the principal verb.

3) *Example:* νομισάντες δὲ αὐτὸν εἶναι ἐν τῇ συνοδίᾳ ἦλθον ἡμέρας ὁδόν = but <u>thinking that he was</u> in the caravan, they went a day's journey (direct discourse: <u>he is</u> in the caravan)

(Lk. 2:44)

(NB: This is basically the same tense usage as with ὅτι and a clause.)

IV. **Exercises:**

A. *Be able to conjugate* the verbs studied so far *in both* the imperative and infinitive moods, the latter having not a true conjugation but a synopsis.

B. *Be able to recognize the forms* of the imperative and infinitive, especially by *comparison and contrast* with the indicative and subjunctive, by identifying those forms which are the same and distinguishing similar ones:

1. *Identical forms:* λύετε (2), λύεσθε (2), λῦσαι (2)

2. *Similar forms:* λύθητε / λυθῆτε, λέλυσαι / λέλυσθαι,
λῦε / λύει, λύεις / λύειν, λύσατε / ἐλύσατε

C. As already indicated on page 65, d, 3 note, attempt to *read, translate,* and *explain* the Lord's Prayer on page 7, which contains abundant examples of the imperative mood used in earnest entreaties and especially prayers.

D. In the following sentences, first *read the passage aloud,* then *translate* it, and finally *explain* the *underlined* imperative and infinitive uses:

1. Ἰωσὴφ δὲ ὁ ἀνὴρ αὐτῆς, δίκαιος ὢν καὶ μὴ θέλων αὐτὴν
Joseph husband being wishing

<u>ματίσαι</u>, <u>ἐβουλήθη</u> λάθρα <u>ἀπολῦσαι</u> αὐτήν.
to disgrace wanted quietly

2. καὶ προσήνεγκα αὐτὸν τοῖς μαθηταῖς σου, καὶ οὐκ ἠδυνήθησαν
I brought (to) they were able

αὐτὸν <u>θεραπεῦσαι</u>.

3. μελλήσετε δὲ <u>ἀκούειν</u> πολέμους καὶ ἀκοὰς πολέμων . . .
(future) rumors

4. καὶ ἔλεγεν, Ὃς ἔχει ὦτα ἀκούειν ἀκουέτω.

he said   has   ears

5. Πάντως ἐρεῖτέ μοι τὴν παραβολὴν . . . Ἰατρέ, θεράπευσον

Surely you will say   Healer

   σεαυτόν.

6. συνήρχοντο ὄχλοι πολλοὶ ἀκούειν καὶ θεραπεύεσθαι . . .

were gathering   great

7. Μὴ φοβοῦ, μόνον πίστευσον, καὶ σωθήσεται.

fear   only   he will be saved

8. ἐν δὲ τῷ πορεύεσθαι αὐτοὺς αὐτὸς εἰσῆλθεν εἰς κώμην τινά . . .

                              entered   village certain

9. ταύτην δὲ θυγατέρα Ἀβραάμ . . . οὐκ ἔδει λυθῆναι . . . ;

            daughter of Abraham   was necessary

10. Ἔχουσι Μωϋσέα καὶ τοὺς προφήτας· ἀκουσάτωσαν αὐτῶν.

They have Moses

11. ἦν γὰρ . . . θέλων ἰδεῖν αὐτὸν διὰ τὸ ἀκούειν περὶ αὐτοῦ . . .

             desiring to see

12. Λύσατε τὸν ναὸν τοῦτον καὶ ἐν τρισὶν ἡμέραις ἐγερῶ αὐτόν.

                              three   I will raise

13. εἰ οὐ ποιῶ τὰ ἔργα τοῦ πατρός μου, μὴ πιστεύετέ μοι . . .

     I do   father

14. λέγει αὐτοῖς . . . , Λύσατε αὐτὸν καὶ ἄφετε αὐτὸν ὑπάγειν.

he says   let   go

15. οὐκ οἶδας ὅτι ἐξουσίαν ἔχω ἀπολῦσαί σε καὶ . . . σταυρῶσαί σε;

    you know   I have   to crucify

16. εἶπεν δὲ αὐτῷ ὁ κύριος, Λῦσον τὸ ὑπόδημα τῶν ποδῶν σου . . .

he said   sandal   feet

17. Τί ἐμὲ ὑπονοεῖτε εἶναι, οὐκ εἰμὶ ἐγώ· ἀλλ' ἰδοὺ ἔρχεται

       you think to be   am   behold one comes

    μετ' ἐμὲ οὗ οὐκ εἰμὶ ἄξιος τὸ ὑπόδημα τῶν ποδῶν λῦσαι.

                          sandal   feet

18. Ἐγένετο δὲ . . . κατὰ τὸ αὐτὸ εἰσελθεῖν αὐτοὺς εἰς τὴν

It happened   at the same time as . . . entered

    συναγωγὴν . . . καὶ λαλῆσαι οὕτως ὥστε πιστεῦσαι . . .

              (that)   spoke

    πολὺ πλῆθος.

great multitude

19. . . . ἐξελέξατο ὁ θεὸς διὰ τοῦ στόματός μου ἀκοῦσαι τὰ ἔθνη

      chose   mouth   gentiles

    τὸν λόγον τοῦ εὐαγγελίου καὶ πιστεῦσαι . . .

20. γένος οὖν ὑπάρχοντες τοῦ θεοῦ οὐκ ὀφείλομεν νομίζειν χρυσῷ

offspring   being   we ought   to think   gold

    ἢ ἀργύρῳ ἢ λίθῳ . . . τὸ θεῖον εἶναι ὅμοιον.

  silver   stone   deity to be

21. Ἐβουλόμην καὶ αὐτὸς τοῦ ἀνθρώπου ἀκοῦσαι.

(Imperfect)

22. Μὴ οὖν βασιλευέτω ἡ ἁμαρτία ἐν τῷ θνητῷ ὑμῶν σώματι εἰς τὸ

      let rule   mortal   body

    ὑπακούειν ταῖς ἐπιθυμίαις αὐτοῦ . . .

              desires

IO Review of the Greek Verb

I. Introduction:

A. WE HAVE NOW STUDIED the regular NT Greek verb in its entirety, except for the participle, which we will address ourselves to as soon as we have prepared ourselves by a knowledge of adjectives of the third declension.

B. ALL OTHER VERB FORMS or patterns of verb forms can now be studied more effectively in comparison and contrast with the regular verb, hence the crucial *necessity* of a thorough knowledge of the *regular Greek verb*.

C. Hence, also, the PURPOSE OF THIS REVIEW, namely to consolidate just as completely as possible what has been presented in the chapters which we have just studied on the forms and usage of the regular NT Greek verb.

D. AFTER OUR REVIEW of the verb, we will then continue with our reading, translation, and explanation of John's Gospel. In view of the wealth of material in these chapters, no further vocabulary will be presented.

II. Review of the regular NT Greek verb:

A. CHAPTER 6: *Formation of the indicative mood—*

   1. *Review:*
   a. **The structure** of the verb: voices, moods, tenses.
   b. **The systems** of the verb, represented by the six principal parts.
   c. **The features** of the verb: stem, pre-stem, post-stem, e.g. endings.

   2. *Be able to:*
   a. **Conjugate** the regular verb λύω in all forms of the *indicative*.
   b. **Recognize** the other regular verbs on p. 46 *in any indicative form.*

B. CHAPTER 7: *Usage of the Indicative Mood—*

   1. *Review:*
   a. **The usage of substantive clauses:** noun and pronoun clauses.

  b. **The usage of adverbial clauses:** causal, comparative,
     conditional, conditional relative, temporal, concessive, and
     result clauses.

  2. *Practice reading aloud, translating, and explaining* the
     underlined expressions in the Exercise on pages 53–55.

C. CHAPTER 8: *Forms and Usage of the Subjunctive Mood*—

  1. *Review:*
  a. **The formation** of the subjunctive, in comparison with the
     indicative.
  b. **The usage** of the subjunctive, especially the following:
     1) *General meaning,* use of the *negative,* and of *tenses.*
     2) *Independent uses:* deliberation, inquiry, exhortation,
        prohibition.
     3) *Dependent uses:* purpose, conditional, conditional relative,
        and temporal clauses.

  2. *Be able to:*
  a. **Conjugate** the regular verb λύω in all forms of the *subjunctive.*
  b. **Recognize** the other regular verbs on p. 46 *in any subjunctive
     form.*

  3. *Practice reading aloud, translating,* and *explaining* the
     underlined expressions in the Exercise on pages 61–62.

D. CHAPTER 9: *The Imperative and Infinitive Moods*—

  1. *Review:*
  a. **The formation of the imperative,** in comparison with the
     subjunctive.
  b. **The formation of the infinitive,** in comparison with the other
     moods.

  2. *Be able to:*
  a. **Conjugate** (or synopsize) the regular verb λύω in all forms of the
     imperative and *infinitive* moods.
  b. **Recognize** the other regular verbs on p. 46 *in any forms of the
     imperative or infinitive* moods.

  3. *Review:*
  a. **The usage of the imperative,** in general and in particular uses.
  b. **The usage of the infinitive,** in general and in particular, e.g.:
     1) The *complementary* infinitive.
     2) The *articular* infinitive.
     3) The *conjunctive* infinitive.
     4) The infinitive of *indirect discourse.*

4. *Practice reading aloud, translating,* and *explaining* the underlined expressions in the Exercise on pages 69–70.

III. **Exercise:** Please *read aloud, translate,* and *explain the underlined portions* of this selection from the continuation of the Gospel of St. John.

Τῇ ἐπαύριον πάλιν εἱστήκει ὁ Ἰωάννης καὶ ἐκ τῶν μαθητῶν αὐτοῦ
next day   was standing   John

δύο, καὶ ἐμβλέψας τῷ Ἰησοῦ περιπατοῦντι λέγει, Ἴδε* ὁ ἀμνὸς
two   seeing   walking   he says Behold   lamb

τοῦ θεοῦ. καὶ <u>ἤκουσαν</u> οἱ δύο μαθηταὶ αὐτοῦ λαλοῦντος καὶ
                                                        speaking

ἠκολούθησαν τῷ Ἰησοῦ. στραφεὶς δὲ ὁ Ἰησοῦς καὶ θεασάμενος
followed   turning   seeing

αὐτοὺς ἀκολουθοῦντας <u>λέγει</u> αὐτοῖς, <u>Τί ζητεῖτε;</u> οἱ δὲ <u>εἶπαν</u> αὐτῷ,
            following   are you seeking   said

Ῥαββί (<u>ὃ λέγεται</u> μεθερμηνευόμενον Διδάσκαλε), <u>ποῦ μένεις;</u>
          is said   translated   are you staying

<u>λέγει αὐτοις</u>, <u>Ἔρχεσθε</u> καὶ <u>ὄψεσθε.</u> ἦλθαν οὖν καὶ <u>εἶδαν</u> ποῦ μένει,
                      come   you will see they went   saw

καὶ παρ' αὐτῷ <u>ἔμειναν</u> τὴν ἡμέραν ἐκείνην· ὥρα <u>ἦν</u> ὡς δεκάτη. Ἦν
                   stayed   the tenth

Ἀνδρέας ὁ ἀδελφὸς Σίμωνος Πέτρου εἷς ἐκ τῶν δύο τῶν <u>ἀκουσάντων</u>
Andrew   Simon   Peter   one   who had heard

παρὰ Ἰωάννου καὶ <u>ἀκολουθησάντων</u> αὐτῷ· <u>εὑρίσκει</u> οὗτος πρῶτον
                          had followed   finds   first

τὸν ἀδελφὸν τὸν ἴδιον Σίμωνα καὶ <u>λέγει</u> αὐτῷ, <u>Εὑρήκαμεν</u> τὸν
                                                           We have found

Μεσσίαν (<u>ὅ ἐστιν</u> μεθερμηνευόμενον Χριστός). ἤγαγεν αὐτὸν πρὸς
Messiah   is   Christ   he led

τὸν Ἰησοῦν. ἐμβλέψας αὐτῷ ὁ Ἰησοῦς <u>εἶπεν</u>, Σὺ εἶ Σίμων ὁ υἱὸς
                 gazing at

Ἰωάννου· σὺ <u>κληθήσῃ</u> Κηφᾶς (<u>ὅ ἑρμηνεύεται</u> Πέτρος). Τῇ ἐπαύριον
                will be called Cephas   means

<u>ἠθέλησεν ἐξελθεῖν</u> εἰς τὴν Γαλιλαίαν, καὶ <u>εὑρίσκει</u> Φίλιππον.
he wanted to leave   finds   Philip

καὶ λέγει αὐτῷ ὁ Ἰησοῦς, <u>Ἀκολούθει</u> μοι. ἦν δὲ ὁ Φίλιππος ἀπὸ
                              follow

Βηθσαϊδά, ἐκ τῆς πόλεως Ἀνδρέου καὶ Πέτρου. <u>εὑρίσκει</u> Φίλιππος
Bethsaida   city   finds

τὸν Ναθαναὴλ καὶ λέγει αὐτῷ, <u>Ὅν ἔγραψεν</u> Μωϋσῆς ἐν τῷ νόμῳ καὶ
Nathaniel   wrote

οἱ προφῆται <u>εὑρήκαμεν</u>, Ἰησοῦν υἱὸν τοῦ Ἰωσὴφ τὸν ἀπὸ Ναζαρέτ.
                we have found   Nazareth

καὶ <u>εἶπεν</u> αὐτῷ Ναθαναήλ, Ἐκ Ναζαρὲτ <u>δύναταί</u> τι ἀγαθὸν <u>εἶναι;</u>
      said   is able   to be

*Ἴδε, though originally an aorist imperative of the verb ὁράω (I see), aor. εἶδον, became an expletive (look! behold!), followed by the *nominative* of the object seen.

λέγει αὐτῷ ὁ Φίλιππος, Ἔρχου καὶ ἴδε. εἶδεν ὁ Ἰησοῦς τὸν
<u>Come</u>   <u>see</u> saw

Ναθαναὴλ ἐρχόμενον πρὸς αὐτὸν καὶ λέγει περὶ αὐτοῦ, Ἴδε ἀληθῶς
<u>coming</u>   truly

Ἰσραηλίτης ἐν ᾧ δόλος οὐκ ἔστιν. λέγει αὐτῷ Ναθαναήλ, Πόθεν με
<u>Israelite</u>   <u>guile</u>

γινώσκεις; ἀπεκρίθη Ἰησοῦς καὶ εἶπεν αὐτῷ, Πρὸ τοῦ σε Φίλιππον
<u>you know</u>   <u>answered</u>

φωνῆσαι ὄντα ὑπὸ τὴν συκῆν εἶδόν σε. ἀπεκρίθη αὐτῷ Ναθαναήλ,
<u>called</u> <u>being</u>   <u>fig tree</u> I saw

Ῥαββί, σὺ εἶ ὁ υἱὸς τοῦ θεοῦ, σὺ βασιλεὺς εἶ τοῦ Ἰσραήλ. ἀπεκρίθη
       are   king

Ἰησοῦς καὶ εἶπεν αὐτῷ, Ὅτι εἶπόν σοι ὅτι εἶδόν σε ὑποκάτω τῆς

συκῆς πιστεύεις; μείζω τούτων ὄψῃ*. καὶ λέγει αὐτῷ, Ἀμὴν ἀμὲν
                    <u>greater</u>   <u>you will see</u>

λέγω ὑμῖν, ὄψεσθε* τὸν οὐρανὸν ἀνεῳγότα καὶ τοὺς ἀγγέλους τοῦ
      <u>you will see</u>   opened

θεοῦ ἀναβαίνοντας καὶ καταβαίνοντας ἐπὶ τὸν υἱὸν τοῦ ἀνθρώπου.
    ascending   descending

(John 1:35–51)

IV. **New Testament Greetings:** The following NT greetings or salutations are used by St. Paul in various letters and sometimes by the Church in her liturgy. They are included here not as an exercise, but for the student's personal information and use. References indicate *substantial agreement* in formula.

1. χάρις ὑμῖν καὶ εἰρήνη ἀπὸ θεοῦ πατρὸς ἡμῶν καὶ κυρίου Ἰησοῦ Χριστοῦ. (Rom. 1:7, I Cor. 1:3, II Cor. 1:2, Gal. 1:3, Eph. 1:2, Phil. 1:2, Col. 1:2, II Thess. 1:2, Phlm. 1:3)
2. χάρις, ἔλεος, εἰρήνη ἀπὸ θεοῦ πατρὸς καὶ χριστοῦ Ἰησοῦ τοῦ κυρίου ἡμῶν. (I Tim. 1:2, II Tim. 1:2)
3. χάρις καὶ εἰρήνη ἀπὸ θεοῦ πατρὸς καὶ Ἰησοῦ Χριστοῦ σωτῆρος ἡμῶν. (Tit. 1:4)
4. χάρις ὑμῖν καὶ εἰρήνη. (I Thess. 1:1)
   (NB: As the references indicate, *all* of the above formulae of greetings are taken from the *opening salutations* of letters attributed to St. Paul. The amount of uniformity among them is quite remarkable. Later, examples will be given of closing formulae, which are much more varied.)

*Note the switch, so characteristic of John's Gospel, from one person to more than one addressed by Jesus, as the verb changes from the singular to the plural.

11 The Third Declension—Part I

Mute Nouns and Adjectives

I. Introduction to the third declension:

A. GENERAL REMARKS:

   1. *Greek has only three declensions,* as compared with Latin's five, but the third declension can seem like such a potpourri of unrelated types that the student can become both confused and discouraged.

   2. It is *encouraging,* then, to know that:

   a. Disordered as it seems, the **third declension does have a definite, beautiful order** which this work will attempt to delineate clearly.

   b. Once learned, the third declension can serve as **the key,** not only to the participle, but also to many of the main types of verbs.

B. THIRD DECLENSION ENDINGS:

   1. As with the endings of the first two declensions and the verb, it is *very important* and *fairly simple* to learn the third declension endings.

   2. Unlike the first two declensions, however, there are *only two sets of endings,* one for masculine *and* feminine forms and one for neuter forms.

   3. *Compare* masculine-feminine with neuter, and singular with plural endings. Note also the *quantity signs* provided here to clarify *ambiguous endings.*

	SINGULAR			PLURAL	
	Mas-Fem.	Neuter		Mas-Fem.	Neuter
Nom.	ς or —	—	*Nom.*	ες	ᾰ
Gen.	ος	ος	*Gen.*	ων	ων
Dat.	ι	ι	*Dat.*	σι	σι
Acc.	ᾰ or ν	—	*Acc.*	ᾰς or νς	ᾰ

C. THIRD DECLENSION TYPES:

    1. The third declension comprises *five principal types*, divided according to the particular *stem ending*, i.e., the *final letter(s) of the stem.*

    2. To determine the proper type of third declension words, *we must observe the genitive form* which, together with the article, is provided in vocabularies and dictionaries, thus indicating both *type and gender.*

    3. *The five principal types,* then, are as follows:
    a. **Mute stems:** which end in one of the mutes or stops (no vowel sound).
    b. **Liquid stems:** which end in one of the liquids or semivowels— λ, μ, ν, ρ.
    c. **Sibilant stems:** which end in the sibilant or "S" sound—σ, ς.
    d. **Vowel stems:** which end in one of the weak vowels—ι, υ.
    e. **Diphthong stems:** which end in a diphthong, usually ευ (αυ, ου).

    4. All of these third declension types will be examined in turn, beginning in this lesson with the *mute stems* and, for the sake of clarity and order, we will also study adjectives, participles, verbs, etc. of the same type before going on to the next type as listed just above.

D. ACCENTUATION: In general, the syllable accented in the *nominative* keeps the accent throughout. (Exceptions will be noted in the proper place.) *All Alpha endings are short.*

II. Nouns of the third declension mute stems:

A. MUTES IN GENERAL:

    1. *Meaning:* Certain consonants are referred to as *mutes or stops* because their pronunciation requires little or no vowel sound.

    2. *Division:*
    a. **Mutes have three classes:** *labial, palatal* (guttural), and *lingual* (dental) according to pronunciation with lips, throat, or tongue.
    b. **These have three orders:** *smooth, middle,* and *rough* according to the amount of effort required in their pronunciation.

c. **This double division** of the mutes may be illustrated as follows:

ORDERS

CLASSES:	**Smooth**	**Middle**	**Rough**	FORMED:
Labial				
(Pi-mute):	π	β	φ	With the *lips.*
Palatal				
(Kappa-mute):	κ	γ	χ	With the *throat.*
Lingual				
(Tau-mute):	τ	δ	θ	With the *tongue.*

B. LABIAL MUTES:

1. *Nouns* and *adjectives* of this type are *so rare in the New Testament* that they need not be declined here.

2. *Verbs* of this type, however, *are more frequent;* we will return to study labial mutes when we examine mute verbs.

C. PALATAL MUTES:

1. *Frequency:* Only *four* palatal mute nouns need be noted in the New Testament:
   a. **Of frequent usage:** σάρξ, -κός, ἡ = flesh (sarcophagus, sarcasm)
   γυνή, -αικός, ἡ = woman, wife (gynecology)
   b. **Less frequently used:** θρίξ, τριχός, ἡ = hair (trichology)
   σάλπιγξ, -γγος, ἡ = trumpet (salpingitis)

2. *Characteristics:*
   a. **All four** are of the *feminine gender.*
   b. **Three** are *regular,* the fourth, γυνή, is *irregular.*
   c. **In the regular declension,** the palatal mute *unites with Sigma* in the nominative singular and dative plural to form the letter ξ.

3. *Declension:* One regular and the other irregular—

	REGULAR			IRREGULAR	
	Sing.	Plural		Sing.	Plural
Nom.	σάρξ	σάρκες	*Nom.*	γυνή	γυναῖκες
Gen.	σαρκός	σαρκῶν	*Gen.*	γυναικός	γυναικῶν
Dat.	σαρκί	σαρξί	*Dat.*	γυναικί	γυναιξί
Acc.	σάρκα	σάρκας	*Acc.*	γυναῖκα	γυναῖκας

4. *Accentuation:* As an exception to the general rule (p. 76), note that third declension *monosyllabic* nouns (and γυνή) normally accent the ultima or final syllable in the *genitive* and *dative* of both singular and plural, e.g. σαρκός, σαρκῶν, γυναικί, -ξί, τριχί, θριξί.

D. LINGUAL MUTES:

    1. *Introduction:* these are *well represented* in the New Testament, especially neuter nouns, which we will study first because of their importance.

    2. *Neuter lingual mutes:*

    a. **Characteristics:**

       1) *Most* of these have nominatives in α with genitives in ατος.

       2) *A few,* however, have *irregular nominatives*, even though the rest of their declension is regular. *(Check the genitive closely!)*

       3) Note that τ always drops before σ and at the *ends of words.*

       4) Note also, as always, that the neuter nominative and accusative are always *exactly the same* in both singular and plural.

    b. **Declension** of two *very common* neuter lingual mute nouns:

       1) **πνεῦμα, ατος, τό**: spirit, wind, breath (pneumatic, pneumonia)

       2) **φῶς, φωτός, τό**: light (photon, photograph, phosphorus, etc.)

	Sing.	Plural		Sing.	Plural
Nom.	πνεῦμα	πνεύματα	*Nom.*	φῶς	φῶτα
Gen.	πνεύματος	πνευμάτων	*Gen.*	φωτός	φώτων
Dat.	πνεύματι	πνεύμασι	*Dat.*	φωτί	φωσί
Acc.	πνεῦμα	πνεύματα	*Acc.*	φῶς	φῶτα

    c. **Vocabulary** (Irregular nominatives indicated by an asterisk *):

       1. **αἷμα**: blood (anemia, hemo-)

       2. **βάπτισμα**: dipping (Baptism)

       3. **γράμμα**: letter (grammar)

       4. **θέλημα**: will (Monothelite)

       5. **κήρυγμα**: message (kerygma)

       6. **κρίμα**: judgment (criticism)

       7. **ὄνομα**: name (anonymous)

       8. **οὖς***, **ὠτός**: ear (otology)

       9. **ῥῆμα**: word (rhetoric)

       10. **σπέρμα**: seed (sperm)

       11. **στόμα**: mouth (stomach)

       12. **σῶμα**: body (psychosomatic)

       13. **ὕδωρ***, **ὕδατος**: water (hydraphobia)

       14. **χάρισμα**: gift (charism)

    d. **Accentuation:** Neuter lingual nouns follow the rules already given, except that *monosyllabic nouns* tend *not to accent* the ultima or final syllable in the genitive plural, e.g. φώτων, ὤτων.

    3. *Feminine lingual mutes:*

    a. **Introduction:** These are *not well represented* in the New Testament, but they do include some very important nouns which deserve special attention.

b. **Characteristics:**

1) These nouns *usually* have a nominative in ις, with genitive in ιτος or ιδος. (Exceptions are *νύξ* and *rare* nouns in -ότης.)
2) By the general rule of orthography, τ or δ drop before σ, ς.
3) There is a *variation* among those nouns with nominative in ις:
   a) Those accenting the ultima take the accusative in α.
   b) Those accenting the penult take the accusative in ν.
4) *νύξ* not only drops τ before σ but unites κ with σ to ξ.

c. **Examples** of feminine lingual mute nouns are these *three common* nouns:

1) *ἐλπίς, ίδος, ἡ:* hope, expectation (very frequent in the New Testament)
2) *χάρις, ιτος, ἡ:* favor, grace, thanks (charity, Eucharist)
3) *νύξ, νυκτός, ἡ:* night (nyctalopia, Lat. *nox:* nocturnal, etc.)

d. **Declension** of the above examples:

	Sing.				Plural		
Nom.	ἐλπίς	χάρις	νύξ	Nom.	ἐλπίδες	χάριτες	νύκτες
Gen.	ἐλπίδος	χάριτος	νυκτός	Gen.	ἐλπίδων	χαρίτων	νυκτῶν
Dat.	ἐλπίδι	χάριτι	νυκτί	Dat.	ἐλπίσι	χάρισι	νυξί
Acc.	ἐλπίδα	χάριν	νύκτα	Acc.	ἐλπίδας	χάριτας	νύκτας

4. *Masculine lingual mutes:*

a. **Introduction:** Though *not well represented* in the New Testament, these nouns are *important*, especially as models for adjectives and participles.

b. **Characteristics:** These nouns fall into *two main classes*, comprising—

1) Those nouns, sometimes originally participles, whose stem ends in ντ, of which the τ drops in the nominative (with a blank ending), and both drop before σ in the dative plural, the preceding vowel (usually o) being lengthened to ω and ου.
2) Those nouns whose stem ends in a mute (usually δ) preceded by a vowel, which drops the mute before σ in the nominative singular and dative plural, the preceding vowel (usually o) being lenghtened—sometimes but not always, e.g. *πούς, ποδός (ποσί).*

c. **Examples** of these nouns are *two very common* words:

1) *ἄρχων, οντος, ὁ:* leader, ruler (anarchy, archangel, hierarchy)
2) *πούς, ποδός, ὁ:* foot (podium, pew, tripod, trapeze, chiropodist)

[See the declension of these two nouns on the following page.]

d. **Declension** of the above examples:

	Sing.	Plural		Sing.	Plural
Nom.	ἄρχων	ἄρχοντες	*Nom.*	πούς	πόδες
Gen.	ἄρχοντος	ἀρχόντων	*Gen.*	ποδός	ποδῶν
Dat.	ἄρχοντι	ἄρχουσι	*Dat.*	ποδί	ποσί
Acc.	ἄρχοντα	ἄρχοντας	*Acc.*	πόδα	πόδας

III. Adjectives of the third declension mute stem:

A. INTRODUCTION to third declension adjectives:

1. We have already studied first and second declension adjectives, by far the largest group, and we will return to them later, especially to examine adjectives of only two terminations and irregular adjectives.

2. Meanwhile, we shall more effectively study third declension adjectives of the different stem groups as we take up the nouns of those groups.

3. Feminines of third declension adjectives (and participles) are declined according to the first declension, also taking a *circumflex on the ultima of the genitive plural.*

4. The *masculine and neuter* follow the third declension, including accentuation, but use the *monosyllabic rule* (p. 77, C, 4) only in the singular.

B. THIRD DECLENSION MUTE ADJECTIVES:

1. Interestingly, the *only* third (and first) declension mute adjective in common use in the New Testament (and very common indeed) is the adjective: πᾶς, πᾶσα, πᾶν: all, whole, every (pantheism, pandemonium, panorama) (NB: An alternate form ἄπας, ἄπασα, ἄπαν is used after consonants.)

2. This adjective is especially important, providing the *model* for the declension of the regular aorist active participle, as we will soon see.

3. *Its declension* includes features from *both* of the masculine lingual mute nouns:

a. **Its stem** ends in ντ like ἄρχων, οντος, ὁ.

b. **Its nominative** uses the ending ς like πούς, ποδός, ὁ.

c. **ντ drops** before σ in the nominative singular and dative plural.

4. *Its accentuation* follows the rules for third declension adjectives already given above in A, 4.

C. DECLENSION

	Sing.				Plural		
	Masc.	**Fem.**	**Neut.**		**Masc.**	**Fem.**	**Neut.**
Nom.	πᾶς	πᾶσα	πᾶν	Nom.	πάντες	πᾶσαι	πάντα
Gen.	παντός	πάσης	παντός	Gen.	πάντων	πασῶν	πάντων
Dat.	παντί	πάσῃ	παντί	Dat.	πᾶσι	πάσαις	πᾶσι
Acc.	πάντα	πᾶσαν	πᾶν	Acc.	πάντας	πάσας	πάντα

D. USAGE:

1. *Introduction:*
a. So common is this adjective that it is helpful at this time to study not only its formation and declension, but also its usage.
b. Its **usage is quite varied,** but in general it tends to parallel our English usage of the adjectives *all, whole,* and *every.*

2. *The usage* of πᾶς can be divided into *two principal ones:*
a. **As an adjective,** it is used:
  1) *Generally before article and noun* (predicative position), e.g. ἡ μήτηρ αὐτοῦ διετήρει πάντα τὰ ῥήματα ἐν τῇ καρδίᾳ αὐτῆς = his mother kept all the words in her heart. (Lk. 2:51)
  2) *Sometimes between article and noun* (attributive position), e.g. Ὑμεῖς ἐπίστασθε . . . πῶς μεθ᾽ ὑμῶν τὸν πάντα χρόνον ἐγενόμην = You know how I came to be (was) with you the whole time. (Acts 20:18)
  3) *Sometimes without the article,* e.g. καὶ ὄψεται πᾶσα σὰρξ τὸ σωτήριον τοῦ θεοῦ = and all flesh will see the salvation of God. (Lk. 3:6)
b. **As a noun,** with or without the article, it can be used:
  1) *Alone,* without any modifiers at all, e.g. καὶ ἐθαύμασαν πάντες = and all were amazed (wondered, were filled with wonder). (Lk. 1:63)
  2) *With a modifying relative clause,* e.g. . . . πάντα ἃ ἤκουσα παρὰ τοῦ πατρός μου ἐγνώρισα ὑμῖν = . . . all things which I heard from my father I (have) made known to you. (Jn. 15:15)

IV. Additional vocabulary:

A. *Introduction:* The following few words were kept until this time, not just for developing vocabulary, but also *specifically* for practice in recognizing the particular stem type to which they belong.

B. Learn these words according to their stem type. (Irregular nominatives are indicated with an asterisk *)

1. **βῆμα, ατος, τό**: tribunal (bema)
2. **βρῶμα, ατος, τό**: food (bromatology)
3. **γόνυ*, ατος, τό**: knee (polygonum)
4. **δράκων, οντος, ὁ**: dragon, devil (draconian)
5. **ἔρις, ιδος, ἡ**: strife (eristic)
6. **λέων, οντος, ὁ**: lion (Leo, leonine)
7. **μερίς, ίδος, ἡ**: part (polymer)
8. **ὀδούς*, όντος, ὁ**: tooth (orthodontic)
9. **πάθημα, ατος, τό**: suffering (pathos)
10. **παῖς, παιδός, ὁ, ἡ**: child, servant (pedagogy, etc.)

V. **Exercises:**

A. *Know thoroughly by memory:*

1. **The endings** and **stem-types** of the third declension.

2. **The classes** and **orders** of mutes (for use now and especially later).

B. *Be able to decline* any of the nouns given as examples or vocabulary.

C. *Learn thoroughly* the declension and usage of the adjective: πᾶς, πᾶσα, πᾶν.

D. *Read aloud, translate,* and *explain the underlined* expressions of the following sentences: (NB: Interrupted underlining refers to previous usage.)

1. μαθητεύσατε πάντα τὰ ἔθνη, βαπτίζοντες αὐτοὺς εἰς τὸ ὄνομα
   teach   peoples   baptizing

   τοῦ πατρὸς καὶ τοῦ υἱοῦ καὶ τοῦ ἁγίου πνεύματος . . .
   father

2. ἐὰν μή τις γεννηθῇ ἐξ ὕδατος καὶ πνεύματος, οὐ δύναται
         is begotten   is able

   εἰσελθεῖν εἰς τὴν βασιλείαν τοῦ θεοῦ.
   enter

3. ἐὰν μὴ φάγητε τὴν σάρκα τοῦ υἱοῦ τοῦ ἀνθρώπου καὶ πίητε
          you eat   drink

   αὐτοῦ τὸ αἷμα, οὐκ ἔχετε ζωὴν ἐν ἑαυτοῖς.
          you have

4. ὁ θεὸς ὁ ποιήσας τὸν κόσμον καὶ πάντα τὰ ἐν αὐτῷ . . . αὐτὸς
         who made

   διδοὺς πᾶσι ζωὴν καὶ πνοὴν καὶ τὰ πάντα ἐποίησέν τε ἐξ ἑνὸς
   giving   breath   made   one

   πᾶν ἔθνος ἀνθρώπων κατοικεῖν ἐπὶ παντὸς προσώπου τῆς
       race   to dwell   face

   γῆς . . .

5. ὃς ἂν ἐσθίῃ τὸν ἄρτον ἢ πίνῃ τὸ ποτήριον τοῦ κυρίου ἀναξίως,
<small>eats   drinks   unworthily</small>

    ἔνοχος ἔσται τοῦ σώματος καὶ τοῦ αἵματος τοῦ κυρίου.
<small>guilty   will be</small>

6. ὁ . . . δοὺς . . . ἐλπίδα ἀγαθὴν ἐν χάριτι, παρακαλέσαι* ὑμῶν
<small>who gave   may he encourage</small>

    τὰς καρδίας καὶ στηρίξαι* ἐν παντὶ ἔργῳ καὶ λόγῳ ἀγαθῷ.
<small>strengthen</small>

7. Οὗτός ἐστιν ὁ ἐλθὼν δι᾽ ὕδατος καὶ αἵματος, Ἰησοῦς Χριστός·
<small>who comes</small>

    οὐκ ἐν τῷ ὕδατι μόνον ἀλλ᾽ ἐν τῷ ὕδατι καὶ ἐν τῷ αἵματι . . .
<small>alone</small>

*These are verbs in the optative mood, *rare in the New Testament,* expressing a wish or desire.

12 The Regular Verb—Part V

The Participle

I. Introduction:

A. We now come to one of NT Greek's favorite parts of speech, the versatile PARTICIPLE, whose use serves to illustrate the genius of the language.

B. Perhaps even more than the infinitive, the NT participle represents *many relationships* which are usually expressed in English by subordinate clauses.

C. The participle is a VERBAL ADJECTIVE (as the infinitive is a verbal noun), hence it has *conjugation* (limited) like a verb, *declension* as an adjective, and *usage* reflecting the characteristics of *both* verbs and adjectives.

D. In our study of the participle, we will first treat its formation, comprising its conjugation and declension, then its usage as a verbal adjective.

II. Formation of the participle:

A. CONJUGATION:
1. *General Remarks:*
   a. **Like** the other verb forms, the participle uses **all three voices.**
   b. **Unlike** some of the others, **four tenses** exist in NT Greek:
      1) The *present* and the *aorist* are the principal tenses used.
      2) The *perfect* tense is used sparingly, mostly in the *passive.*
      3) The *future* is rare in the active and middle, *unused* in the passive.
   c. **Pre-stem characteristics:**
      1) *Augment* is absent, as always outside of the indicative.
      2) *Reduplication* is used *only* in the perfect.
   d. **Post-stem characteristics:**
      1) *System signs:* Only these four appear—
         a) *Future:* σ- in active and middle only, and *rarely.*
         b) *Aorist:* σα- in active and middle voices.

c) *Perfect:* κ- in active only (middle-passive has no system sign).

d) *Passive:* θε- in aorist only (no future passive)

2) *Variable vowels:* Unlengthened, these are used only in the *present* and *rare future* participles, ο/ε.

3) *Participial signs:* After stem (system sign) and/or variable vowels—

a) *ντ:* present, future, aorist active, and aorist passive.

b) *οτ:* perfect active only.

c) *μεν:* all middle and passive participles except the aorist passive.

4) *Endings* will be treated under the declension of the participle.

e. **Accentuation:** Generally recessive, like most verb forms, but—

1) *Also follows rules of adjectives* (pp. 15, 76, 80), e.g. genitive plural.

2) *Perfect middle and passive* take an acute accent on the penult.

3) *Perfect active and aorist passive* accent the penult or the ultima. (*Note especially* the accentuation of the perfect active *feminine*.)

2. *Synopsis of the conjugation* of the participle of λύω (loose, destroy):

a. **The active voice:**

1) *Present* active: λυ + ο + ντ + endings.

2) *Future* active: λυ + σ + ο + ντ + endings.

3) *Aorist* active: λυ + σα + ντ + endings.

4) *Perfect* active: λε + λυ + κ + οτ + endings.

b. **The middle and passive:**

1) *Present* middle and passive: λυ + ο + μεν + endings.

2) *Future* middle: λυ + σ + ο + μεν + endings.

3) *Aorist* middle: λυ + σα + μεν + endings.

4) *Perfect* middle and passive: λε + λυ + μεν + endings.

5) *Aorist* passive: λυ + θε + ντ + endings.

B. DECLENSION:

1. *General remarks:* declension according to *gender*—

a. **Masculine and neuter:**

1) *Follow the third declension* (lingual mute) in the *active voice of all tenses* and the *aorist passive,* which has active endings.

2) *Follow the second declension* in the *middle and passive of all tenses* except the aorist passive, which has active endings.

b. **Feminine:** *Follows the first declension* in *all* tenses and voices.

2. *Formation and declension* of the *present active participle:*
a. **Formation:**
   1) *Masculine-neuter* adds ντ to the *present stem* to form a lingual mute stem declined like ἄρχων, ἄρχοντος = leader, p. 80.
   2) The *feminine* may have added ντι which evolved into ντσ, the ντ then dropping before σ and the vowel lengthened to ου.
b. **Declension:** (NB: Designations of *masculine, feminine,* and *neuter* are omitted as unnecessary.)

	Sing.				Plural		
N.	λύων	λύουσα	λῦον	N.	λύοντες	λύουσαι	λύοντα
G.	λύοντος	λυούσης	λύοντος	G.	λυόντων	λυουσῶν	λυόντων
D.	λύοντι	λυούσῃ	λύοντι	D.	λύουσι	λυούσαις	λύουσι
A.	λύοντα	λύουσαν	λῦον	A.	λύοντας	λυούσας	λύοντα

3. *Formation and declension* of the *future active participle:* about to loose—
a. **Formation:** Just like the present participle in the regular verb, *with the addition of the system sign* σ of the future.
b. **Declension:**

	Sing.				Plural		
N.	λύσων	λύσουσα	λῦσον	N.	λύσοντες	λύσουσαι	λύσοντα
G.	λύσοντος	λυσούσης	λύσοντος	G.	λυσόντων	λυσουσῶν	λυσόντων
D.	λύσοντι	λυσούσῃ	λύσοντι	D.	λύσουσι	λυσούσαις	λύσουσι
A.	λύσοντα	λύσουσαν	λῦσον	A.	λύσοντας	λυσούσας	λύσοντα

4. *The aorist active participle:* having loosed (single action in past time)—
a. **Formation:**
   1) It adds ντ to the *aorist stem* to form a lingual mute stem declined like the adjective πᾶς, πᾶσα, πᾶν = all, whole, every (p. 81).
   2) ντ drops before σ in the nominative singular and dative plural of the masculine and neuter, and throughout the feminine.
b. **Declension:**

	Sing.				Plural		
N.	λύσας	λύσασα	λῦσαν	N.	λύσαντες	λύσασαι	λύσαντα
G.	λύσαντος	λυσάσης	λύσαντος	G.	λυσάντων	λυσασῶν	λυσάντων
D.	λύσαντι	λυσάσῃ	λύσαντι	D.	λύσασι	λυσάσαις	λύσασι
A.	λύσαντα	λύσασαν	λῦσαν	A.	λύσαντας	λυσάσας	λύσαντα

5. *The perfect active participle:* having loosed (past action continued in the present; completed, perfect)—
a. **Formation:**
   1) It adds στ to the *perfect active stem* to form a lingual mute stem declined much like φῶς, φωτός, τό = light (p. 78). (*Note accents!*)
   2) τ drops before σ in the nominative singular and dative plural of the masculine and neuter, the feminine adding υι throughout.
b. **Declension:**

	Sing.				Plural		
N.	λελυκώς	λελυκυῖα	λελυκός	N.	λελυκότες	λελυκυῖαι	λελυκότα
G.	λελυκότος	λελυκυίας	λελυκότος	G.	λελυκότων	λελυκυιῶν	λελυκότων
D.	λελυκότι	λελυκυίᾳ	λελυκότι	D.	λελυκόσι	λελυκυίαις	λελυκόσι
A.	λελυκότα	λελυκυῖαν	λελυκός	A.	λελυκότας	λελυκυίας	λελυκότα

6. *The aorist passive participle:* having been loosed (single past action)—
a. **Formation:**
   1) It adds ντ to the *aorist passive stem* to form a lingual mute stem declined somewhat like πᾶς, πᾶσα, πᾶν, with obvious differences.
   2) ντ drops before σ in the nominative singular and dative plural of the masculine and neuter, and throughout the feminine.
b. **Declension:**

	Sing.				Plural		
N.	λυθείς	λυθεῖσα	λυθέν	N.	λυθέντες	λυθεῖσαι	λυθέντα
G.	λυθέντος	λυθείσης	λυθέντος	G.	λυθέντων	λυθεισῶν	λυθέντων
D.	λυθέντι	λυθείσῃ	λυθέντι	D.	λυθεῖσι	λυθείσαις	λυθεῖσι
A.	λυθέντα	λυθεῖσαν	λυθέν	A.	λυθέντας	λυθείσας	λυθέντα

7. *The middle and passive participles:*
a. **Formation:** They add μεν to their respective stems, then the *endings of the 1st and 2nd declensions*, being declined like μόνος, η, ον = only. (p. 16)
b. **Declensions** (summarized):
   1) *Present middle and passive:* {loosing oneself, etc.
      λυόμενος, η, ον = {being loosed
   2) *Future middle:* λυσόμενος, η, ον = about to loose oneself.
   3) *Aorist middle:* λυσάμενος, η, ον = having loosed oneself.
   4) *Perfect middle and passive:* {having loosed oneself
      λελυμένος, η, ον = {having been loosed

III. Usage of the NT Greek participle:

A. INTRODUCTION:

1. As already indicated, the use of the NT Greek participle is extremely *varied* and interesting, but not necessarily confusing and discouraging if we keep in mind that, as a verbal adjective, it partakes of the uses of both a verb and an adjective.

2. Each of these uses we will examine in turn, but before doing so, *three important considerations* need to be addressed:

   a. **The use of tenses:**

   1) *As an oblique mood,* the participle does not use tenses in exactly the same way as the indicative, but on the other hand *participial tenses do not refer simply to aspect* as in other oblique moods.

   2) Rather, *tenses in the participle indicate relative time,* that is, present, past, or future time in relation to that of the main verb. (cf. VERBAL AND ADVERBIAL USE, p. 89)

   b. **The negative:**

   1) *As an oblique mood,* the participle normally uses the negative μή rather than οὐ.

   2) However, the negative οὐ is *sometimes* used for the sake of special *emphasis* or for *stylistic reasons.*

   c. **Translation:**

   1) It is perfectly legitimate and perhaps helpful to first translate a participle with the familiar English participial *ending "-ing."*

   2) However, we must then interpret the *meaning of the participle in context* and express it with the "-ing" ending or, more often, with some form of *adjectival or adverbial clause.*

B. ADJECTIVAL USE:

1. *Introduction:*

   a. As we have already seen on page 17, **NT Greek adjectives are used in three ways:** attributively, predicatively, and substantively.

   b. This is also true of NT Greek participles when they are **used as adjectives,** i.e. modifying nouns or pronouns.

2. *Attributive use:*
   Used after the article, a participle is often equivalent to a *relative clause,* e.g. ὁ πιστεύων ἄνθρωπος (ὁ ἄνθρωπος ὁ πιστεύων) = The believing man, *or:* The man who believes.

3. *Predicative use:*

a. **Used apart from the article,** the predicative participle makes a statement about the subject with a connecting verb expressed or understood, e.g. ὁ ἄνθρωπός (ἐστι) πιστεύων /πιστεύων (ἐστιν) ὁ ἄνθρωπος = The man is believing, believes, is a believer.

b. This kind of *periphrastic* (or "roundabout") expression *is very common* in the New Testament, for it reflects a Semitic (especially Aramaic) usage, though it was not unknown among the Greeks as well, e.g. Καὶ αὐτὸς ἦν Ἰησοῦς ἀρχόμενος ὡσεὶ ἐτῶν τριάκοντα . . . = And Jesus himself was beginning about thirty years (of age). (Lk. 3:23)

4. *Substantive use:*

a. The participle is frequently used in the New Testament, often with an article, **simply as a noun,** e.g. οἱ πιστεύοντες = the believers.

b. In a usage referred to by some as *supplementary*, by others as a form of *indirect discourse*, the participle is not infrequently **used after verbs of perception** (seeing, hearing, feeling) **and cognition** (learning, knowing, proving), e.g. καὶ εὐθὺς ὁ Ἰησοῦς ἐπιγνοὺς ἐν ἑαυτῷ τὴν ἐξ αὐτοῦ δύναμιν ἐξελθοῦσαν . . . ἔλεγεν . . . = and immediately Jesus, knowing in himself that power had gone out from him . . . said . . . (Mk. 5:30)

C. VERBAL AND ADVERBIAL USE:

1. *Verbal:*

a. **As part of the verb,** of course, the participle can have a *subject* and *object* much as does the verbal noun, the infinitive.

b. However, it may be more accurate to regard the participle as *agreeing with or modifying* the subject and *governing* an object.

2. *Adverbial:* More importantly, the participle is used as equivalent to an adverbial clause (i.e. modifying the *verb*, not the subject) in a variety of ways, best interpreted from the context and translated as *clauses:*

a. **Dependent circumstantial usage:** The participle, used in an adverbial manner, may be understood in several ways, as exemplified in the introduction to the Sermon on the Mount (Mt. 5:1): Ἰδὼν δὲ τοὺς ὄχλους ἀνέβη εἰς τὸ ὄρος . . . can be translated—

1) But seeing the crowds he went up into the mountain . . .

(general)

2) But when he saw the crowds he went up into the mt . . .

(temporal)

3) But <u>because he saw the crowds</u> he went up into the mt . . .

(causal)

4) But <u>although he saw the crowds</u> he went up into the mt . . .

(concessive)

b. **Independent circumstantial usage** (genitive absolute):

1) This is the Greek equivalent of the English nominative absolute and the Latin ablative absolute, combining a noun or pronoun (other than the subject) in the genitive with a participle of the same case, and best translated by a clause.

2) A perfect example occurs immediately following the above text: καὶ *καθίσαντος αὐτοῦ προσῆλθαν αὐτῷ οἱ μαθηταὶ αὐτοῦ* = and <u>when he had sat down</u> his disciples approached him. (Mt. 5 : 1)

c. **Semitic or "dramatic" usage:**

1) In a manner characteristic of Biblical Greek (Septuagint and New Testament) *the participle is often used as the equivalent of Semitic expressions* (Jesus spoke Aramaic), especially for authenticity and dramatic effect.

2) Again, a perfect example occurs immediately after the text above: καὶ *ἀνοίξας τὸ στόμα αὐτοῦ ἐδίδασκεν αὐτοὺς λέγων* . . . = and <u>opening his mouth</u> he taught them, <u>saying</u> . . .

(Mt. 5 : 2)

(Note how precisely Greek uses participial tenses, e.g. employing the aorist participle to mean literally: "<u>having opened</u> his mouth" or "when he <u>had opened</u> his mouth," i.e. <u>before</u> he began to teach.)

IV. Exercises:

A. *Be able to conjugate and decline the participle* of any of the regular verbs studied so far in *all tenses and voices* (cf. pages 38 and 43–44).

B. *Be able to recognize* participial forms, especially by comparison with other moods, by means of *identification* or *distinction* from other forms:

1. *Identify* these forms, *multiple* in their *possible meanings:* λύουσι (3), λῦσον (3), λύσουσι (3)

2. *Distinguish* these forms, which look the same, but are not: λελυκόσι (2) + λελύκασι, λελυμένη + λελύμεθα, λυθείσῃ + λυθήσῃ, λυόμενον + λυσόμενον, λῦον + ἔλυον (2), λύοντι + λύονται, λύσασαι + λῦσαι (2), λυσάσῃ + λύσῃ (3).

C. Please *read aloud, translate,* and *explain the underlined words* of the following (The interrupted underlining refers to previous usage for review.):

1. καὶ μακαρία ἡ πιστεύσασα ὅτι ἔσται τελείωσις
   will be   fulfillment

   τοῖς λελαλημένοις αὐτῇ παρὰ κυρίου.
   for the things spoken

2. καὶ γυναῖκές τινες αἳ ἦσαν τεθεραπευμέναι ἀπὸ πνευμάτων
   some   were   spirits

   πονηρῶν καὶ ἀσθενειῶν, Μαρία ἡ καλουμένη Μαγδαληνή . . .
   illnesses   called

3. Καὶ πορευομένων αὐτῶν ἐν τῇ ὁδῷ εἶπεν τις πρὸς αὐτόν . . .
   said

4. Πᾶς ὁ ἀπολύων τὴν γυναῖκα αὐτοῦ καὶ γαμῶν ἑτέραν μοιχεύει,
   marries   commits adultery

   καὶ ὁ ἀπολελυμένην ἀπὸ ἀνδρὸς γαμῶν μοιχεύει.
   man

5. ἀπελθόντες δὲ οἱ ἀπεσταλμένοι εὗρον καθὼς εἶπεν αὐτοῖς.
   departing   sent   found   told

   λυόντων δὲ αὐτῶν τὸν πῶλον εἶπαν οἱ κύριοι αὐτοῦ πρὸς αὐτούς,
   donkey   said   masters

   Τί λύετε τὸν πῶλον;

6. ᾔδει γὰρ ἐξ ἀρχῆς ὁ Ἰησοῦς τίνες εἰσὶν οἱ μὴ πιστεύοντες καὶ
   knew   are

   τίς ἐστιν ὁ παραδώσων αὐτόν.
   is   will betray

7. Ἔλεγεν οὖν ὁ Ἰησοῦς πρὸς τοὺς πεπιστευκότας αὐτῷ Ἰουδαίους,
   said   Jews

   Ἐὰν ὑμεῖς μείνητε ἐν τῷ λόγῳ τῷ ἐμῷ . . . μαθηταί μού
   remain

   ἐστε . . .
   you are

8. ἐλεύσεται ὃν τρόπον ἐθεάσασθε αὐτὸν πορευόμενον εἰς . . .
   he will come   manner   you saw

   οὐρανόν.

9. Ἦσαν δὲ εἰς Ἰερουσαλὴμ κατοικοῦντες Ἰουδαῖοι . . . γενομένης
   there were   in   Jerusalem   dwelling   happened

   δὲ τῆς φωνῆς ταύτης συνῆλθεν τὸ πλῆθος καὶ συνεχύθη, ὅτι
   gathered   crowd   was confused

   ἤκουον εἰς ἕκαστος τῇ ἰδίᾳ διαλέκτῳ λαλούντων αὐτῶν.
   one   each   speaking

10. πολλοὶ δὲ τῶν ἀκουσάντων τὸν λόγον ἐπίστευσαν . . .
    many

11. τόν τε ἄνθρωπον βλέποντες σὺν αὐτοῖς ἑστῶτα τὸν
    seeing   standing

    τεθεραπευμένον οὐδὲν εἶχον ἀντειπεῖν.
    nothing   they had   to say against

13 Mute Verbs and Their Changes

I. **Introduction:**

A. Just as the Greek third declension comprises various types according to their stems, so also the Greek verbs, which include the same general types: mute, liquid, sibilant, vowel, and diphthong stems.

B. So far, we have studied only certain vowel and diphthong verbs with stems ending in the unchanging vowel Upsilon (*v*) and therefore called "regular" because they have minimum changes.

C. Now it is time to look at some other types, beginning with the MUTE VERBS, for which we have prepared ourselves by examining the mute changes (the "mutations") in third declension nouns, adjectives, and participles.

D. As an immediate preparation for this lesson, the student would do well to *review and clinch memorization of the brief chart* on the classes and orders of the mutes on pages 77–78.

II. **Changes in mute verbs:**

A. IN GENERAL:

    1. In many forms, e.g. those of the present system with its variable vowel, *mute verbs are conjugated exactly like the regular verb* we have studied.

    2. *But whenever the stem mute meets a consonant,* mute changes ("mutations") occur, for example when the mute encounters:

    a. **The system signs** of the future, aorist, perfect, and passive systems.

    b. The **endings** of the perfect middle system, which has no system signs.

    3. *The examples of the three classes of mutes* which we will use are:

    a. **Labial:** πέμπω (πεμπ) = send, commission (apopemptic).

b. **Palatal:** διώκω (διωκ) = pursue, persecute, seek, strive for, etc.
c. **Lingual:** πείθω (πειθ) = persuade, reassure, trust, obey.

B. IN PARTICULAR: We need to examine the *specific changes* ("mutations") which occur when mute stems encounter the consonants of system signs or endings—

1. *Mute stem changes before system signs:*
a. **With the system sign** σ of the **future** and **aorist** systems:
   1) A *labial* mute unites with σ to form ψ: πέμψω, ἔπεμψα.
   2) A *palatal* mute unites with σ to form ξ: διώξω, ἐδίωξα.
   3) A *lingual* mute is simply dropped before σ: πείσω, ἔπεισα.
b. **With the system sign** κ of the **perfect active** system:
   1) A *labial* mute usually drops* κ and "roughens": πέπομφα.
   2) A *palatal* mute usually drops* κ and "roughens": δεδίωχα.
   3) A *lingual* mute is usually dropped (or drops κ): πέπεικα, πέποιθα.
   *NB: A perfect active without the κ is called a "second perfect."
c. **With the system sign** θ of the *aorist passive* system:
   1) A *labial* mute usually coordinates ("roughens"): ἐπέμφθην.
   2) A *palatal* mute usually coordinates ("roughens"): ἐδιώχθην.
   3) A *lingual* mute usually changes to σ before θ: ἐπείσθην.

2. *Alternate changes* in mute verbs encountering system signs:
a. **Introduction:** many mute verbs, instead of changing in the manner just described, follow an alternate route by forming what are traditionally called "second aorists" and "second perfects."
b. **The second aorist system** (aorist active and middle):
   1) Is formed by dropping the system sign σα and using the variable vowel with regular secondary endings, thus *resembling* the imperfect in the indicative and the present in the oblique moods, e.g. λείπω (λιπ): ἔλιπον, λίπω, λίπε, λίπειν, λίπων.
   2) However, it can be *distinguished* from these tenses *by the use of a different stem*, usually the more basic verb stem, as distinct from the present stem which is usually in a developed state, e.g. φεύγω (φυγ): ἔφυγον, φύγω, κτλ.
              (Imperfect ἔφευγον)
c. **The second perfect system** (perfect and pluperfect active):
   1) Is formed by dropping the system sign κ, but retaining the vowel α or ει and usually "roughening" the mute, e.g. διώκω (διωκ): δεδίωχα, ἐδεδιώχειν.
   2) Some verbs also *strengthen the vowel* in the middle of the stem, usually from ε to ο, e.g. πέμπω (πεμπ): πέπομφα.

d. **The second passive system** (aorist and future passive):
1) Is formed by dropping the system sign θ, but retaining the vowel η, ε, e.g. γράφω (γραφ): ἐγράφην, γραφήσομαι.
2) It *usually retains an already rough mute,* but sometimes changes the vowel in the middle of the stem, e.g. στρέφω: ἐστράφην.

3. *Mute stem changes before endings:* Occurring in the perfect middle system and constituting the most difficult, but also *the least frequent*—

a. With $\mu\alpha\iota$ and $\mu\varepsilon\theta\alpha$ of the **1st person singular and plural:**
1) A *labial* mute changes to μ: πέπεμμαι, πεπέμμεθα. (NB: When three of the same letter occur in a row, one is dropped.)
2) A *palatal* mute changes to γ: δεδίωγμαι, δεδιώγμεθα.
3) A *lingual* mute changes to σ: πέπεισμαι, πεπείσμεθα.

b. With $\sigma\alpha\iota$ and $\tau\alpha\iota$ of the **2nd and 3rd persons singular,** the same changes occur as with the system signs σ and θ, but coordination results in a smooth mute: π, κ, (τ).
1) A *labial* mute changes to ψ and π: πέπεμψαι, πέπεμπται.
2) A *palatal* mute changes to ξ and κ: δεδίωξαι, δεδίωκται.
3) A *lingual* mute drops before σ and changes to σ before τ, e.g.: πέπεισαι, πέπεισται.

c. With $\sigma\theta\varepsilon$ of the **2nd person plural,** the σ is dropped between the two mutes and the stem mute changes before θ as before the system sign θ:
1) A *labial* mute coordinates (rough here): πέπεμφθε.
2) A *palatal* mute coordinates (rough here): δεδίωχθε.
3) A *lingual* mute changes to σ: πέπεισθε. (NB: Lingual mute changes *always* result in a σ in every form of the perfect middle and passive, a good indicator to keep in mind.)

d. With $\nu\tau\alpha\iota$ of the **3rd person plural,** the resulting word would be unpronounceable, so Greek wisely *takes a different route,* namely:
1) The regular ending is replaced by a *periphrastic* or "roundabout" form, consisting of:
a) The perfect middle and passive participle, nominative plural endings: μένοι, αι, α.
b) The 3rd person plural present indicative of the verb ("to be"): εἰσί(ν) ("Nu-Movable" is frequently used, p. 7)
2) There are still *mute changes,* of course, but they are simply the mute changes before μ that we have already studied.

3) The *result,* then, for the three kinds of mutes *looks like this:* πεπεμμένοι, αι, α / δεδιωγμένοι, αι, α / πεπεισμένοι, αι, α εἰσί(ν).

C. The foregoing mute changes can be *summarized* in the following doggerel "bone rules" which are easier to remember because they are somewhat silly:

1. A **Pi-mute** with a Mu will be Another Mu; with Sigma, Psi. With Tau-mutes it coordinates, But, dropping Kappa, aspirates.*

2. A **K-mute** with a Mu will be A Gamma; with a Sigma, Xi. With Tau-mutes it coordinates, But, dropping Kappa, aspirates.*

3. A **Tau-mute,** when before a Mu, Will be (as with a Tau-mute too) A Sigma; while before a K Or Sigma, it just fades away.

(*In verses 1 and 2, the word "aspirates" means "roughens")

III. Synopsis of the three mute verbs used as examples:

A. PRINCIPAL PARTS, which show the changes before system signs:

1. **πέμπω,** πέμψω, ἔπεμψα, (πέπομφα),** (πέπεμμαι),** ἐπέμφθην.

2. **διώκω,** διώξω, ἐδίωξα, (δεδίωχα),** δεδίωγμαι, ἐδιώχθην.

3. **πείθω,** πείσω, ἔπεισα, πέποιθα, πέπεισμαι, ἐπείσθην.

(**Forms in parentheses are legitimate forms which do *not* happen to be *used* in the New Testament, except perhaps in their compound forms.)

B. CONJUGATION of the three mute verbs in the perfect middle and passive: (The pluperfect occurs too seldom to warrant conjugating here.)

πέμπω:	**διώκω:**	**πείθω:**
Sing.	Sing.	Sing.
1. πέπεμμαι	δεδίωγμαι	πέπεισμαι
2. πέπεμψαι	δεδίωξαι	πέπεισαι
3. πέπεμπται	δεδίωκται	πέπεισται
Plural	Plural	Plural
1. πεπέμμεθα	δεδιώγμεθα	πεπείσμεθα
2. πέπεμφθε	δεδίωχθε	πέπεισθε
3. πεπεμμένοι, αι, α εἰσί(ν)	δεδιωγμένοι, αι, α εἰσί(ν)	πεπεισμένοι, αι, α εἰσί(ν)

IV. Vocabulary of mute verbs:

A. INTRODUCTION:

1. The mute verbs are rather numerous, hence we will select only a small representative number, *based on frequency of use* and *comparatively regular formation,* leaving less frequent, less regular verbs until later.

2. For easier learning, these mute verbs are divided into *two main groups:*

a. The first group comprises mute verbs which are **more varied** and, on the whole, **more frequently used,** especially **in compounds.**

b. The second group contains mute verbs which follow the same pattern of formation and are **common in the New Testament,** but **not in compounds.**

3. *Some practical reminders:*

a. **Defective verbs** are those which lack one or more principal parts.

b. **Deponent verbs** are those which generally have only a middle and/or passive form, *but an active meaning.*

c. Forms in parentheses are genuine but not found in the New Testament.

B. MUTE VERBS OF GREATER VARIETY AND FREQUENCY:
(verb stem given when needed)

ἄγω, ἄξω, ἤγαγον, (ἦχα), ἦγμαι, ἤχθην: lead, do (agent, synagogue)

ἀνοίγω,* ἀνοίξω, ἀνέῳξα, ἀνέῳγα, ἀνέῳγμαι, ἀνεῴχθην: open

ἄρχω, ἄρξω, ἦρξα: be first, rule; *middle:* begin (patriarch, archangel)

βλέπω, βλέψω, ἔβλεψα: see (blepharitis); **ἀναβλέπω:** receive sight

γράφω, γράψω, ἔγραψα, γέγραφα, γέγραμμαι, ἐγράφην: write (telegraph, telegram)

δέχομαι, δέξομαι, ἐδεξάμην, δέδεγμαι, ἐδέχθην: receive (synecdoche)

διδάσκω (διδαχ), διδάξω, ἐδίδαξα, ἐδιδάχθην: teach (didactic)

*This verb also has *two alternate forms* in the aorist, perfect middle and passive, and aorist passive systems, to which the student needs to advert: ἤνοιξα, ἠνέῳξα — ἤνοιγμαι, ἠνέῳγμαι — ἠνοίχθην, ἠνεῴχθην.

κηρύσσω (κηρυκ), κηρύξω, ἐκήρυξα, (κεκήρυχα, κεκήρυγμαι),
　　ἐκηρύχθην: herald, preach (kerygma)

-κόπτω (κοπ), κόψω, ἔκοψα, κέκομμαι, ἐκόπην: cut (pericope,
　　capon)

κράζω (κραγ), κράξω, ἔκραξα, κέκραγα: cry out (onomatopoeia,
　　i.e., the sound suggests the meaning)

-λείπω (λιπ), λείψω, ἔλιπον, (λέλοιπα), λέλειμμαι, ἐλείφθην: leave
　　(eclipse, ellipse)

πράσσω (πραγ), πράξω, ἔπραξα, πέπραχα, πέπραγμαι,
　　ἐπράχθην: do, accomplish (pragmatic)

προσεύχομαι, προσεύξομαι, ἐπροσηυξάμην: pray, entreat

στρέφω, (στρεψω), ἔστρεψα, (ἔστραμμαι), ἐστράφην: turn,
　　change (strope, apostrophe, catastrophe)

-τάσσω (ταγ), τάξω, ἔταξα, τέταχα, τέταγμαι: arrange (tactic)

φεύγω (φευγ, φυγ), φεύξομαι, ἔφυγον, πέφευγα: flee (fugue,
　　centrifugal)

φυλάσσω (φυλακ), φυλάξω, ἐφύλαξα, πεφύλαχα, ἐφυλάχθην:
　　guard, watch (phylactery, prophylactic)

C.　MUTE AND PSEUDO-MUTE VERBS OF LESSER VARIETY AND FREQUENCY:

1. *Formation:* Usually formed by adding ζω to the stem of a noun,
   adjective, or adverb, *thus creating a verb of action*, with stem
   in δ (or γ).

2. *Model:* **πειράζω** (πειραδ), (πειράσω), ἐπείρασα, (πεπείρακα),
   πεπείρασμαι, ἐπειράσθην: try, test, tempt, experiment
   (πειρασμός)

ἁγιάζω: sanctify, hallow (ἅγιος)	**ἐργάζομαι**: work, labor (ἔργον)
ἀγοράζω: buy, purchase (ἄγορα)	**ἑτοιμάζω**: prepare, destine (ἕτοιμος)
ἁρπάζω (-αγ): grasp, rob (ἅρπαξ)	**εὐαγγελίζω**: evangelize (εὐαγγέλιον)
ἀσπάζομαι: greet (ἀσπασμός)	**θαυμάζω**: wonder, admire (θαῦμα)
βαπτίζω: baptize, dip (βάπτισμα)	**καθίζω**: seat, cause to sit (καθέδρα)
βαστάζω (-αγ): carry, bear	**λογίζομαι**: count, consider (λόγος)
γνωρίζω: make known (γνῶσις)	**νομίζω**: think, suppose (νόημα)
δοκιμάζω: prove, test (δόγμα)	**ποτίζω**: give to drink, water (πόσις)
δοξάζω: glorify, praise (δόξα)	

σκανδαλίζομαι: scandalize (σκάνδαλον)

σώζω*/σώζω** (σω): save, cure (σωτήρ)

χαρίζομαι: give, donate (χάρις)

*A pseudo-mute verb—a vowel stem resembling a mute in the present system.

**Omission of Iota subscript when not needed for inflection/ meaning, see page 3.

V. Exercises:

A. BE ABLE TO:

1. *Give* and *explain* the *principal parts* of: πέμπω, διώκω, πείθω.

2. *Conjugate* and *explain* the *perfect middle and passive* of the same verbs.

B. BE ABLE TO:

1. *Recognize* the meaning and principal parts of the verbs on pages 96 and 97.

2. *Recognize* the meaning of the verbs on pages 97 and 98, especially by going back to the noun, adjective, or adverb from which they are derived.

C. *Read aloud, translate,* and *explain* the *underlined* words in these sentences:

1. Τότε ὁ Ἰησοῦς ἀνήχθη εἰς τὴν ἔρημον . . . πειρασθῆναι . . .

was led up

2. ἤρξατο ὁ Ἰησοῦς κηρύσσειν καὶ λέγειν . . . Ἤγγικεν ἡ

to say   is near
   βασιλεία . . .

3. μακάριοι οἱ δεδιωγμένοι . . . μακάριοί ἐστε ὅταν . . . ὑμᾶς . . .

you are
   διώξωσιν . . . οὕτως γὰρ ἐδίωξαν τοὺς προφήτας τοὺς πρὸ ὑμῶν.

4. Οὕτως οὖν προσεύχεσθε ὑμεῖς . . . ἁγιασθήτω τὸ ὄνομά
   σου . . .

5. Πορευθέντες ἀπαγγείλατε Ἰωάννῃ ἃ ἀκούετε καὶ βλέπετε·

announce
   τυφλοὶ ἀναβλέπουσιν . . . πτωχοὶ εὐαγγελίζονται· καὶ

poor
   μακάριός ἐστιν ὃς ἐὰν μὴ σκανδαλισθῇ ἐν ἐμοί.

is

6. ἀπόλυσον τοὺς ὄχλους, ἵνα . . . ἀγοράσωσιν ἑαυτοῖς βρώματα.

7. Ἄλλους ἔσωσεν, ἑαυτὸν οὐ δύναται σῶσαι . . .

8. Ὃς ἂν ἓν τῶν τοιούτων παιδίων δέξηται . . . ἐμὲ δέχεται.

9. ἰδόντες δὲ ἐγνώρισαν περὶ τοῦ ῥήματος τοῦ λαληθέντος αὐτοῖς
seeing   spoken

περὶ τοῦ παιδίου τούτου. καὶ πάντες οἱ ἀκούσαντες

ἐθαύμασαν . . .

10. ὡς γέγραπται ἐν βίβλῳ λόγων Ἡσαΐου τοῦ προφήτου, Φωνὴ
Isaiah

βοῶντος ἐν τῇ ἐρήμῳ, Ἑτοιμάσατε τὴν ὁδὸν κυρίου . . .
sounding

11. Καὶ πάντες ἐμαρτύρουν αὐτῷ καὶ ἐθαύμαζον ἐπὶ τοῖς λόγοις τῆς
bore witness

χάριτος τοῖς ἐκπορευομένοις ἐκ τοῦ στόματος αὐτοῦ . . .

12. μὴ βαστάζετε βαλλάντιον, μὴ πήραν, μὴ ὑποδήματα, καὶ
purse   bag   sandals

μηδένα κατὰ τὴν ὁδὸν ἀσπάσησθε.
no one

13. καὶ στραφεὶς ὁ κύριος ἐνέβλεψεν τῷ Πέτρῳ . . .
looked at   Peter

14. ἔκραξεν οὖν ἐν τῷ ἱερῷ διδάσκων ὁ Ἰησοῦς καὶ λέγων, Κἀμὲ
Jesus   saying

οἴδατε καὶ οἴδατε πόθεν εἰμί.
you know   I am

15. ἡμᾶς δεῖ ἐργάζεσθαι τὰ ἔργα τοῦ πέμψαντός με ἕως ἡμέρα
while

ἐστίν· ἔρχεται νὺξ ὅτε οὐδεὶς δύναται ἐργάζεσθαι.
comes   no one

16. Νῦν ἐδοξάσθη ὁ υἱὸς τοῦ ἀνθρώπου, καὶ ὁ θεὸς ἐδοξάσθη ἐν

αὐτῷ καὶ ὁ θεὸς δοξάσει αὐτὸν ἐν αὐτῷ.

17. ἁγίασον αὐτοὺς ἐν τῇ ἀληθείᾳ . . . ὑπὲρ αὐτῶν ἐγὼ ἁγιάζω

ἐμαυτόν, ἵνα ὦσιν καὶ αὐτοὶ ἡγιασμένοι ἐν ἀληθείᾳ.
may be

18. ἐγὼ δὲ κατελαβόμην μηδὲν ἄξιον αὐτὸν θανάτου πεπραχέναι,
found   nothing

αὐτοῦ δὲ τούτου ἐπικαλεσαμένου τὸν Σεβαστὸν ἔκρινα
appealed   Emperor   I decided

πέμπειν.

19. Ἐπίστευσεν δὲ Ἀβραὰμ τῷ θεῷ, καὶ ἐλογίσθη αὐτῷ εἰς

δικαιοσύνην. τῷ δὲ ἐργαζομένῳ ὁ μισθὸς οὐ λογίζεται κατὰ
reward

χάριν . . .

20. Πεποιθὼς τῇ ὑπακοῇ σου ἔγραψά σοι . . . ἅμα δὲ καὶ ἑτοίμαζέ
<u>obedience</u>   at the same time

    μοι ξενίαν, ἐλπίζω γὰρ ὅτι διὰ τῶν προσευχῶν ὑμῶν
      lodging   I hope   prayers

    χαρισθήσομαι ὑμῖν. Ἀσπάζεταί σε Ἐπαφρᾶς . . .
                                                     Epaphras

VI. It is fitting to conclude this lesson with one of Paul's farewell greetings, one which will be easily recognizable because of its use in the Liturgy:

Ἡ χάρις τοῦ κυρίου Ἰησοῦ Χριστοῦ καὶ ἡ ἀγάπη τοῦ θεοῦ καὶ ἡ κοινωνία τοῦ ἁγίου πνεύματος μετὰ πάντων ὑμῶν. (II Cor. 13:13)

14 Liquid or Semivowel Stems

Nouns, Adjectives, Pronouns, Numerals, Verbs

I. Introduction:

A. We have completed the study of the first type of third declension stems, that is, the mute stems, as we see them in nouns, adjectives, and verbs.

B. Now we are ready to examine the second type, namely the LIQUID OR SEMIVOWEL STEMS, as found in nouns, adjectives, pronouns, numerals, and verbs.

II. Liquid nouns of the third declension:

A. GENERAL REMARKS:

1. *The Greek liquids* or semivowels are λ, μ, ν, ρ, but only the latter two, ν, ρ, are used to form noun stems in NT Greek, e.g. μήν, ἀνήρ.

2. *The nominative* normally *ends in the liquid itself* (blank ending, p. 75) with the *preceding vowel lengthened*, e.g. εἰκών, ποιμήν, πατήρ.

3. *The genitive* indicates not only the *liquid stem* but also whether the *vowel preceding* the liquid is *long or short*, e.g. μηνός, ποιμένος.

4. *The gender* of liquid nouns is *predominantly masculine*, e.g. πατήρ, ὁ, with some notable (often natural) exceptions, e.g. μήτηρ, ἡ; πῦρ, τό.

5. *Accentuation is generally regular,* the same syllable being stressed as in the nominative, and monosyllabic nominatives accenting the ultima in the genitive and dative of both numbers, e.g. αἰών, ὧνος; μήν, μηνός.

B. LIQUID STEMS IN ν:

1. *Remarks:*

a. **The nominative,** using the blank form, ends in ν, e.g. ἀγών, μήν.

b. **In the dative plural,** ν is regularly dropped before σ, but the preceding vowel is not lengthened, e.g. ἡγεμόσι, ποιμέσι.

c. **Accentuation is regular** and almost always begins with an acute accent on the ultima of the nominative, e.g. μήν, εἰκών, ἀμπελών.

2. *Examples:*

a. **ἡγεμών, όνος, ὁ:** leader, ruler, governor, prince (hegemony, exegete)

b. **μήν, μηνός, ὁ:** month (moon, menopause, menstrual)

3. *Sample declension:*

	Sing.	Plur.		Sing.	Plur.
Nom.	ἡγεμών	ἡγεμόνες	Nom.	μήν	μῆνες
Gen.	ἡγεμόνος	ἡγεμόνων	Gen.	μηνός	μηνῶν
Dat.	ἡγεμόνι	ἡγεμόσι	Dat.	μηνί	μησί
Acc.	ἡγεμόνα	ἡγεμόνας	Acc.	μῆνα	μῆνας

4. *Select vocabulary:*

ἀγών, ῶνος, ὁ: struggle (agony)

αἰών, ῶνος, ὁ: age, era (eon)

ἀμπελών, ῶνος, ὁ: vineyard

εἰκών, όνος, ἡ: image (ikon)

Ἕλλην, ηνος, ὁ: Greek, gentile (Helen)

ποιμήν, ένος, ὁ: shepherd (poimenic)

πυλών, ῶνος, ὁ: gate, porch (pylon)

χιτών, ῶνος, ὁ: tunic, shirt (chiton)

C. LIQUID STEMS IN ρ:

1. *Remarks:*

a. These are divided into two groups: **simple** and **syncopated** liquids—

   1) **Simple stems** are declined more or less regularly, exceptions being indicated in connection with the vocabulary.

   2) **Syncopated stems** (from Greek: to cut short) *drop the vowel* preceding the liquid in some cases, as will be seen when declined.

b. With few exceptions (which will be pointed out) stems in ρ:

   1) **End the nominative** with the liquid itself, e.g. ἀστήρ, ἀνήρ.

   2) Retain the liquid in the **dative plural,** e.g. ἀστέρσι, χέρσι.

   3) **Accent** the ultima in the nominative and the rest regularly.

2. *Simple stems:* examples, declension, and vocabulary—
a. **Examples:**
   1) **σωτήρ, ῆρος, ὁ:** savior, redeemer, deliverer (soteriology)
   2) **χείρ, χειρός, ἡ:** hand (chiropodist, chiropractor, surgeon)
b. **Sample declension:**

	Sing.	Plur.		Sing.	Plur.
Nom.	σωτήρ	σωτῆρες	*Nom.*	χείρ	χεῖρες
Gen.	σωτῆρος	σωτήρων	*Gen.*	χειρός	χειρῶν
Dat.	σωτῆρι	σωτῆρσι	*Dat.*	χειρί	χερσι*
Acc.	σωτῆρα	σωτῆρας	*Acc.*	χεῖρα	χεῖρας

c. **Select vocabulary:**

ἀλέκτωρ, ορος, ὁ: cock, rooster

ἀστήρ, έρος, ὁ: star (astronomy)

μάρτυς,* υρος, ὁ: witness (martyr) *Note spelling of the nominative.*

παντοκράτωρ, ορος, ὁ: almighty

πῦρ, πυρός, τό: fire (pyre, pyro-)

*NB: χείρ drops ι and μάρτυς drops ρ in the dative plural.

3. *Syncopated stems:* examples, declension, and vocabulary:
a. **Examples:**
   1) **πατήρ, τρός, ὁ:** father (patriarch, patriot, patronym, patrology)
   2) **ἀνήρ, δρός, ὁ:** man, male, husband (philander, polyandry, android)
b. **Sample declension:**

	Sing.	Plur.		Sing.	Plur.
Nom.	πατήρ	πατέρες	*Nom.*	ἀνήρ	ἄνδρες
Gen.	πατρός	πατέρων	*Gen.*	ἀνδρός	ἀνδρῶν
Dat.	πατρί	πατράσι	*Dat.*	ἀνδρί	ἀνδράσι
Acc.	πατέρα	πατέρας	*Acc.*	ἄνδρα	ἄνδρας

c. **Select vocabulary** (Other words declined like *πατήρ*):

γαστήρ, τρός, ἡ: womb (gastric)

θυγάτηρ, τρός, ἡ: daughter (daughter)

μήτηρ, τρός, ἡ: mother (metropolis)

Note accents of these words.

III. Liquid adjectives, pronouns, and numerals:

A. INTRODUCTION: A limited number of these parts of speech also have liquid stems, and for that reason it is helpful to study them at this time, as we do on the following two pages.

B.   LIQUID ADJECTIVES: *Very few* in NT Greek, usually composite, and always of *two terminations*, i.e. the masculine and feminine have the same form, e.g., **ἄφρων, ον** (ἀ + φρήν = without a brain): foolish, senseless, unlearned.

	Sing. Masc.-Fem.	Neut.		Plur. Masc.-Fem.	Neut.
Nom.	ἄφρων	ἄφρον	*Nom.*	ἄφρονες	ἄφρονα
Gen.	ἄφρονος	ἄφρονος	*Gen.*	ἀφρόνων	ἀφρόνων
Dat.	ἄφρονι	ἄφρονι	*Dat.*	ἄφροσι	ἄφροσι
Acc.	ἄφρονα	ἄφρον	*Acc.*	ἄφρονας	ἄφρονα

C.   LIQUID PRONOUNS: These are the *interrogative and indefinite pronouns*, already mentioned on pp. 47–50, and the *indefinite relative pronoun*, which is a combination of the relative plus the indefinite (pp. 18, 50, 52, 60).

1. *Declension* of the *interrogative* pronoun: *who, which, what, why, how?*

	Sing. Masc.-Fem.	Neut.		Plur. Masc.-Fem.	Neut.
Nom.	τίς	τί	*Nom.*	τίνες	τίνα
Gen.	τίνος	τίνος	*Gen.*	τίνων	τίνων
Dat.	τίνι	τίνι	*Dat.*	τίσι	τίσι
Acc.	τίνα	τί	*Acc.*	τίνας	τίνα

NOTE that these acute accents *never* change to the grave.

2. *Declension* of the *indefinite* pronoun: *someone/-thing, anyone/-thing.*

	Sing. Masc.-Fem.	Neut.		Plur. Masc.-Fem.	Neut.
Nom.	τις	τι	*Nom.*	τινές	τινά
Gen.	τινός	τινός	*Gen.*	τινῶν	τινῶν
Dat.	τινί	τινί	*Dat.*	τισί	τισί
Acc.	τινά	τι	*Acc.*	τινάς	τινά

NOTE that the only *difference* from the interrogative is in accents.

3. *Declension* of the *indefinite relative* pronoun: *whoever, whatever.*

	Sing. Masc.	Fem.	Neut.		Plur. Masc.	Fem.	Neut.
N.	ὅστις	ἥτις	ὅτι	*N.*	οἵτινες	αἵτινες	ἅτινα
G.	οὗτινος	ἧστινος	οὗτινος	*G.*	ὧντινων	ὧντινων	ὧντινων
D.	ᾧτινι	ᾗτινι	ᾧτινι	*D.*	οἷστισι	αἷστισι	οἷστισι
A.	ὅντινα	ἥντινα	ὅτι	*A.*	οὕστινας	ἅστινας	ἅτινα

NOTE the following with regard to the indefinite relative
pronoun:

1) ὅτι is often written ὅ τι to distinguish it from ὅτι: *that, because.*
2) The indefinite pronoun does *not* affect accents on the
relative.

D. LIQUID NUMERALS:

1. *Explanation:* of the declinable numerals, two are liquids,
   namely the number *one* (with its compounds) and the number
   four, which are—
   a. **εἷς, μία, ἕν:** *one, a, an, single* (hyphen, hendiadys, henotheism)
   b. **τέσσαρες, τέσσαρα:** *four* (diatesseron, tetrarch, tetragrammaton)

2. *Declension* of the simple liquid numerals: *one* and *four*—

	Masc.	Fem.	Neut.		Masc.-Fem.	Neut.
Nom.	εἷς	μία	ἕν	Nom.	τέσσαρες	τέσσαρα
Gen.	ἑνός	μιᾶς	ἑνός	Gen.	τεσσάρων	τεσσάρων
Dat.	ἑνί	μιᾷ	ἑνί	Dat.	τέσσαρσι	τέσσαρσι
Acc.	ἕνα	μίαν	ἕν	Acc.	τέσσαρας	τέσσαρα

3. *Declension* of compound (negative) liquid numerals: *no one,
   nothing*—

	Masc.	Fem.	Neut.		Masc.	Fem.	Neut.
N.	οὐδείς	οὐδεμία	οὐδέν	N.	μηδείς	μηδεμία	μηδέν
G.	οὐδένος	οὐδεμίας	οὐδένος	G.	μηδένος	μηδεμίας	μηδένος
D.	οὐδένι	οὐδεμίᾳ	οὐδένι	D.	μηδένι	μηδεμίᾳ	μηδένι
A.	οὐδένα	οὐδεμίαν	οὐδέν	A.	μηδένα	μηδεμίαν	μηδέν

NOTE: These are simply the negatives οὐ and μή plus the numeral
εἷς, μία, ἕν, with δ or δε added for pronunciation. Do not confuse
with οὐδέ, μηδέ: *neither/nor, and not, not even* (adverb or
adverbial conjunction).

IV. Liquid verbs:

A. INTRODUCTION:

1. *Liquid verbs* are those whose *verb stem* (and usually the
   present stem) ends in a liquid: λ, ν, ρ and, very rarely, μ.

2. While this *affects all six* verb systems, the ones most affected
   are the future, aorist, perfect active, and perfect middle and
   passive.

B.   FORMATION of liquid verbs *according to systems:* *

1. *Present system:* The present stem is almost always a *strengthened form* of the verb stem (given in parentheses), but the conjugation is regular, e.g. ἀποστέλλω (στελ): send out (apostle), φαίνω (φαν): show (Epiphany), σπείρω (σπερ): sow, broadcast (diaspora).

2. *Future system:*

a. The liquid stem **adds to the verb stem** the system sign ε instead of σ, then **contracts** the ε with the variable vowel or developed endings according to the following pattern:
   1) ε is *absorbed* into a following ⌠ ω, η
      long vowel or diphthong: ⌡ ου, ει
   2) ε + o = ου, ε + ε = ει.
   3) The resulting *contraction* is indicated by the *circumflex accent.*

b. Hence, the **synopsis** of the above-mentioned verbs in the **future:**
   1) **ἀποστελῶ** (ἀπο + στελ + ε + ω), **ἀποστελοῦμαι** (ἀπο + στελ + ε + o + μαι)
   2) **φανῶ** (φαν + ε + ω), **φανοῦμαι** (φαν + ε + o + μαι)
   3) **σπερῶ** (σπερ + ε + ω), **σπεροῦμαι** (σπερ + ε + o + μαι)

c. **Sample conjugation** of the liquid future of: **βάλλω** (βαλ): throw.

	ACTIVE			MIDDLE	
	Sing.	Plur.		Sing.	Plur.
1)	βαλῶ	βαλοῦμεν	1)	βαλοῦμαι	βαλούμεθα
2)	βαλεῖς	βαλεῖτε	2)	βαλῇ	βαλεῖσθε
3)	βαλεῖ	βαλοῦσι	3)	βαλεῖται	βαλοῦνται

3. *Aorist system:*

a. The liquid aorist uses a **strengthened form** of the verb stem (α to long α or η, ε to ει), e.g. ἀπέστειλα, ἔφανα, ἔσπειρα.

b. To the strengthened verb stem **it adds** α instead of σα, but is then conjugated regularly, e.g. ἔφανα, ας, ε — ἐφάναμεν, ατε, αν.

4. *Perfect system:*

a. The perfect **characteristic** κα **is retained,** but before it ν is either dropped or becomes gamma nasal, while λ and ρ remain as they are, e.g. ἀπέσταλκα, κέκρικα, πέφαγκα, ἦρκα.

b. **Conjugation is regular,** but ε in the stem is usually strengthened to α, e.g. ἀπέσταλκα.

*For complete vocabulary of verbs used as examples, see pages 108–109, V, B.

5. *Perfect middle-passive system:* difficult but easier than the mutes—
a. As in the perfect active, ε in the stem **is strengthened** to α.
b. When the liquids λ, ν, ρ encounter the middle-passive endings:
   1) λ and ρ usually remain **intact** throughout the system.
   2) ν varies, being **assimilated** to μ or **changed** to σ or simply **dropped,** e.g. ἐξήραμμαι (ξηραίνω), πέφασμαι (φαίνω), κέκριμαι (κρίνω).
   3) **With all three liquids:**
      a) The σ of σθε and the infinitive σθαι is **dropped** between the two consonants involved, e.g. ἔσταλθε, ἐστάλθαι.
      b) νται of the 3rd person plural is almost always **discarded** and a **periphrastic form,** consisting of participial endings and the verb "to be," is used as in the mute verbs.
c. **Sample conjugation** of the perfect middle-passive of: **ἀποστέλλω.**

	Sing.		Plur.
1)	ἀπέσταλμαι	1)	ἀπεστάλμεθα
2)	ἀπέσταλσαι	2)	ἀπέσταλθε
3)	ἀπέσταλται	3)	ἀπεσταλμένοι, αι, α εἰσί

d. **Sample conjugation** of the perfect middle-passive of: **κρίνω, αἴρω.**

	Sing.			Plur.	
1)	κέκριμαι	ἦρμαι	1)	κεκρίμεθα	ἤρμεθα
2)	κέκρισαι	ἦρσαι	2)	κέκρισθε	ἦρθε
3)	κέκριται	ἦρται	3)	κέκρινται	ἠρμένοι, αι, α εἰσί

6. *(Aorist) passive system:* **Regular,** except for the usual *strengthening* of the stem and the frequent omission of θ, thus forming a *second passive aorist:* ἀπεστάλην, ἤρθην, ἐφάνην, ἐκρίθην, ἐσπάρην; and *future:* ἀποσταλήσομαι, ἀρθήσομαι, φανήσομαι, κριθήσομαι, σπαρήσομαι.

V. **Select vocabulary of liquid and pseudo-liquid verbs:**

A. INTRODUCTION: *All* these verbs are *important,* being divided not according to frequency and importance but *according to quality* as liquid verbs.

B. GENUINE LIQUID VERBS more or less regular and complete:
αἴρω (ἀρ), ἀρῶ, ἦρα, ἦρκα, ἦρμαι, ἤρθην: take up, take away, conquer.
ἀπαγγέλλω (ἀγγελ), ἀπαγγελῶ, ἀπήγγειλα, ἀπηγγέλην: tell, inform; proclaim; call upon, command; acknowledge, confess (angel).

ἀποκτείνω (κτεν), ἀποκτενῶ, ἀπέκτεινα, ἀπεκτάνθην: kill,
     murder.

ἀποστέλλω (στελ), ἀποστελῶ, ἀπέστειλα, ἀπεσταλκα,
     ἀπέσταλμαι, ἀπεστάλην: send, send out, send away
     (apostle).

βάλλω (βαλ, βλα), βαλῶ, ἔβαλον*, βέβληκα, βέβλημαι, ἐβλήθην:
     throw; put; give (ball?, ballistic, parable, hyperbole,
     symbol).

ἐγείρω (ἐγερ), ἐγερῶ, ἤγειρα, ἐγήγερμαι, ἠγέρθην: raise, rouse.

κρίνω (κριν), κρινῶ, ἔκρινα, κέκρικα, κέκριμαι, ἐκρίθην: judge,
     condemn; decide; consider, think; prefer (critic, crisis, etc.)

μένω (μεν), μενῶ, ἔμεινα, μεμένηκα: stay, dwell: await (remain).

σπείρω (σπερ), σπερῶ, ἔσπειρα, ἔσπαρμαι, ἐσπάρην: sow
     (sperm).

φαίνω (φαν), φανοῦμαι, ἔφανα, (πέφαγκα, πέφασμαι), ἐφάνην:
     shine; show; appear (Epiphany, theophany, diaphanous,
     phenomenon).

C. GENUINE LIQUID VERBS more or less irregular and incomplete
    (defective):

ἀποκρίνομαι (κριν), ἀπεκρινάμην, ἀπεκρίθην: answer; declare.

βούλομαι (βουλ, βουλε), ἐβουλήθην: want, will (boule, abulia).

γίνομαι (γεν, γενε), γενήσομαι, ἐγενόμην,* γέγονα, γεγένημαι,
     ἐγενήθην: become, be; happen (gene, genesis, oxygen,
     cosmogony).

θέλω (θελ, θελε), θελήσω, ἐθέλησα: wish, desire, will
     (Monothelite).

μέλλω (μελ, μελε), μελλήσω: be about to, intend; delay; future,
     coming.

ὀφείλω (ὀφελ): owe; ought, must, be bound or obligated; sin
     against.

χαίρω (χαρ, χαρε), χαρήσομαι, ἐχάρην: rejoice, be glad;
                                   also "greetings!"

*This is a second aorist, cf. page 93.

D. PSEUDO-LIQUID VERBS apparently liquid in present or future, but
    not stem:

ἁμαρτάνω (ἁμαρτα), ἁμαρτήσω, ἡμάρτησα/ἥμαρτον,* ἡμάρτηκα,
     (ἡμάρτημαι, ἡμαρτήθην): miss the mark, go astray;
     sin.

-βαίνω (βα), βήσομαι, ἐβήν,** βέβηκα: go (acrobat, anabasis,
     diabetes).

*This is an *athematic aorist*, which will be studied in chapter 18.

ἐγγίζω (ἐγγιδ), ἐγγιῶ,*** ἤγγισα, ἤγγικα: draw near, approach (ἐγγύς).

ἐλπίζω (ἐλπιδ), ἐλπιῶ,*** ἤλπισα, ἤλπικα: hope, hope in/for (ἐλπίς).

καθαρίζω (καθαριδ), καθαριῶ,** ἐκαθάρισα, κεκαθάρισμαι, cleanse, ἐκαθαρίσθην: make or declare clean (καθαρός).

λαμβάνω (λαβ), λήμψομαι, ἔλαβον, εἴληφα, εἴλημμαι, ἐλήμφθην: take; receive; obtain; remove (syllable, epilepsy, astrolabe).

μανθάνω (μαθ, μαθε), ἔμαθον,* μεμάθηκα: learn, discover (mathematics).

πίνω (πι, πο), πίομαι, ἔπιον,* πέπωκα: drink (potion, potable, symposium).

**These are technically "Attic futures" but conjugated like liquid futures.

VI. Exercises:

A. BE ABLE TO:

1. *Decline* the following liquid nouns: εἰκών, μάρτυς, μήτηρ.

2. *Decline* the indefinite relative pronoun: ὅστις, ἥτις, ὅτι.

3. *Decline* the negative liquid numeral: οὐδείς, οὐδεμία, οὐδέν.

4. *Conjugate* the future, aorist, and { ἀποστέλλω,
   perfect middle of: { αἴρω, κρίνω

B. *Read aloud, translate,* and *explain the underlined terms* of:

1. ἄρατε τὸν ζυγόν μου ἐφ᾽ ὑμᾶς καὶ μάθετε ἀπ᾽ ἐμοῦ . . .
   yoke

2. ἔρχεται ὁ πονηρὸς καὶ ἁρπάζει τὸ ἐσπαρμένον ἐν τῇ καρδίᾳ
   comes

   αὐτοῦ· οὗτός ἐστιν ὁ παρὰ τὴν ὁδὸν σπαρείς.
   is

3. καὶ λαβόντες αὐτὸν ἐξέβαλον ἔξω τοῦ ἀμπελῶνος καὶ

   ἀπέκτειναν.

4. ἐπερωτήσω ὑμᾶς ἕνα λόγον, καὶ ἀποκρίθητέ μοι . . .
   I will ask

5. ὁ δὲ ἀρχιερεὺς διαρρήξας τοὺς χιτῶνας αὐτοῦ λέγει, Τί ἔτι
   high priest   tearing

   χρείαν ἔχομεν μαρτύρων; ἠκούσατε τῆς βλασφημίας· τί ὑμῖν
   we have   blasphemy

   φαίνεται; οἱ δὲ πάντες κατέκριναν αὐτὸν ἔνοχον εἶναι
                                          deserving   to be

   θανάτου.

6. διαμερίζονται τὰ ἱμάτια αὐτοῦ, βάλλοντες κλῆρον ἐπ᾽ αὐτὰ τίς

they divide   garments   lot
   τί ἄρῃ.

7. καὶ οὐδενὶ ἀπήγγειλαν ἐν ἐκείναις ταῖς ἡμέραις οὐδὲν . . .

8. πῦρ ἦλθον βαλεῖν ἐπὶ τὴν γῆν, καὶ τί θέλω εἰ ἤδη ἀνήφθη.

    I came   kindled

9. οὐ γὰρ ἀπέστειλεν ὁ θεὸς τὸν υἱὸν εἰς τὸν κόσμον ἵνα κρίνῃ τὸν

   κόσμον, ἀλλ᾽ ἵνα σωθῇ ὁ κόσμος δι᾽ αὐτοῦ.

10. εἰ ἠγαπᾶτέ με ἐχάρητε ἄν, ὅτι πορεύομαι πρὸς τὸν πατέρα . . .

    you loved

11. Ἐὰν μὴ ἴδω ἐν ταῖς χερσὶν αὐτοῦ τὸν τύπον τῶν ἥλων καὶ βάλω

        I see   print   nails
    τὸν δάκτυλόν μου εἰς τὸν τύπον τῶν ἥλων καὶ βάλω μου τὴν

    finger
    χεῖρα εἰς τὴν πλευρὰν αὐτοῦ, οὐ μὴ πιστεύσω.

                   side

12. Μηδενὶ μηδὲν ὀφείλετε, εἰ μὴ τὸ ἀλλήλους ἀγαπᾶν . . .

                                   to love

13. ἀστὴρ γὰρ ἀστέρος διαφέρει ἐν δόξῃ. οὕτως καὶ ἡ ἀνάστασις

               differs from   resurrection
    τῶν νεκρῶν . . . σπείρεται ἐν ἀτιμίᾳ, ἐγείρεται ἐν δόξῃ . . .

                             dishonor

14. Ὁ θεὸς ἀγάπη ἐστίν, καὶ ὁ μένων ἐν τῇ ἀγάπῃ ἐν τῷ θεῷ μένει

           is
    καὶ ὁ θεὸς ἐν αὐτῷ μένει.

15   Review and Development

I. Introduction:

A.   We have now COMPLETED THREE QUARTERS of our enterprise and can afford to pause a moment to contemplate what we have covered so far:

    1.   First, we have studied almost the entire *first and second declensions,* and *over half of the third,* in nouns, adjectives, pronouns, and numerals.

    2.   In addition, we have also learned a large number of *important "little words"*—the *indeclinable* adverbs, conjunctions, and prepositions.

    3.   Finally, but most essentially, we have studied the *entire regular verb* as well as the very valuable categories of *mute* and *liquid verbs.*

B.   LOOKING AHEAD, there remains before us only the task of:

    1.   *Finishing* our study of the *third declension nouns and adjectives* with an examination of the sibilant, vowel, and diphthong stems.

    2.   *Finalizing* our treatment of the verb by learning the formation and conjugation of two special groups: the *contract* and *athematic verbs.*

    3.   *Completing* our study with a final look at some adjectives, adverbs, and numerals not yet studied, as well as some *principal Semitic uses.*

C.   But before we undertake our "stretch run" or "final ascent," it will be helpful to REVIEW immediate past chapters, with vocabulary and practice.

II. Review of past chapters:

A. CHAPTER 11: Third Declension, Part I, Mute Nouns and Adjectives—

    1. *Review* and clinch knowledge of third declension endings and types.

    2. *Review* carefully the salient points regarding mute stems:
    a. The **classes** and **orders** of the mutes.
    b. The **formation** and declension of **palatal** and **lingual** mute nouns.
    c. The **formation,** declension, and usage of the **adjective:** πᾶς, πᾶσα, πᾶν.

    3. *Review* and test knowledge of the *vocabulary* of this chapter.

B. CHAPTER 12: The Regular Verb, Part V, The Participle—

    1. *Review* the formation, conjugation, and declension of the participle.

    2. *Review* the *usage* of the participle as adjective, verb, and adverb.

    3. *Check understanding* of this uniquely versatile part of speech in NT Greek by *again reading, translating,* and *explaining* the sentences.

C. CHAPTER 13: Mute Verbs and Their Changes (or: "mutations")—

    1. *Review* the effects upon *mute verb stems* of their encounter with the system signs, variable vowels, and endings of the verbal conjugation.

    2. *Check* knowledge of the *alternate or "second" forms* of the aorist, perfect, and passive systems employed in many of the most common verbs.

    3. *Consolidate knowledge* of mute verbs by reviewing:
    a. The vocabulary of the more **common** and more **varied** mute verbs.
    b. The vocabulary of the **less frequent** and **varied** verbs in -ζω.

D. CHAPTER 14: The Liquid or Semivowel Stems—

    1. *Review* the formation, declension, and vocabulary of:
    a. Liquid or semivowel **nouns** with stems ending in ν.
    b. **Simple** and **syncopated** liquid nouns with stems in ρ.

    2. *Review* the formation and declension of liquid **adjectives.**

3. *Review* by comparison the liquid *pronouns:*
a. The **interrogative** and **indefinite** pronouns: τίς, τί and τις, τι.
b. The **indefinite relative** pronoun: ὅστις, ἥτις, ὅτι (ὅ τι).

4. *Check* knowledge of the *liquid numerals:*
a. The **positive** numerals *one* and *four:* εἷς, μία, ἕν and τέσσαρες, α.
b. The **negative** numerals *no one, nothing:* οὐ/μηδείς, -δεμία, -δέν.

5. *Review* the formation of liquid *verbs,* especially:
a. The liquid **future** and **aorist** active and middle.
b. The liquid **perfect active** and **middle-passive.**
c. The liquid **passive** system (aorist and future).

6. *Review* the vocabulary of these *very important verbs:*
a. The more **regular** and **complete** liquid verbs.
b. The more **irregular** and **incomplete** liquid verbs.
c. The **pseudo-liquid** verbs.

III. Additional vocabulary:

A. INTRODUCTION:

1. *Vocabulary building* is one of the keys to any language, Greek included. In fact, it is *especially true of Greek,* which is a "word rich" language and justifies the saying: "The Greeks have a word for it!"

2. However, we must maintain a *balance* between neglecting to build a sound vocabulary of important words on the one hand and, on the other, attempting the impossible by trying to learn too many seldom-used words.

3. In this course, we have tried to keep this balance and will continue to try to do so:
a. **Later on,** in our final review and development chapter, we will provide a number of Greek words which are helpful but not essential.
b. **In this chapter,** we are listing some *extremely important verbs,* which the student should make every effort to learn and learn well.

B. VERY COMMON IRREGULAR VERBS, mostly mute and liquid:

1. *Comment:* These twelve verbs might well be affectionately designated the "Dirty Dozen" because, as is true of commonly used verbs in most languages, they have developed *irregular forms* which challenge the mind.

2. *Directions* for learning:
a. It is **essential** to pay careful attention to the **verb stem(s),** which will be provided in parentheses and which will indicate according to what type of stem the various **systems** are to be conjugated.
b. Ultimately, there is **no substitute for memorization,** and this is feasible since the number of these verbs is kept here at twelve.

3. *Twelve very common irregular verbs*—the "Dirty Dozen":
   ἀποθνῄσκω (θαν) (or -θνη), **ἀποθανοῦμαι, ἀπέθανον:** die, face death, be mortal (Athanasius, euthanasia, Thanatopsis)
   γινώσκω (γνο), **γνώσομαι, ἔγνων,* ἔγνωκα, ἔγνωσμαι, ἐγνώσθην:** know, learn, discern (Gnostic, agnostic, diagnosis, prognosis)
   ἔρχομαι (ἐρχ, ἐλθ, ἐλευθ, ἐλυθ), **ἐλεύσομαι, ἦλθον, ἐλήλυθα:** come, go, appear, return (proselyte)
   ἐσθίω/ἔσθω (ἐσθ, φαγ), **φάγομαι, ἔφαγον:** eat, consume (esophagus, sarcophagus; akin to Latin edo, edere/esse: edible, etc.)
   εὑρίσκω (εὑρ, εὑρε), **εὑρήσω, εὗρον, εὕρηκα, εὑρέθην:** find, obtain, receive (eureka!, heuristic)
   ἔχω (ἐχ, ἑχ, ἐσχ, σχε), **ἕξω, ἔσχον, ἔσχηκα:** have, receive, regard, can, must (epoch, eunuch, hectic, monk, scheme, schema, school)
   λέγω (λεγ, ἐρ, ἐπ), **ἐρῶ, εἶπον, εἴρηκα, εἴρημαι, ἐρρέθην/ήθην:** say, speak, tell, call, intend (dialect, eclectic, prolegomena)
   μιμνῄσκομαι (μνα) (or -μνη), **μέμνημαι, ἐμνήσθην:** remember, keep in mind, care about (amnesia, amnesty, anamnesis, mnemonics)
   ὁράω** (ὁρα, ὀπ, ἰδ), **ὄψομαι, εἶδον/δα, ἑώρακα/ἑόρακα, ὤφθην:** see, understand, visit (panorama, optic, synopsis, autopsy, idol)
   πάσχω (παθ, πενθ), **(πείσομαι), ἔπαθον, πέπονθα:** suffer, endure, feel, experience (pathos, apathy, antipathy, sympathy, telepathy)
   πίπτω (πετ, πτ, πτο), **πεσοῦμαι, ἔπεσον/σα, πέπτωκα:** fall, bow, fall down, die (symptom, proptosis, feather)
   φέρω (φερ, οἰ, ἐνεκ, ἐνεγκ), **οἴσω, ἤνεγκον/κα, ἐνήνοχα, ἠνέχθην:** bring, bear, lead (Christopher, euphoria, metaphor, phosphorus)

*An *athematic aorist* (like ἔβην, p. 106), to be studied in chapter 18.
**Partial or complete *contract verbs,* to be studied in chapter 17.

C. COMPOUND OR COMPOSITE VERBS of special importance:

1. **Compound verbs** from some of the "Twelve" listed above:
   (NOTE: Read across page)

   ἀναγινώσκω: read (esp. aloud)   *ἐπιγινώσκω*: know well, understand

   ἀνέρχομαι: go/come up, ascend   *ἀπέρχομαι*: go away, depart, be over

   διέρχομαι: pass through/over   *εἰσέρχομαι*: go into, enter, share in

   ἐξέρχομαι: come out, escape   *κατέρχομαι*: go/come down, arrive

   παρέρχομαι: pass by/away, leave   *προέρχομαι*: go ahead, precede, lead

   προσέρχομαι: go to, approach   *συνέρχομαι*: come together, assemble

   ἀνέχομαι: endure, be patient   *ἀπέχω*: be distant, free from, avoid

   κατέχω: hold fast/back, restrain   *παρέχω*: cause, do; grant, give, offer

   προσέχω: attend to, hold on to   *συνέχω*: hem in, control, guard

   ἀπολογέομαι:** speak for oneself   *διαλέγομαι*: discuss, debate, address (dialect, dialogue)

   ἐκλέγομαι: choose, select (eclectic)   *εὐλογέω*:** praise, bless, be kind to (eulogy)

   ἀναπίπτω: sit, lean (at table)   *ἐπιπίπτω*: fall/come upon, press

   ἀναφέρω: offer, bear, remove   *διαφέρω*: be superior, differ from

   προσφέρω: offer, do a service   *συμφέρω*: be better/useful, profit

2. *Compound verbs* from mute verbs listed on pages 96 to 98;

   ἀνάγω: lead; bring up, before   *ἀπάγω*: lead away, astray; arrest

   εἰσάγω: lead; bring in, into   *ἐξάγω*: lead out, bring out

   παράγω: pass by, on; disappear   *προάγω*: go before, go too far

   συνάγω: gather, assemble, welcome   *ὑπάγω*: go away, go home, return

   ὑπάρχω: be at one's disposal   *κατεργάζομαι*: produce, prepare

**Partial or complete *contract verbs*, to be studied in chapter 17.

ἐμβλέπω: look straight at, see

ἐκκόπτω: cut off, down; remove

καταλείπω: leave behind, neglect

ἀναστρέφω: return, stay, live

ὑποστρέφω: return, go home

ἐπιτάσσω: command, order

ἀναβλέπω: receive one's sight

διαλογίζομαι: discuss, wonder

ἐγκαταλείπω: abandon, neglect

ἐπιστρέφω: turn back, around, to

διατάσσω: order, instruct, arrange

ὑποτάσσω: subject, be subject to

3. *Compound verbs* from liquid/pseudo-liquid verbs listed on pages 107 to 109:

ἀναγγέλλω: proclaim, report

ἐπαγγέλλομαι: promise, profess

καταγγέλλω: teach, advocate

ἀναβαίνω: go up, aboard; grow

καταβαίνω: go down, fall down

ἐκβάλλω: drive, lead out, expel

περιβάλλω: put on, clothe, dress

ἀνακρίνω: examine, judge

διακρίνω: discern, dispute

ἀποκτείνω:* kill, put to death

ἀναλαμβάνω: take up, carry

καταλαμβάνω: grasp, overcome

προσλαμβάνομαι: welcome, receive

ἐπιμένω: remain, continue, persist

ἀπαγγέλλω:* tell, command, confess

εὐαγγελίζω:* preach the good news

παραγγέλλω: command, order, direct

ἐμβαίνω: get into, embark

μεταβαίνω: leave, move, cross over

ἐπιβάλλω: lay (hands) on, throw on

παραγίνομαι: arrive, appear, defend

ἀποκρίνομαι: reply, declare, go on

κατακρίνω: condemn, pass judgement

ἐκτείνω: stretch out, arrest

ἐπιλαμβάνομαι: take hold of, seize

παραλαμβάνω: receive, accept, learn

συλλαμβάνω: conceive, catch, arrest

ὑπομένω: endure, persevere, hold out

*Verbs already listed but repeated here in the context of other compounds.

IV. **Reading exercise:** Having completed the first chapter of John's Gospel, we now turn to the first chapter of Luke's Gospel for the *Infancy Narrative* from v. 26:

Ἐν δὲ τῷ μηνὶ τῷ ἕκτῳ ἀπεστάλη ὁ ἄγγελος Γαβριὴλ ἀπὸ τοῦ θεοῦ

(sixth) (Gabriel)

εἰς πόλιν τῆς Γαλιλαίας ᾗ ὄνομα Ναζαρὲθ πρὸς παρθένον

(city) (Galilee) (Nazareth)

ἐμνηστευμένην ἀνδρὶ ᾧ ὄνομα Ἰωσὴφ ἐξ οἴκου Δαυίδ, καὶ τὸ ὄνομα

(betrothed) (Joseph) (David)

τῆς παρθένου Μαριάμ. καὶ εἰσελθὼν πρὸς αὐτὴν εἶπεν, Χαῖρε,

(Mary)

κεχαριτωμένη, ὁ κύριος μετὰ σοῦ. ἡ δὲ ἐπὶ τῷ λόγῳ διεταράχθη καὶ

(fully favored) (was troubled)

διελογίζετο ποταπὸς εἴη** ὁ ἀσπασμὸς οὗτος. καὶ εἶπεν ὁ ἄγγελος

(what kind might be) (greeting)

αὐτῇ, Μὴ φοβοῦ, Μαριάμ, εὗρες γὰρ χάριν παρὰ τῷ θεῷ· καὶ ἰδοὺ

(fear) (behold)

συλλήμψῃ ἐν γαστρὶ καὶ τέξῃ υἱόν, καὶ καλέσεις τὸ ὄνομα αὐτοῦ

(womb) (will bear) (you will call)

Ἰησοῦν. οὗτος ἔσται μέγας καὶ υἱὸς ὑψίστου κληθήσεται, καὶ

(will be) (great) (of the Most High) (will be called)

δώσει αὐτῷ κύριος ὁ θεὸς τὸν θρόνον Δαυὶδ τοῦ πατρὸς αὐτοῦ, καὶ

(will give) (of David)

βασιλεύσει ἐπὶ τὸν οἶκον Ἰακὼβ εἰς τοὺς αἰῶνας, καὶ τῆς βασιλείας

(he will rule) (Jacob)

αὐτοῦ οὐκ ἔσται τέλος. εἶπεν δὲ Μαριὰμ πρὸς τὸν ἄγγελον, Πῶς

(an end)

ἔσται τοῦτο, ἐπεὶ ἄνδρα οὐ γινώσκω; καὶ ἀποκριθεὶς ὁ ἄγγελος

εἶπεν αὐτῇ, Πνεῦμα ἅγιον ἐπελεύσεται ἐπὶ σέ, καὶ δύναμις

(power)

ὑψίστου ἐπισκιάσει σοι· διὸ καὶ τὸ γεννώμενον ἅγιον κληθήσεται,

(will overshadow) (hence) (one born)

υἱὸς θεοῦ. καὶ ἰδοὺ Ἐλισάβετ ἡ συγγενίς σου καὶ αὐτὴ συνείληφεν

(Elizabeth) (kinswoman)

υἱὸν ἐν γήρει αὐτῆς, καὶ οὗτος μὴν ἕκτος ἐστὶν αὐτῇ τῇ καλουμένῃ

(old age) (sixth) (called)

στείρᾳ ὅτι οὐκ ἀδυνατήσει παρὰ τοῦ θεοῦ πᾶν ῥῆμα. εἶπεν δὲ

(sterile) (will be impossible)

Μαριάμ, Ἰδοὺ ἡ δούλη κυρίου· γένοιτό* μοι κατὰ τὸ ῥῆμά σου.

(slave) (let it be (done))

καὶ ἀπῆλθεν ἀπ᾽ αὐτῆς ὁ ἄγγελος. Ἀναστᾶσα δὲ Μαριὰμ ἐν ταῖς

(rising)

ἡμέραις ταύταις ἐπορεύθη εἰς τὴν ὀρεινὴν μετὰ σπουδῆς εἰς πόλιν

(hill country) (with haste) (a city)

*The present *optative*, third person singular, of the verb εἰμί
= I am.

**This is the aorist *optative* 3rd person singular of γίνομαι
= I become, am made, am done.

Ἰούδα, καὶ <u>εἰσῆλθεν</u> εἰς τὸν οἶκον Ζαχαρίου καὶ <u>ἠσπάσατο</u> τὴν
of Juda   of Zachary

Ἐλισάβετ. καὶ ἐγένετο <u>ὡς</u> ἤκουσεν τὸν ἀσπασμὸν τῆς Μαρίας ἡ
Elizabeth   it happened that   greeting

Ἐλισάβετ, <u>ἐσκίρτησεν</u> τὸ <u>βρέφος</u> ἐν τῇ <u>κοιλίᾳ</u> αὐτῆς, καὶ <u>ἐπλήσθη</u>
          moved   baby   womb   was filled

<u>πνεύματος</u> ἁγίου ἡ Ἐλισάβετ, καὶ <u>ἀνεφώνησεν κραυγῇ μεγάλη</u> καὶ
                          exclaimed   cry   great

<u>εἶπεν</u>, <u>Εὐλογημένη</u> σὺ <u>ἐν γυναιξίν</u>, καὶ <u>εὐλογημένος</u> ὁ καρπὸς τῆς
     Blessed   blessed

κοιλίας σου. καὶ <u>πόθεν μοι τοῦτο ἵνα ἔλθη ἡ μήτηρ</u> τοῦ κυρίου μου
womb

<u>πρὸς ἐμέ</u>; <u>ἰδοὺ</u> γὰρ <u>ὡς ἐγένετο</u> ἡ φωνὴ τοῦ <u>ἀσπασμοῦ</u> σου <u>εἰς τὰ</u>
                               greeting

<u>ὦτά</u> μου, ἐσκίρτησεν <u>ἐν ἀγαλλιάσει</u> τὸ <u>βρέφος</u> ἐν τῇ κοιλίᾳ μου.
     moved, leaped   great joy   baby

καὶ <u>μακαρία ἡ πιστεύσασα</u> <u>ὅτι ἔσται τελείωσις τοῖς λελαλημένοις</u>
                                fulfillment   things spoken

αὐτῇ παρὰ κυρίου . . . Ἔμεινεν δὲ Μαριὰμ σὺν αὐτῇ ὡς <u>μῆνας</u>

<u>τρεῖς</u>, καὶ <u>ὑπέστρεψεν</u> εἰς τὸν οἶκον αὐτῆς.
three

CLOSING GREETING from Eph. 6:23–24: Εἰρήνη τοῖς ἀδελφοῖς
καὶ ἀγάπη μετὰ πίστεως ἀπὸ θεοῦ πατρὸς καὶ κυρίου Ἰησοῦ
Χριστοῦ. ἡ χάρις μετὰ πάντων τῶν ἀγαπώντων τὸν κύριον ἡμῶν
Ἰησοῦν Χριστὸν ἐν ἀφθαρσίᾳ (with undying . . . , the word "love"
being understood).

16 The Third Declension Concluded

Sibilant, Vowel, Diphthong Stems

I. **Introduction:**

A. Having studied the mute and liquid stems of the third declension, let us now conclude our examination of this important declension with a careful study of the remaining three types, namely the SIBILANT OR SIGMA STEMS, the (WEAK) VOWEL STEMS, and the DIPHTHONG STEMS, in that order.

B. There is a *special value* in treating all of these *together* because all three, including the sibilant stems, involve the *use and contraction of vowels* in a special and extensive manner.

II. **Sibilant or sigma stems:**

A. INTRODUCTION: Sibilant stems exist in **two forms:** nouns and adjectives—

B. SIBILANT NOUNS:

　1. *Formation:*
　a. The **original stem** ended in $\varepsilon\sigma$, which is **strengthened** to os in the nominative and accusative singular.
　b. In **other cases,** σ is dropped as usual between two vowels (with resulting **contractions:** $\varepsilon + o = ov$, $\varepsilon + \iota = \varepsilon\iota$, $\varepsilon + \alpha = \eta$, $\varepsilon + \omega = \omega$).
　c. In the **dative plural,** σ is still dropped but no contractions occur because the ending $\sigma\iota$ begins with a consonant.
　2. *Characteristics:*
　a. **Gender:** with rare exceptions, **neuter.**
　b. **Syllables:** almost universally, of **two syllables.**
　c. **Accentuation:** normally on the **penult,** except for the genitive plural which accents the ultima for reasons clear from the declension.
　3. *Example:* τέλος, ους, τό: end, completion, fulfillment, tax, duty (toll, philately, teleology, telegraph, telephone, telescope, telepathy, television)

4. *Sample declension* (analytical):

	Sing.			Plur.	
Nom.	τέλος	(τέλεσ + –)	*Nom.*	τέλη	(τέλεσ + α)
Gen.	τέλους	(τέλεσ + ος)	*Gen.*	τελῶν	(τελέσ + ων)
Dat.	τέλει	(τέλεσ + ι)	*Dat.*	τέλεσι	(τέλεσ + σι)
Acc.	τέλος	(τέλεσ + –)	*Acc.*	τέλη	(τέλεσ + α)

5. *Select vocabulary* of sibilant nouns, all of them declined like τέλος, ους, τό.

γένος: race, kind (genus, genocide)

ἔθνος: nation, people (ethnic)

ἔθος: custom, usage (ethics)

ἔτος: year (etesian: annual wind)

κράτος: power (democrat, aristocrat)

μέλος: limb, member; song (melody)

μέρος: part, piece (polymer)

ὄρος: mountain, hill (orology)

πλῆθος: multitude, crowd (plethora)

σκεῦος: vessel; plural— goods

σκότος: darkness (scotia = molding)

ψεῦδος: lie, falsehood (pseudonym, pseudepigraphy)

C. SIBILANT ADJECTIVES: Important though less frequent than the nouns, and *usually* found in *compound or composite* form.

1. *Formation:*

a. They have **only two terminations:** *masculine-feminine* and *neuter.*

b. The **nominative singular** strengthens ες to ης in the *masculine-feminine* but leaves it *unchanged* in the *neuter.*

c. The **other cases,** dropping σ, follow the same general rules about **contractions** as do the nouns, plus *one additional rule:* ε + ε = ει.

2. *Accentuation:* **Usually** on the ultima throughout the declension.

3. *Example:* **ἀληθής, ές** (ἀ + λανθάνω = not to hide): true, truthful, real, honest, genuine.

4. *Sample declension* (partially analytical):

	Sing.			Plur.	
	Masc.-Fem.	*Neut.*		*Masc.-Fem.*	*Neut.*
N.	ἀληθής	ἀληθές	N.	ἀληθεῖς (έσ + ες)	ἀληθῆ
G.	ἀληθοῦς	ἀληθοῦς	G.	ἀληθῶν	ἀληθῶν
D.	ἀληθεῖ	ἀληθεῖ	D.	ἀληθέσι	ἀληθέσι
A.	ἀληθῆ (έσ + α)	ἀληθές	A.	ἀληθεῖς (έσ + ν̥ς)	ἀληθῆ

5. *Select vocabulary* of sibilant adjectives, all of them declined like ἀληθής, ές.

ἀσθενής: weak, ill (neurasthenia)

μονογενής: only-begotten, unique

πλήρης: full, full-grown (complete)

συγγενής: related; as noun: relative

ὑγιής: healthy, sound (hygiene)

III. Vowel stems:

A. INTRODUCTION:

1. In the first and second declensions, we studied nouns and adjectives whose stems end in the *strong vowels:* α, η, ο.

2. Now, *in the third declension,* we will study nouns and adjectives with stems ending in the *weak vowels:* ι, υ.

B. VOWEL NOUNS:

1. *Division:* weak vowel nouns comprise *two main types* of unequal frequency:

a. **Rather frequent:** *feminine* nouns, mostly abstract, with stems in ι.

b. **Very infrequent:** *masculine* (and feminine) nouns with stems in υ.

2. *Formation* is sometimes the same, sometimes different in the two groups:

a. **The same:** both take *basically the same endings,* including ς, ν in the nominative and accusative singular, and ες in the nominative plural, but there are **exceptions:**

1) Nouns in ι lengthen the genitive singular ending to ως and use the νς ending in the accusative plural. (ως, ων *do not absorb.*)

2) Nouns in υ retain the genitive singular ending as it is: ος, and use the ας ending in the accusative plural (unlike Attic Greek).

b. **Different:**

1) *Stem vowel:* nouns in ι change it to ε in all but the nominative and accusative singular; nouns in υ retain it through all cases.

2) *Accentuation:* nouns in ι have an unusual kind of "recessive accent," accenting the antepenult with a long ultima; nouns in υ accent the ultima in the nominative and accentuate regularly thereafter.

3. *Examples* of weak vowel nouns:
a. **πίστις, εως, ἡ:** faith, trust, belief, conviction, conscience (πιστεύω).
b. **ἰχθύς, ύος, ὁ:** fish (ichthyology, ichthyosis).

4. *Sample declension* of vowel nouns:

	Sing.		Plur.		Sing.	Plur.
N.	πίστις	(ι + ς)	πίστεις	(ε + ες)	ἰχθύς	ἰχθύες
G.	πίστεως	(ε + ως)	πίστεων	(ε + ων)	ἰχθύος	ἰχθύων
D.	πίστει	(ε + ι)	πίστεσι	(ε + σι)	ἰχθύϊ	ἰχθύσι
A.	πίστιν	(ι + ν)	πίστεις	(ε + ϝς)	ἰχθύν	ἰχθύας

5. *Select vocabulary* of vowel nouns in ι, all of them declined like
   πίστις, εως, ἡ: (NB: Of vowel stems in υ, the only frequent
   NT Greek representative is ἰχθύς, but they are important as
   models for the vowel adjectives.)

ἀνάστασις: r(a)ising (Anastasia)

ἀποκάλυψις: unveiling (Apocalypse)

ἄφεσις: pardon, release (aphesis)

γνῶσις: knowledge (prognosis, gnostic)

δύναμις: power, miracle (dynamic, dynamite)

κρίσις: judgment, justice (crisis, critical)

παράδοσις: betrayal, tradition

παράκλησις: comfort, encouragement (Paraclete)

πόλις: city, town (acro/metro/necropolis, police, policy, politic)

φύσις: nature (physics, metaphysics)

C. VOWEL ADJECTIVES: Important though less frequent than nouns in ι—

1. *Formation:*
a. These are of **three terminations:** masculine, feminine, neuter.
b. Their **stem** ends in υ, which, however, **changes** as follows:
   1) In the *masculine* and *neuter,* to ε (like stems in ι) in all but the nominative and accusative singular.
   2) In the *feminine,* to ει, to which are added, as expected, the first declension endings in α.
c. The **endings** are regular for this stem, including:
   1) *Long vowels* in all genitives of the masculine and neuter.
   2) ς, ν and ες, νς in the nominative and accusative of the masculine, singular and plural (unlike ἰχθύας, above).
d. **Contractions** occur **neither** in the masculine and neuter genitive **nor** in the neuter nominative and accusative plural— έως, έων, έα.

e. **Accentuation** generally follows the pattern of ἰχθύς, rather than that of πίστις with its very unusual "recessive accent."

2. *Sample declension of* **βαθύς, εῖα, ύ** deep (bathos, bathysphere):

	Sing.				Plur.		
	Masc.	Fem.	Neut.		Masc.	Fem.	Neut.
N.	βαθύς	βαθεῖα	βαθύ	N.	βαθεῖς	βαθεῖαι	βαθέα
G.	βαθέως	βαθείας	βαθέως	G.	βαθέων	βαθειῶν	βαθέων
D.	βαθεῖ	βαθείᾳ	βαθεῖ	D.	βαθέσι	βαθείαις	βαθέσι
A.	βαθύν	βαθεῖαν	βαθύ	A.	βαθεῖς	βαθείας	βαθέα

3. *Select vocabulary* of vowel adjectives, all of them declined like βαθύς, εῖα, ύ.

βαρύς: heavy, hard (baritone)   **πραῦς:** meek, gentle

γλυκύς: sweet (glucose)   **ταχύς:** swift, quick

εὐθύς: straight, right, upright   (tachometer)

πλατύς: wide (plate, place)

IV. Diphthong stems:

A. INTRODUCTION: These comprise *only nouns* and almost only those with stems ending in ευ, plus some rare nouns with stems ending in ου or αυ.

B. DIPHTHONG NOUNS with stems in ευ:

1. *General description:* These are *masculine* and usually denote some kind of title, profession, calling, or role.

2. *Formation:*

a. They regularly drop the υ of ευ before vowels and ν and then are **declined** more or less like vowel stems in ι, e.g. Gen. in ως.

b. However, they use the ending α instead of ν in the accusative singular, **not contracting** the resulting combination εα.

3. *Accentuation:* They are accented more like υ stems than ι stems, beginning with an *acute accent on the ultima,* then accenting regularly.

4. *Sample declension* of **ἱερεύς, έως, ὁ** = priest (hierarchy, hieroglyphics):

	Sing.			Plur.	
Nom.	ἱερεύς	(ἱερεύ + ς)	Nom.	ἱερεῖς	(ἱερέϝ + ες)
Gen.	ἱερέως	(ἱερέϝ + ως)	Gen.	ἱερέων	(ἱερέϝ + ων)
Dat.	ἱερεῖ	(ἱερέϝ + ι)	Dat.	ἱερεῦσι	(ἱερεῦ + σι)
Acc.	ἱερέα	(ἱερέϝ + α)	Acc.	ἱερεῖς	(ἱερέϝ + ϝς)

5. *Select vocabulary* of diphthong nouns in ευ, declined like
   ἱερεύς.

   ἀρχιερεύς: high or chief   **γονεύς:** parent (gonad,
   priest   cosmogony)
   βασιλεύς: king (basilica,   **γραμματεύς:** scribe
   basil)   (grammarian)

C. DIPHTHONG NOUNS with stems in ου:

1. *General description:*
a. Though **rare** in the New Testament, these are included for
   completeness' sake.
b. They are **all masculine** and **all monosyllabic** in the nominative
   case.

2. *Formation:*
a. They regularly drop the *υ* of ου before vowels, then are declined
   somewhat like vowel stems in *υ* or diphthong stems in ευ.
b. However, they use the ending *ν* in the accusative singular and
   ας in the accusative plural, with **no contractions** and **regular
   accents.**

3. *Sample declension* of **νοῦς, νοός, ὁ** = mind (noosphere,
   paranoia, metanoia):

	Sing.			Plur.	
Nom.	νοῦς	(νοῦ + ς)	Nom.	νόες	(νόϝ + ες)
Gen.	νοός	(νοϝ + ός)	Gen.	νοῶν	(νοϝ + ῶν)
Dat.	νοῖ	(νοϝ + ι)	Dat.	νουσί	(νου + σί)
Acc.	νοῦν	(νοῦ + ν)	Acc.	νόας	(νόϝ + ας)

4. *Select vocabulary* of diphthong nouns in ου, declined like νοῦς,
   νοός:

   βοῦς: ox (Bucephalus,   **πλοῦς:** voyage (πλέω = sail,
   bucolic)   swim)

D. DIPHTHONG NOUNS with stems in αυ:

1. *Apparently, the only* diphthong noun in αυ found in the New
   Testament is that of **ναῦς, νεώς, ἡ:** ship (nausea, nautical,
   Argonaut, aeronautics; akin to Latin *navis*, whence navy, nave,
   navigation, etc.).

2. *It is found only* in the nominative ναῦς, genitive νεώς, and
   accusative singular ναῦν, hence there is no need to give a full
   declension.

V. Verbs with sibilant, vowel, or diphthong stems:

A. INTRODUCTION:

1. *In previous lessons,* we studied together the nouns, adjectives, pronouns, and verbs with the same stem type, e.g. mute, liquid, etc.

2. *Hence, in this lesson,* it will be helpful to examine any verbs formed with *sibilant, vowel,* or *diphthong* stems.

3. Our task is made easier, of course, because we have already studied, under the category of *"regular verbs"* those with stems in v, εv, ov, e.g. λύω, θεραπεύω, πιστεύω, πορεύομαι, ἀκούω, ἀπολύω, ὑπακούω (cf. p. 45).

4. Here, then, we will content ourselves with:
a. A brief treatment of **sibilant verbs.**
b. **Additional vocabulary** of vowel and diphthong verbs.

B. SIBILANT VERBS:

1. *Introduction:*
a. At one time, Greek had a number of verbs with at least one stem in σ, but in **NT Greek** they are all treated as **contract verbs** (which we will study next), sometimes with a liquid future, e.g. τελέω (τελεσ, τελε), (τελέσω/τελῶ), ἐτέλεσα, τετέλεκα, τετέλεσμαι, ἐτελέσθην: end, complete (telemetry, teletype, etc.).
b. For our purposes, we may safely assume that **the only common** sibilant verb in NT Greek is the very popular athematic verb εἰμί: "to be."

2. *Conjugation* of the indicative mood of **εἰμί** (ἐσ), **ἔσομαι**: I am, exist, happen, live, stay, be possible (ontic, ontology, parousia; essence, etc.).

	Sing.				*Plur.*		
	Pres.	Impf.	Fut.		Pres.	Impf.	Fut.
1)	εἰμί	ἤμην	ἔσομαι	1)	ἐσμέν	ἦμεν	ἐσόμεθα
2)	εἶ	ἦς	ἔσῃ	2)	ἐστέ	ἦτε	ἔσεσθε
3)	ἐστί	ἦν	ἔσται	3)	εἰσί	ἦσαν	ἔσονται

(NB: The conjugation of εἰμί will be presented more visually in chapter 18, when we compare the conjugations of short athematic verbs.)

3. *Other important forms* of εἰμί are:
   a. The **subjunctive:** ὦ, ᾖς, ᾖ — ὦμεν, ἦτε, ὦσι.
   b. The **imperative:** ἴσθι, ἔστω — ἔστε, ἔστωσαν.
   c. The **infinitive:** εἶναι, ἔσεσθαι (Fut.).
   d. The **participle:** ὤν, οὖσα, ὄν — ὄντος, οὔσης, ὄντος.

C. ADDITIONAL VOCABULARY of vowel and diphthong verbs:
   (NB: Principal parts and conjugation are generally like the regular verbs λύω, πιστεύω, etc., though *many are defective* to some extent.)

1. *Weak vowel verbs* in υ (conjugated more or less like λύω):
   δείκνυμι (δεικ): show (cf. p. 141)
   ἐνδύω: dress; wear (indusium)
   θύω: sacrifice, kill (thurible)
   ἰσχύω: be strong, healthy (ἔχω)
   καταλύω: tear down; lodge (catalyst)
   κωλύω: hinder; withhold; forbid
   ὀμνύω (ὀμο): swear, vow (cf. p. 141)
   ῥύομαι: save, rescue, deliver

2. *Diphthong verbs* in αυ (some with present stem αι, verb stem αυ):
   ἀναπαύω: give relief, rest
   καίω (καυ): light, burn (caustic)
   κατακαίω (-καυ): burn up, burn down
   κλαίω (κλαυ): weep, cry, bewail
   παύομαι: cease, desist (pause)

3. *Diphthong stems* in ει (rare):
   κλείω: shut, lock (clef, clitoris, cleistogamy)

4. *Diphthong stems* in ευ (conjugated more or less like πιστεύω):
   βασιλεύω: rule, reign (basilica)
   γεύομαι: taste (gusto, disgust)
   δουλεύω: serve as slave (dulia)
   εἰσπορεύομαι: go in, enter (pore)
   ἐκπορεύομαι: go out, set out (pore)
   κελεύω: order, command, direct
   λατρεύω: worship (idolatry, latria)
   μνημονεύω: remember, mention (mnemonics)
   μοιχεύω: commit adultery
   νηστεύω: fast, go without food
   παιδεύω: instruct, correct (pedagogy)
   περισσεύω: be left over, increase
   προφητεύω: speak for, prophesy
   σαλεύω: shake, stir up, be confused (rel. to ἅλλομαι: leap, sally)

VI. Exercises:

A. Before anything else, learn the meaning attached by the earliest Christians to the SYMBOL OF THE FISH ('ΙΧΘΥΣ/ἰχθύς), whose letters form the initial letters of this *basic statement of Christian Faith:* Ἰησοῦς Χριστὸς Θεοῦ Υἱὸς Σωτήρ.

B. *Translate and decline,* in both singular and plural, these three phrases:

  1. ὁ πραῢς βασιλεύς:

  2. ἡ κρίσις ἡ ἀληθής:

  3. τὸ βαθὺ σκότος:

C. *Read aloud, translate,* and *explain the underlined passages* of the following sentences from the New Testament:

  1. Ὑμεῖς ἐστε τὸ φῶς τοῦ κόσμου. οὐ δύναται πόλις κρυβῆναι

is able   to be hidden

  ἐπάνω ὄρους κειμένη· οὐδὲ καίουσιν λύχνον καὶ τιθέασιν αὐτὸν

atop   lying   lamp   put

  ὑπὸ τὸν μόδιον ἀλλ᾽ ἐπὶ τὴν λυχνίαν . . .

basket   lampstand

  2. Ἄφετε τὰ παιδία ἔρχεσθαι πρός με, μὴ κωλύετε αὐτά, γὰρ

let children

  τοιούτων ἐστὶν ἡ βασιλεία τοῦ θεοῦ.

  3. Καὶ ἔρχονται Σαδδουκαῖοι πρὸς αὐτόν, οἵτινες λέγουσιν

     Sadducees

  ἀνάστασιν μὴ εἶναι, καὶ ἐπηρώτων αὐτὸν λέγοντες, . . . ἐν

          they asked

  τῇ ἀναστάσει τίνος αὐτῶν ἔσται γυνή;

  4. ὡς δὲ ἤγγισεν τῇ πύλῃ τῆς πόλεως, καὶ ἰδοὺ ἐξεκομίζετο

     gate   behold was carried out

  τεθνηκὼς μονογενὴς υἱὸς τῇ μητρὶ αὐτοῦ, καὶ αὐτὴ ἦν

dead

  χήρα . . .

widow

  5. καὶ ἰδὼν αὐτὴν ὁ κύριος ἐσπλαγχνίσθη ἐπ᾽ αὐτῇ καὶ εἶπεν

         was moved with pity

  αὐτῇ, Μὴ κλαῖε . . . καὶ εἶπεν, Νεανίσκε,* σοί λέγω, ἐγέρθητι.

          Young man

  6. Νῦν ἐγνώκαμεν ὅτι δαιμόνιον ἔχεις. Ἀβραὰμ ἀπέθανεν καὶ οἱ

  προφῆται, καὶ σὺ λέγεις, Ἐάν τις τὸν λόγον μου τηρήσῃ, οὐ μὴ

              keeps

  γεύσηται θανάτου εἰς τὸν αἰῶνα. μὴ σὺ μείζων εἶ τοῦ πατρὸς

            greater

  ἡμῶν Ἀβραάμ, ὅστις ἀπέθανεν;

  *The vocative of *νεανίσκος, ου, ὁ* = young man.

7. ἐκέλευσεν συνελθεῖν τοὺς ἀρχιερεῖς καὶ πᾶν τὸ συνέδριον, καὶ

καταγαγὼν τὸν Παῦλον ἔστησεν εἰς αὐτούς.
he set

8. Καθάπερ γὰρ τὸ σῶμα ἕν ἐστιν καὶ μέλη πολλὰ ἔχει, πάντα δὲ
Just as   many

τὰ μέλη τοῦ σώματος πολλὰ ὄντα ἕν ἐστιν σῶμα, οὕτως καὶ ὁ

Χριστός . . . καὶ γὰρ τὸ σῶμα οὐκ ἔστιν ἓν μέλος ἀλλὰ πολλά.

9. Ἔχομεν δὲ τὸν θησαυρὸν τοῦτον ἐν ὀστρακίνοις σκεύεσιν, ἵνα
treasure   clay

ἡ ὑπερβολὴ τῆς δυνάμεως ᾖ τοῦ θεοῦ καὶ μὴ ἐξ ἡμῶν . . .
excellence

10. Ὑμεῖς δὲ γένος ἐκλεκτόν, βασίλειον ἱεράτευμα, ἔθνος ἅγιον,
chosen   royal   priesthood

λαὸς εἰς περιποίησιν, ὅπως τὰς ἀρετὰς ἐξαγγείλητε τοῦ ἐκ
possession   saving acts   you may proclaim

σκότους ὑμᾶς καλέσαντος εἰς τὸ θαυμαστὸν αὐτοῦ φῶς . . .
of him who called   wonderful

11. ὃ ἑωράκαμεν καὶ ἀκηκόαμεν ἀπαγγέλλομεν καὶ ὑμῖν, ἵνα καὶ
announce

ὑμεῖς κοινωνίαν ἔχητε μεθ᾽ ἡμῶν.

12. Παιδία, ἐσχάτη ὥρα ἐστίν, καὶ καθὼς ἠκούσατε ὅτι

ἀντίχριστος ἔρχεται, καὶ νῦν ἀντίχριστοι πολλοὶ
antichrist

γεγόνασιν . . .

13. ὃς δ᾽ ἂν ἔχῃ τὸν βίον τοῦ κόσμου καὶ θεωρῇ τὸν ἀδελφὸν αὐτοῦ
life   sees

χρείαν ἔχοντα καὶ κλείσῃ τὰ σπλάγχνα αὐτοῦ ἀπ᾽ αὐτοῦ, πῶς ἡ
bowels (heart)

ἀγάπη τοῦ θεοῦ μένει ἐν αὐτῷ;

14. Τεκνία, μὴ ἀγαπῶμεν λόγῳ μηδὲ τῇ γλώσσῃ ἀλλὰ ἐν ἔργῳ καὶ
let us love

ἀληθείᾳ.

17 Strong Vowel Verbs—Part I

Contract Verbs

I. **Introduction:**

A. We have now concluded our study of the three declensions as well as of most of the verbs, including weak vowel, diphthong, and consonant verbs.

B. Now, in a sense, we come full circle as we take up those verbs which have stems ending in the strong vowels α, ε, o and therefore correspond to the first and second declension of nouns, adjectives, and pronouns.

C. STRONG VOWEL VERBS in NT Greek are conjugated in one of three ways:

    1. *As contract verbs:* which, in the present system, use the variable vowel and *contract it with the strong vowel,* regularly *lengthening* the strong vowel in the *other systems.* These will be treated in this chapter.

    2. *As athematic verbs:* which, in the present system, omit the variable or thematic vowel, are often reduplicated, and use some primitive endings, with other variations in the other tenses. (These will be treated in the next chapter.)

    3. *As pseudo-mute or pseudo-liquid verbs,* especially in the present system. (Please check the stems and alternate stems on pages 97–98, 108–109, and 114–116.)

II. **Guiding principles of contract verbs:**

A. First, let us remember that CONTRACTIONS occur ONLY IN THE PRESENT SYSTEM, i.e. the present tense in all its forms, and the imperfect indicative.

B. IN ALL OTHER TENSES, the vowel in which the stem ends (called the *contract vowel*) is normally *lengthened,* as follows:

    1. α to η or (after ε, ι, ρ) long α, e.g. ἀγαπήσω, ἰασάμην.

    2. ε to η and o to ω, e.g. λαλήσω, πληρώσω.

C. THE CONTRACTIONS in the present system follow these rules which will be clearer when applied on the following pages:

1. *Contractions of Alpha:*
    a. α plus any E-Sound (ε, ει; η, ῃ) becomes long α, e.g.: ἀγαπᾶτε, ἀγαπᾷς; ἀγαπᾶτε, ἀγαπᾷς.
    b. α plus any O-Sound (o, ου, ω) becomes ω, e.g.: ἀγαπῶμεν, ἠγαπῶ, ἀγαπῶ.
    c. *If an Iota is involved, it is subscribed* (written under) except in the infinitive, where it is omitted, e.g. ἀγαπᾷς, ἀγαπᾶν.

2. *Contractions of Epsilon:*
    a. ε plus any long vowel or diphthong (ω, η, ου, ει, ῃ) is absorbed, e.g. λαλῶ, λαλῆτε, ἐλαλοῦ, λαλεῖ, λαλῇ, (infinitive) λαλεῖν.
    b. ε plus ε becomes ει, e.g. λαλεῖτε, ἐλάλει.
    c. ε plus o becomes ου, e.g. λαλοῦμεν, ἐλαλοῦμεν.

3. *Contractions of Omicron:*
    a. o plus any long vowel (ω, η) becomes ω, e.g. πληρῶ, πληρῶτε.
    b. o plus any Iota-diphthong (ει, ῃ) becomes οι, except in the infinitive, which omits the Iota, e.g. πληροῖ, πληροῖ, πληροῦν.
    c. o plus any other vowel or diphthong (o, ε, ου) becomes ου, e.g. πληροῦμεν, πληροῦτε; ἐπλήρου, ἐπληροῦ; πλήρου, πληροῦ.

D. The contractions described occur BETWEEN THE CONTRACT VOWEL AND THE DEVELOPED ENDINGS, i.e. the endings which result from the interaction of the variable vowel and the primitive endings, as seen in regular verbs, e.g.: λύω, λύεις, λύει; λύομεν, λύετε, λύουσι, κτλ.

E. AN IMPORTANT CLUE to contract verbs is the ACCENT, usually circumflex, ON THE CONTRACTION if either of the contracting vowels had an accent, e.g. ἀγαπῶ, ἀγαπᾷς, ἀγαπᾷ; ἀγαπῶμεν, ἀγαπᾶτε, ἀγαπῶσι, κτλ., but: ἠγάπων, ἀγαπώμεθα, ἀγαπάτω, κτλ.

III. Contract verbs in α:

A. EXAMPLE: **ἀγαπάω** (ἀγαπα): love (spiritually), show love, long for (agape).

B. PRINCIPAL PARTS: ἀγαπῶ, ἀγαπήσω, ἠγάπησα, ἠγάπηκα, ἠγάπημαι, ἠγαπήθην.

C. CONJUGATION OF THE PRESENT SYSTEM:

<table>
<tr><td colspan="2">PRESENT INDICATIVE ACTIVE</td><td colspan="2">IMPERFECT INDICATIVE ACTIVE</td></tr>
<tr><td colspan="2" align="center">Sing.</td><td colspan="2" align="center">Sing.</td></tr>
<tr><td>1. ἀγαπῶ</td><td>(ἀγαπά + ω)</td><td>1. ἠγάπων</td><td>(ἠγάπα + ον)</td></tr>
<tr><td>2. ἀγαπᾷς</td><td>(ἀγαπά + εις)</td><td>2. ἠγάπας</td><td>(ἠγάπα + ες)</td></tr>
<tr><td>3. ἀγαπᾷ</td><td>(ἀγαπά + ει)</td><td>3. ἠγάπα</td><td>(ἠγάπα + ε)</td></tr>
<tr><td colspan="2" align="center">Plur.</td><td colspan="2" align="center">Plur.</td></tr>
<tr><td>1. ἀγαπῶμεν</td><td>(ἀγαπά + ομεν)</td><td>1. ἠγαπῶμεν</td><td>(ἠγάπα + ομεν)</td></tr>
<tr><td>2. ἀγαπᾶτε</td><td>(ἀγαπά + ετε)</td><td>2. ἠγαπᾶτε</td><td>(ἠγάπα + ετε)</td></tr>
<tr><td>3. ἀγαπῶσι</td><td>(ἀγαπά + ουσι)</td><td>3. ἠγάπων</td><td>(ἠγάπα + ον)</td></tr>
<tr><td colspan="2">PRESENT INDIC. MID. & PASS.</td><td colspan="2">IMPERFECT INDIC. MID. & PASS.</td></tr>
<tr><td colspan="2" align="center">Sing.</td><td colspan="2" align="center">Sing.</td></tr>
<tr><td>1. ἀγαπῶμαι</td><td>(ἀγαπά + ομαι)</td><td>1. ἠγαπώμην</td><td>(ἠγάπα + ομην)</td></tr>
<tr><td>2. ἀγαπᾷ</td><td>(ἀγαπά + ῃ)</td><td>2. ἠγαπῶ</td><td>(ἠγάπα + ου)</td></tr>
<tr><td>3. ἀγαπᾶται</td><td>(ἀγαπά + εται)</td><td>3. ἠγαπᾶτο</td><td>(ἠγάπα + ετο)</td></tr>
<tr><td colspan="2" align="center">Plur.</td><td colspan="2" align="center">Plur.</td></tr>
<tr><td>1. ἀγαπώμεθα</td><td>(ἀγαπα + όμεθα)</td><td>1. ἠγαπώμεθα</td><td>(ἠγάπα + όμεθα)</td></tr>
<tr><td>2. ἀγαπᾶσθε</td><td>(ἀγαπά + εσθε)</td><td>2. ἠγαπᾶσθε</td><td>(ἠγάπα + εσθε)</td></tr>
<tr><td>3. ἀγαπῶνται</td><td>(ἀγαπά + ονται)</td><td>3. ἠγαπῶντο</td><td>(ἠγάπα + οντο)</td></tr>
<tr><td colspan="2">PRESENT SUBJUNCTIVE ACTIVE</td><td colspan="2">PRESENT IMPERATIVE ACTIVE</td></tr>
<tr><td colspan="2" align="center">Sing.</td><td colspan="2" align="center">Sing.</td></tr>
<tr><td>1. ἀγαπῶ</td><td>(ἀγαπά + ω)</td><td>2. ἀγάπα</td><td>(ἀγάπα + ε)</td></tr>
<tr><td>2. ἀγαπᾷς</td><td>(ἀγαπά + ῃς)</td><td>3. ἀγαπάτω</td><td>(ἀγαπα + έτω)</td></tr>
<tr><td>3. ἀγαπᾷ</td><td>(ἀγαπά + ῃ)</td><td colspan="2" align="center">Plur.</td></tr>
<tr><td colspan="2" align="center">Plur.</td><td>2. ἀγαπᾶτε</td><td>(ἀγαπά + ετε)</td></tr>
<tr><td>1. ἀγαπῶμεν</td><td>(ἀγαπά + ωμεν)</td><td>3. ἀγαπάτωσαν</td><td>(ἀγαπα + έτωσαν)</td></tr>
<tr><td>2. ἀγαπᾶτε</td><td>(ἀγαπά + ητε)</td><td colspan="2">PRESENT IMPERATIVE</td></tr>
<tr><td>3. ἀγαπῶσι</td><td>(ἀγαπά + ωσι)</td><td colspan="2">MID. & PASS.</td></tr>
<tr><td colspan="2">PRESENT SUBJUNC. MID. & PASS.</td><td colspan="2" align="center">Sing.</td></tr>
<tr><td colspan="2" align="center">Sing.</td><td>2. ἀγαπῶ</td><td>(ἀγαπά + ου)</td></tr>
<tr><td>1. ἀγαπῶμαι</td><td>(ἀγαπά + ωμαι)</td><td>3. ἀγαπάσθω</td><td>(ἀγαπα + έσθω)</td></tr>
<tr><td>2. ἀγαπᾷ</td><td>(ἀγαπά + ῃ)</td><td colspan="2" align="center">Plur.</td></tr>
<tr><td>3. ἀγαπᾶται</td><td>(ἀγαπά + ηται)</td><td>2. ἀγαπᾶσθε</td><td>(ἀγαπά + εσθε)</td></tr>
<tr><td colspan="2" align="center">Plur.</td><td>3. ἀγαπάσθωσαν</td><td>(ἀγαπα + έσθωσαν)</td></tr>
<tr><td>1. ἀγαπώμεθα</td><td>(ἀγαπα + ώμεθα)</td><td colspan="2">PRESENT INFINITIVE ACTIVE</td></tr>
<tr><td>2. ἀγαπᾶσθε</td><td>(ἀγαπά + ησθε)</td><td>ἀγαπᾶν</td><td>(ἀγαπά + ειν)</td></tr>
<tr><td>3. ἀγαπῶνται</td><td>(ἀγαπά + ωνται)</td><td colspan="2">PRESENT INFINITIVE</td></tr>
<tr><td colspan="2">PRESENT PARTICIPLE ACTIVE</td><td colspan="2">MID. & PASS.</td></tr>
<tr><td>ἀγαπῶν, ῶσα, ῶν</td><td>(ἀγαπά + ων, ουσα, ον)</td><td>ἀγαπᾶσθαι</td><td>(ἀγαπά + εσθαι)</td></tr>
<tr><td colspan="2">PRESENT PARTICIPLE</td><td colspan="2"></td></tr>
<tr><td colspan="2">MID. & PASS.</td><td colspan="2"></td></tr>
<tr><td>ἀγαπώμενος, η, ον</td><td>(ἀγαπα + όμενος)</td><td colspan="2"></td></tr>
</table>

IV. **Contract verbs** in ε:

A. EXAMPLE: **λαλέω** (λαλε): speak, say; address; converse (glossolalia).

B. PRINCIPAL PARTS: λαλῶ, λαλήσω, ἐλάλησα, λελάληκα, λελάλημαι, ἐλαλήθην.

C. CONJUGATION OF THE PRESENT SYSTEM:

PRESENT INDICATIVE ACTIVE
Sing.
1. λαλῶ   (λαλέ + ω)
2. λαλεῖς   (λαλέ + εις)
3. λαλεῖ   (λαλέ + ει)

Plur.
1. λαλοῦμεν   (λαλέ + ομεν)
2. λαλεῖτε   (λαλέ + ετε)
3. λαλοῦσι   (λαλέ + ουσι)

PRESENT INDIC. MID. & PASS.
Sing.
1. λαλοῦμαι   (λαλέ + ομαι)
2. λαλῇ   (λαλέ + η)
3. λαλεῖται   (λαλέ + εται)

Plur.
1. λαλούμεθα   (λαλε + όμεθα)
2. λαλεῖσθε   (λαλέ + εσθε)
3. λαλοῦνται   (λαλέ + ονται)

PRESENT SUBJUNCTIVE ACTIVE
Sing.
1. λαλῶ   (λαλέ + ω)
2. λαλῇς   (λαλέ + ης)
3. λαλῇ   (λαλέ + η)

Plur.
1. λαλῶμεν   (λαλέ + ωμεν)
2. λαλῆτε   (λαλέ + ητε)
3. λαλῶσι   (λαλέ + ωσι)

PRESENT SUBJUNC. MID. & PASS.
Sing.
1. λαλῶμαι   (λαλέ + ωμαι)
2. λαλῇ   (λαλέ + η)
3. λαλῆται   (λαλέ + ηται)

Plur.
1. λαλώμεθα   (λαλε + ώμεθα)
2. λαλῆσθε   (λαλέ + ησθε)
3. λαλῶνται   (λαλέ + ωνται)

PRESENT PARTICIPLE ACTIVE
λαλῶν, οῦσα, οῦν   (λαλέ + ων, ουσα, ον)

PRESENT PARTICIPLE MID. & PASS.
λαλούμενος, η, ον (λαλε + όμενος)

IMPERFECT INDICATIVE ACTIVE
Sing.
1. ἐλάλουν   (ἐλάλε + ον)
2. ἐλάλεις   (ἐλάλε + ες)
3. ἐλάλει   (ἐλάλε + ε)

Plur.
1. ἐλαλοῦμεν   (ἐλαλέ + ομεν)
2. ἐλαλεῖτε   (ἐλαλέ + ετε)
3. ἐλάλουν   (ἐλάλε + ον)

IMPERFECT INDIC. MID. & PASS.
Sing.
1. ἐλαλούμην   (ἐλαλε + όμην)
2. ἐλαλοῦ   (ἐλαλέ + ου)
3. ἐλαλεῖτο   (ἐλαλέ + ετο)

Plur.
1. ἐλαλούμεθα   (ἐλαλε + όμεθα)
2. ἐλαλεῖσθε   (ἐλαλέ + εσθε)
3. ἐλαλοῦντο   (ἐλαλέ + οντο)

PRESENT IMPERATIVE ACTIVE
Sing.
2. λάλει   (λάλε + ε)
3. λαλείτω   (λαλε + έτω)

Plur.
2. λαλεῖτε   (λαλέ + ετε)
3. λαλείτωσαν   (λαλε + έτωσαν)

PRESENT IMPERATIVE MID. & PASS.
Sing.
2. λαλοῦ   (λαλέ + ου)
3. λαλείσθω   (λαλε + έσθω)

Plur.
2. λαλεῖσθε   (λαλέ + εσθε)
3. λαλείσθωσαν   (λαλε + έσθωσαν)

PRESENT INFINITIVE ACTIVE
λαλεῖν   (λαλέ + ειν)

PRESENT INFINITIVE MID. & PASS.
λαλεῖσθαι   (λαλέ + εσθαι)

V. Contract verbs in o:

A. EXAMPLE: **πληρόω** (πληρο): fill, fulfill; complete; elapse (pleroma)

B. PRINCIPAL PARTS: πληρῶ, πληρώσω, ἐπλήρωσα, πεπλήρωκα, πεπλήρωμαι, ἐπληρώθην.

C. CONJUGATION OF THE PRESENT SYSTEM:

PRESENT INDICATIVE ACTIVE

Sing.
1. πληρῶ   (πληρό + ω)
2. πληροῖς   (πληρό + εις)
3. πληροῖ   (πληρό + ει)

Plur.
1. πληροῦμεν   (πληρό + ομεν)
2. πληροῦτε   (πληρό + ετε)
3. πληροῦσι   (πληρό + ουσι)

PRESENT INDIC. MID. & PASS.

Sing.
1. πληροῦμαι   (πληρό + ομαι)
2. πληροῖ   (πληρό + ῃ)
3. πληροῦται   (πληρό + εται)

Plur.
1. πληρούμεθα   (πληρο + όμεθα)
2. πληροῦσθε   (πληρό + εσθε)
3. πληροῦνται   (πληρό + ονται)

PRESENT SUBJUNCTIVE ACTIVE

Sing.
1. πληρῶ   (πληρό + ω)
2. πληροῖς   (πληρό + ῃς)
3. πληροῖ   (πληρό + ῃ)

Plur.
1. πληρῶμεν   (πληρό + ωμεν)
2. πληρῶτε   (πληρό + ητε)
3. πληρῶσι   (πληρό + ωσι)

PRESENT SUBJUNC. MID. & PASS.

Sing.
1. πληρῶμαι   (πληρό + ωμαι)
2. πληροῖ   (πληρό + ῃ)
3. πληρῶται   (πληρό + ηται)

Plur.
1. πληρώμεθα   (πληρο + ώμεθα)
2. πληρῶσθε   (πληρό + ησθε)
3. πληρῶνται   (πληρό + ωνται)

PRESENT PARTICIPLE ACTIVE

πληρῶν, οῦσα, οῦν (πληρό + ων, ουσα, ον)

PRESENT PARTICIPLE
MID. & PASS.

πληρούμενος, η, ον (πληρο + όμενος)

IMPERFECT INDICATIVE ACTIVE

Sing.
1. ἐπλήρουν   (ἐπλήρο + ον)
2. ἐπλήρους   (ἐπλήρο + ες)
3. ἐπλήρου   (ἐπλήρο + ε)

Plur.
1. ἐπληροῦμεν   (ἐπλήρό + ομεν)
2. ἐπληροῦτε   (ἐπλήρό + ετε)
3. ἐπλήρουν   (ἐπλήρο + ον)

IMPERFECT INDIC. MID. & PASS.

Sing.
1. ἐπληρούμην   (ἐπληρο + όμην)
2. ἐπληροῦ   (ἐπληρό + ου)
3. ἐπληροῦτο   (ἐπληρό + ετο)

Plur.
1. ἐπληρούμεθα   (ἐπληρο + όμεθα)
2. ἐπληροῦσθε   (ἐπληρό + εσθε)
3. ἐπληροῦντο   (ἐπληρό + οντο)

PRESENT IMPERATIVE ACTIVE

Sing.
2. πλήρου   (πλήρο + ε)
3. πληρούτω   (πληρο + έτω)

Plur.
2. πληροῦτε   (πληρό + ετε)
3. πληρούτωσαν   (πληρο + έτωσαν)

PRESENT IMPERATIVE
MID. & PASS.

Sing.
2. πληροῦ   (πληρό + ου)
3. πληρούσθω   (πληρο + έσθω)

Plur.
2. πληροῦσθε   (πληρό + εσθε)
3. πληρούσθωσαν   (πληρο + έσθωσαν)

PRESENT INFINITIVE ACTIVE

πληροῦν   (πληρό + ειν)

PRESENT INFINITIVE
MID. & PASS.

πληροῦσθαι   (πληρό + εσθαι)

VI. **Select vocabulary** of contract verbs:

A. CONTRACT VERBS in α (fairly frequent):

γεννάω: beget, bear (genetics)
ἐπερωτάω: ask for, demand
ἐπιτιμάω: command, rebuke
ἐρωτάω: ask about, request
ζάω: live, be alive (zodiac)
θεάομαι: see, behold (theater)
ἰάομαι: heal (pediatrics)

καυχάομαι: boast, take pride
νικάω: conquer (Nicholas, Nicaea)
ὁράω: see (panorama) cf. p. 79
πλανάω: mislead; wander (planets)
τιμάω: honor, prize (Timothy)

B. CONTRACT VERBS in ε (most frequent of all contract verbs):

αἰτέω: ask for, require, demand
ἀκολουθέω: follow, obey (acolyte)
βλασφημέω: blaspheme, insult
δέω: bind (diadem), δεῖ, p. 67
δοκέω: think (dogma), δοκεῖ, p. 67
εὐλογέω: bless, praise (eulogy)
εὐχαριστέω: thank (Eucharist)
ζητέω: seek, try, ask for, expect
θεωρέω: see, watch (theory)
καλέω: call, name (ecclesial)
κατοικέω: inhabit (ecumenical)
κρατέω: hold, take, restrain (autocrat)

μαρτυρέω: testify, approve (martyr)
μετανοέω: be converted (metanoia)
μισέω: hate, love less (misogynist)
παρακαλέω: urge, encourage (Paraclete)
περιπατέω: walk about (peripatetic)
ποιέω: make, do, cause, provide (poem)
προσκυνέω: kneel, bow, kiss, worship
τηρέω: keep, guard, observe, reserve
φιλέω: love (as a friend), like (bibliophile)
φοβέομαι: fear, dread, worship (phobia)

C. CONTRACT VERBS in o (least frequent of all contract verbs):

δικαιόω: make right, justify
ζηλόω: be zealous/jealous (Zealot)
θανατόω: put to death (Thanatos, thanatology)
κοινόω: make/call common, unclean (Koine)
ὁμοιόω: make/be like (homoiousian)

σταυρόω: crucify (staurolite, to steer)
ταπεινόω: level, humble
τελειόω: perfect, complete (talisman)
ὑψόω: lift up, exalt (hypsography)
φανερόω: reveal, manifest (diaphanous)

NOTE that verbs ending in όω usually contain the idea of *doing or making*, much like verbs ending in -ζω (δοξάζω) and like Latin verbs ending in -*ficio*, from *facio* (*perficio*—to perfect).

VII. Exercises:

A. RECOGNITION EXERCISES:

1. *Explanation:*
   a. As has been mentioned, contract verbs are usually recognizable from the extensive use of the **circumflex accent.**
   b. **Another characteristic,** however, and one that can be a help or hindrance, is the *identity* of many forms and the *similarity* of others.
   c. The following exercise, then, is designed to help the student to **identify** those forms which are the same **and distinguish** those which are similar and easily mistaken for one another.

2. *Contract forms identical* in different parts of the *present system:* (Numerals in parentheses indicate the number of identical forms.)

ἀγαπᾶτε (3)	ἀγαπῶσι (4)	λαλῇ (3)	πληροῖ (4)
ἀγαπᾶσθε (3)	ἀγαπᾷ (4)	λαλοῦσι (3)	πληροῦν (3)
ἀγαπῶ (3)	λαλεῖτε (2)	ἐλάλουν (2)	πληροῦσι (3)

3. *Contract forms so similar* they must be carefully *distinguished:*

   a. ἀγαπᾷ   b. ἀγαπῶν   c. λαλεῖ   d. λαλεῖτε   e. πλήρου
      ἀγάπα   ἠγάπων   λάλει   ἐλαλεῖτε   πληροῦ
      ἠγάπα   ἀγαπᾶν   ἐλάλει   λαλῆτε   ἐπλήρου
                                                        ἐπληροῦ

B. *Read aloud, translate,* and *explain the underlined forms* in the following:

1. Φωνὴ <u>βοῶντος</u> ἐν τῇ ἐρήμῳ, Ἑτοιμάσατε τὴν ὁδὸν κυρίου,
   _{of one calling}

   εὐθείας <u>ποιεῖτε</u> τὰς τρίβους αὐτοῦ. πᾶσα φάραγξ <u>πληρωθήσεται</u>
              _{paths}   _{valley}

   καὶ πᾶν ὄρος καὶ βουνὸς <u>ταπεινωθήσεται</u>, καὶ ἔσται τὰ σκολιὰ
              _{hill}   _{crooked}

   εἰς εὐθείαν καὶ αἱ τραχεῖαι εἰς ὁδοὺς λείας· καὶ <u>ὄψεται</u> πᾶσα
              _{rough}   _{smooth}

   σὰρξ τὸ σωτήριον τοῦ θεοῦ.

2. Πάτερ* ἅγιε,* <u>τήρησον</u> αὐτοὺς ἐν τῷ ὀνόματί σου ᾧ <u>δέδωκάς</u>
                                                          _{you gave}

   μοι, ἵνα <u>ὦσιν ἓν</u> καθὼς ἡμεῖς. ὅτε <u>ἤμην</u> μετ᾽ αὐτῶν ἐγὼ <u>ἐτήρουν</u>
                                             _{I was}

   αὐτοὺς ἐν τῷ ὀνόματί σου ᾧ δέδωκάς μοι, καὶ <u>ἐφύλαξα</u>, καὶ

   *All words with a single asterisk (*) are vocatives of the masculine gender.

οὐδεὶς ἐξ αὐτῶν ἀπώλετο εἰ μὴ ὁ υἱὸς τῆς ἀπωλείας, ἵνα ἡ γραφὴ
_{perished} _{perdition}

πληρωθῇ. νῦν δὲ πρὸς σὲ ἔρχομαι, καὶ ταῦτα λαλῶ ἐν τῷ κόσμῳ

ἵνα ἔχωσιν τὴν χαρὰν τὴν ἐμὴν πεπληρωμένην ἐν αὐτοῖς. ἐγὼ
_{joy}

δέδωκα αὐτοῖς τὸν λόγον σου, καὶ ὁ κόσμος ἐμίσησεν αὐτούς,
_{have given}

ὅτι οὐκ εἰσὶν ἐκ τοῦ κόσμου καθὼς ἐγὼ οὐκ εἰμὶ ἐκ τοῦ κόσμου.

οὐκ ἐρωτῶ ἵνα ἄρῃς αὐτοὺς ἐκ τοῦ κόσμου ἀλλ' ἵνα τηρήσῃς

αὐτοὺς ἐκ τοῦ πονηροῦ.

3. Ὅτε οὖν ἠρίστησαν λέγει τῷ Σίμωνι Πέτρῳ ὁ Ἰησοῦς, Σίμων
_{had breakfast}

Ἰωάννου, ἀγαπᾷς με πλέον τούτων; λέγει αὐτῷ, Ναί, κύριε,* σὺ
_{Son of John} _{Yes}

οἶδας ὅτι φιλῶ σε. λέγει αὐτῷ, Βόσκε τὰ ἀρνία μου. λέγει αὐτῷ
_{know} _{Feed} _{lambs}

πάλιν δεύτερον, Σίμων Ἰωάννου, ἀγαπᾷς με; λέγει αὐτῷ, Ναί,
_{a second time}

κύριε,* σὺ οἶδας ὅτι φιλῶ σε. λέγει αὐτῷ, Ποίμαινε τὰ πρόβατά
_{Shepherd} _{sheep}

μου. λέγει αὐτῷ τὸ τρίτον, Σίμων Ἰωάννου, φιλεῖς με; ἐλυπήθη
_{the third time} _{was saddened}

ὁ Πέτρος ὅτι εἶπεν αὐτῷ τὸ τρίτον, Φιλεῖς με; καὶ λέγει αὐτῷ,

Κύριε,* πάντα σὺ οἶδας, σὺ γινώσκεις ὅτι φιλῶ σε. λέγει αὐτῷ,

Βόσκε τὰ πρόβατά μου. ἀμὴν ἀμὴν λέγω σοι, ὅτε ἦς νεώτερος,
_{younger}

ἐζώννυες σεαυτὸν καὶ περιεπάτεις ὅπου ἤθελες·** ὅταν δὲ
_{you girded}

γηράσῃς, ἐκτενεῖς τὰς χεῖράς σου, καὶ ἄλλος σε ζώσει καὶ
_{you grow old} _{will gird}

οἴσει ὅπου οὐ θέλεις. τοῦτο δὲ εἶπεν σημαίνων ποίῳ θανάτῳ
_{signifying}

δοξάσει τὸν θεόν· καὶ τοῦτο εἰπὼν λέγει αὐτῷ, Ἀκολούθει μοι.

** This is the imperfect indicative (with irregular augment) of
θέλω: I will.

18 Strong Vowel Verbs—Part II

Athematic Verbs

I. Introduction:

A. In the previous lesson, we studied strong vowel verbs which contract the stem vowel α, ε, ο with the variable vowel or developed ending.

B. IN THIS LESSON, we will examine those strong vowel verbs *which do not use a variable vowel* (except in the futures) and do use more *primitive endings*.

C. For these reasons, they are called ATHEMATIC (i.e. without thematic vowels) verbs; and PRIMITIVE OR MI-VERBS, in reference to their unusual endings.

D. Our study will comprise THREE KINDS of athematic verbs: 1) regular and complete, 2) regular but incomplete, and 3) irregular athematic verbs.

II. Regular and complete athematic verbs:

A. IMPORTANCE: These verbs are *few but extremely important* for their usage in compounds, their Latin counterparts, and their many English derivatives.

B. PRINCIPAL PARTS, meaning, Latin counterparts, and English derivatives of:

δίδωμι (δο), δώσω, ἔδωκα, δέδωκα, δέδομαι, ἐδόθην: give, grant (L. do = give; E. anecdote, antidote, dose, dosage, overdose, etc.).

ἵστημι (στα), στήσω, ἔστησα/ἔστην, ἔστηκα, (ἔσταμαι), ἐστάθην: set, stand (L. sto = stand, E. (ec)static, statistic, apostasy, system).

τίθημι (θε), θήσω, ἔθηκα, τέθεικα, τέθειμαι, ἐτέθην: put, place (L. thema, thesis; E. anathema, apothecary, hypothesis, parenthesis).

C. SOME COMPOUNDS of these verbs, chosen for frequency in the New Testament:

1. *Compounds of* δίδωμι: **ἀποδίδωμι** = give back, (re)pay, reward.
   παραδίδωμι = hand on/over
   (παράδοσις = tradition, p. 122).

2. *Compounds of* ἵστημι: **ἀνίστημι** = raise; rise (ἀνάστασις = resurrection, p. 122).
   παρίστημι = be present, stand by; present!

3. *Compound of* τίθημι: **ἐπιτίθημι** = lay (hands) on; add (to).

D. CHARACTERISTIC FORMATION, primarily in the present and aorist systems:

1. *Reduplication in the present system:* δ̲ίδωμι, (σ)ἵστημι, τ̲ίθημι.

2. *Lengthening of the stem vowel:* α to η, but $\begin{cases} \varepsilon \text{ to } \eta \text{ or } \varepsilon\iota. \\ o \text{ to } \omega \text{ or } o\upsilon. \end{cases}$
   a. In the **present/imperfect ind., act., sing.:** ω/ου, η/η, η/η-ει.
   b. In the **entire aorist indicative active:** ἔδ̲ωκα, ἔστ̲ησα/ην, ἔθηκα.
   c. In the **formation of most of the other tenses:** ω-ο, η-α, η-ει-ε̣.

3. *Contraction* in the present/aorist subjunctive: ῶ-ῷ, ῶ-ῇ-ῇ, ῶ-ῇ-ῇ.

4. *Change or omission* of the aorist system sign: κα, σα/-, κα.

5. *Different endings* only in the present and aorist active systems:
   a. The **present indicative:** μι, ς, σι — μεν, τε, ασι (sing.-plur.).
   b. The **imperfect indicative, third person plural:** σαν.
   c. The **present/aorist imperative,** 2nd. pers. sing.: ε/ς-θι (present contracts).
   d. The **present/aorist infinite:** ναι/έναι (aor. contracts).
   e. The **present/aorist participle:** (ντ)ς, (ντ)σα, (ντ).

E. CONJUGATION of the present system of:

	δίδωμι (δο)		ἵστημι (στα)		τίθημι (θε)	
	ACTIVE	MID-PASS.	ACTIVE	MID-PASS.	ACTIVE	MID-PASS.
	present indicative		present indicative		present indicative	
S. 1.	δίδωμι	δίδομαι	ἵστημι	ἵσταμαι	τίθημι	τίθεμαι
2.	δίδως	δίδοσαι	ἵστης	ἵστασαι	τίθης	τίθεσαι
3.	δίδωσι	δίδοται	ἵστησι	ἵσταται	τίθησι	τίθεται
P. 1.	δίδομεν	διδόμεθα	ἵσταμεν	ἱστάμεθα	τίθεμεν	τιθέμεθα
2.	δίδοτε	δίδοσθε	ἵστατε	ἵστασθε	τίθετε	τίθεσθε
3.	διδόασι	δίδονται	ἱστᾶσι	ἵστανται	τιθέασι	τίθενται

	ACTIVE	MID-PASS.	ACTIVE	MID-PASS.	ACTIVE	MID-PASS.
	imperfect indicative		imperfect indicative		imperfect indicative	
S. 1.	ἐδίδουν	ἐδιδόμην	ἵστην	ἱστάμην	ἐτίθην	ἐτιθέμην
2.	ἐδίδους	ἐδίδοσο	ἵστης	ἵστασο	ἐτίθεις	ἐτίθεσο
3.	ἐδίδου	ἐδίδοτο	ἵστη	ἵστατο	ἐτίθει	ἐτίθετο
P. 1.	ἐδίδομεν	ἐδιδόμεθα	ἵσταμεν	ἱστάμεθα	ἐτίθεμεν	ἐτιθέμεθα
2.	ἐδίδοτε	ἐδίδοσθε	ἵστατε	ἵστασθε	ἐτίθετε	ἐτίθεσθε
3.	ἐδίδοσαν	ἐδίδοντο	ἵστασαν	ἵσταντο	ἐτίθεσαν	ἐτίθεντο
	present subjunctive		present subjunctive		present subjunctive	
S. 1.	διδῶ	(διδῶμαι)	ἱστῶ	(ἱστῶμαι)	τιθῶ	(τιθῶμαι)
2.	διδῷς	(διδῷ)	ἱστῇς	(ἱστῇ)	τιθῇς	(τιθῇ)
3.	διδῷ	(διδῶται)	ἱστῇ	(ἱστῆται)	τιθῇ	(τιθῆται)
P. 1.	διδῶμεν	(διδώμεθα)	ἱστῶμεν	(ἱστώμεθα)	τιθῶμεν	(τιθώμεθα)
2.	διδῶτε	(διδῶσθε)	ἱστῆτε	(ἱστῆσθε)	τιθῆτε	(τιθῆσθε)
3.	διδῶσι	(διδῶνται)	ἱστῶσι	(ἱστῶνται)	τιθῶσι	(τιθῶνται)
	present imperative		present imperative		present imperative	
S. 2.	δίδου	δίδοσο	ἵστη	ἵστασο	τίθει	τίθεσο
3.	διδότω	διδόσθω	ἱστάτω	ἱστάσθω	τιθέτω	τιθέσθω
P. 2.	δίδοτε	δίδοσθε	ἵστατε	ἵστασθε	τίθετε	τίθεσθε
3.	διδότωσαν	διδόσθωσαν	ἱστάτωσαν	ἱστάσθωσαν	τιθέτωσαν	τιθέσθωσαν
	present infinitive		present infinitive		present infinitive	
	διδόναι	δίδοσθαι	ἱστάναι	ἵστασθαι	τιθέναι	τίθεσθαι
	present participle		present participle		present participle	
	ACTIVE		ACTIVE		ACTIVE	
S. N.	διδούς, οῦσα, όν		ἱστάς, ᾶσα, άν		τιθείς, εῖσα, έν	
G.	διδόντος, ούσης, όντος		ἱστάντος, άσης, άντος		τιθέντος, είσης, έντος	
	MID-PASS.		MID-PASS.		MID-PASS.	
S. N.	διδόμενος, η, ον		ἱστάμενος, η, ον		τιθέμενος, η, ον	
G.	διδομένου, ης, ου		ἱσταμένου, ης, ου		τιθεμένου, ης, ου	

F. CONJUGATION of the aorist of:

	δίδωμι		ἵστημι*		τίθημι	
	ACTIVE—MID.		FIRST—SECOND		ACTIVE—MID.	
	Indicative		Indicative		Indicative	
S. 1.	ἔδωκα	ἐδόμην	ἔστησα	ἔστην	ἔθηκα	ἐθέμην
2.	ἔδωκας	ἔδου	ἔστησας	ἔστης	ἔθηκας	ἔθου
3.	ἔδωκε	ἔδοτο	ἔστησε	ἔστη	ἔθηκε	ἔθετο
P. 1.	ἐδώκαμεν	ἐδόμεθα	ἐστήσαμεν	ἔστημεν	ἐθήκαμεν	ἐθέμεθα
2.	ἐδώκατε	ἔδοσθε	ἐστήσατε	ἔστητε	ἐθήκατε	ἔθεσθε
3.	ἔδωκαν	ἔδοντο	ἔστησαν	ἔστησαν	ἔθηκαν	ἔθεντο
	Subjunctive		Subjunctive		Subjunctive	
S. 1.	δῶ	δῶμαι	στῶ		θῶ	θῶμαι
2.	δῷς	δῷ	στῇς		θῇς	θῇ
3.	δῷ	δῶται	στῇ		θῇ	θῆται

	ACTIVE—MID.		FIRST—SECOND	ACTIVE—MID.	
	Subjunctive		Subjunctive	Subjunctive	
P. 1.	δῶμεν	δώμεθα	στῶμεν	θῶμεν	θώμεθα
2.	δῶτε	δῶσθε	στῆτε	θῆτε	θῆσθε
3.	δῶσι	δῶνται	στῶσι	θῶσι	θῶνται
	Imperative		Imperative	Imperative	
S. 2.	δός	δοῦ	στῆθι	θές	θοῦ
3.	δότω	δόσθω	στήτω	θέτω	θέσθω
P. 2.	δότε	δόσθε	στῆτε	θέτε	θέσθε
3.	δότωσαν	δόσθωσαν	στήτωσαν	θέτωσαν	θέσθωσαν
	Infinitive		Infinitive	Infinitive	
	δοῦναι	δόσθαι	στῆναι	θεῖναι	θέσθαι
	Participle		Participle	Participle	
	ACTIVE		ACTIVE	ACTIVE	
S. N.	δούς, δοῦσα, δόν		στάς, στᾶσα, στάν	θείς, θεῖσα, θέν	
G.	δόντος, ούσης, όντος		στάντος, άσης, άντος	θέντος, είσης, έντος	
	MIDDLE			MIDDLE	
S. N.	δόμενος, η, ον			θέμενος, η, ον	
G.	δομένου, ης, ον			θεμένου, ης, ον	

*IMPORTANT NOTE about the forms and meanings of ἵστημι—

1. **Forms:** Both the aorist and perfect active have first and second forms—
a. The *first aorist form* appears *only in the indicative* (cf. above).
b. The *first perfect* appears in the *indicative* (ἕστηκα) and *participle*** (ἑστηκώς); *the second*, in ἑστάναι (infinitive), ἑστώς (participle).

2. **Meanings:**
a. The *pres., impf., fut.,* and *1st aor. act.* are *transitive:* I set, etc.
b. The *2nd aor.* and *perf. act.* and *all mid-pass.* are *intransitive:* I stand.
c. The *perfect active* in both forms has a *present* meaning: I am standing.

**The rough breathing in the perfect (and present) systems is for reduplication.

III. **Regular but incomplete athematic verbs:**

A. EXPLANATION: These are divided into:

1. *Deponent athematic verbs*, i.e. athematic verbs with no active voice.

2. *Thematic verbs* with one or more athematic systems.

B. DEPONENT ATHEMATIC VERBS: are principally these—

δύναμαι (δυνα), δυνήσομαι, ἐδυνάμην/ἠδυνάμην, ἠδυνήθην/άσθην: be able, can (dynamic, dynamite, dynasty, teledyne, thermodynamic).

ἐπίσταμαι (ἐπιστα): know, understand (epistemic, epistemology, history) (not to be confused with the compound of ἵστημι, ἐφίστημι: stand by).

κάθημαι (καθη, καθησ), καθήσομαι: be seated, sit, originally used as the perfect of καθέζομαι: be seated (ex cathedra, cathedral).

κεῖμαι (κει, κε): lie, be laid (in death, burial); be, exist, stand; be destined (related to κοιμάομαι: sleep, whence cemetery).

Also the compounds: **ἀνάκειμαι** = recline at meals, be a dinner guest; **κατάκειμαι** = lie down, lie sick; recline at meals.

C. THEMATIC VERBS with an athematic present system:

1. *Explanation:*

a. Some verbs are **athematic only in the present system,** but otherwise are conjugated like vowel, mute, or liquid verbs.

b. A few of these verbs have **two forms for the present system,** an older athematic and a later thematic form, the latter usually being more popular in Koine Greek and in the New Testament.

2. *Principal thematic verbs* with an athematic present system:

ἀπόλλυμι/ἀπολλύω (ἀπολε), ἀπολήσω/ἀπολῶ, ἀπώλεσα, ἀπόλωλα: destroy; perish, be lost, related to λύω: loose, destroy (Apollyon).

δείκνυμι/δεικνύω (δεικ), δείξω, ἔδειξα, (δέδειχα), δέδειγμαι, ἐδείχθην: show, prove, reveal, explain (apodictic, deictic).

ὄμνυμι/ὀμνύω (ὀμο), (ὀμοῦμαι), ὤμοσα: swear, vow, take an oath.

πίμπλημι (πλη/πλα), (πλήσω), ἔπλησα, ἐπλήσθην: fill, fulfill.

3. *Conjugation of thematic verbs* with an athematic present system:

a. **Verbs in** α (πίμπλημι) form their present system like ἵστημι.

b. **Verbs in** υ (ἀπόλλυμι, δείκνυμι, ὄμνυμι) have *no contractions* and *can be synopsized* in the present system as follows:

ACTIVE

Pres. Ind. ὄμνυμι	*Impf. Ind.* ὤμνυν	*Pres. Subj.* ὀμνύω
Pres. Imp. ὄμνυ	*Pres. Inf.* ὀμνύναι	*Pres. Part.* ὀμνύς, ύσα, ύν

MID-PASS.

Pres. Ind. ὄμνυμαι	*Impf. Ind.* ὠμνύμην	*Pres. Subj.* ὀμνύωμαι
Pres. Imp. ὄμνυσο	*Pres. Inf.* ὄμνυσθαι	*Pres. Part.* ὀμνύμενος, η, ον

c. **Synopsis** of the present and imperfect indicative active is:

Pres.: S. 1. ὄμνυμι P. 1. ὄμνυμεν *Imperf.:* S. 1. ὤμνυν P. 1. ὤμνυμεν
      2. ὄμνυς   2. ὄμνυτε   2. ὤμνυς   2. ὤμνυτε
      3. ὄμνυσι   3. ὀμνύασι   3. ὤμνυ   3. ὤμνυσαν

D. THEMATIC VERBS with an athematic aorist system:

  1. *Explanation:*

    a. So far, we have studied **five kinds** of aorists:

      1) (Thematic) first (or regular) aorists in σα: ἔλυσα

      2) (Thematic) second (usually mute) aorists in ον: ἔλιπον

      3) (Thematic) liquid aorists in α: ἀπέστειλα

      4) Athematic (first) aorists in κα: ἔδωκα

      5) Athematic second aorists in ν: ἔστην

    b. Now, we must examine: **thematic verbs** with **athematic second aorists—**

  2. *Principal* thematic verbs with athematic second aorists are:

    -βαίνω (βα), βήσομαι, <u>ἔβην</u>, βέβηκα: go (p. 106; compounds, p. 116).

    γινώσκω (γνο), γνώσομαι, <u>ἔγνων</u>, κτλ.: know (p. 114; compounds, p. 115).

  3. *Conjugation* of the athematic second aorists: **ἔστην, ἔβην, ἔγνων,** in the *active voice,* the only voice in which they are used:

	ἔστην		ἔβην		ἔγνων	
	Sing.	*Plur.*	*Sing.*	*Plur.*	*Sing.*	*Plur.*
	Indicative		Indicative		Indicative	
1.	ἔστην	ἔστημεν	ἔβην	ἔβημεν	ἔγνων	ἔγνωμεν
2.	ἔστης	ἔστητε	ἔβης	ἔβητε	ἔγνως	ἔγνωτε
3.	ἔστη	ἔστησαν	ἔβη	ἔβησαν	ἔγνω	ἔγνωσαν
	Subjunctive		Subjunctive		Subjunctive	
1.	στῶ	στῶμεν	(βῶ)	(βῶμεν)	γνῶ	γνῶμεν
2.	στῇς	στῆτε	(βῇς)	(βῆτε)	γνῷς	γνῶτε
3.	στῇ	στῶσι	(βῇ)	(βῶσι)	γνῷ	γνῶσι
	Imperative		Imperative		Imperative	
2.	στῆθι	στῆτε	βῆθι	βῆτε	γνῶθι	γνῶτε
3.	στήτω	στήτωσαν	βήτω	βήτωσαν	γνώτω	γνώτωσαν
	Inf.	Part.	Inf.	Part.	Inf.	Part.
	στῆναι	στάς, ᾶσα, άν	βῆναι	βάς, ᾶσα, άν	γνῶναι	γνούς, οὖσα, όν

IV. **Irregular athematic verbs:** Finally, there are some short and mostly irregular verbs which, to avoid confusion, are best studied by comparison and contrast—

εἰμί (ἐσ), **ἔσομαι**: be, exist; happen; live (L. *esse:* to be, hence essence; E. ontic, ontology, ontogenesis; homoousian),
    πάρειμι: be present (Parousia).

-εἶμι (ἰ): go (L. *ire:* to go, hence ion, itinerary), **εἴσειμι**: go in, enter; **ἔξειμι**: go away, leave, head for; **σύνειμι**: gather, assemble.

-ἵημι (ἑ), **-ἥσω**, **-ἧκα**, **-εἷκα**, **-εἷμαι**, **-ἕθην**: send (catheter, enema, etc.), **ἀφίημι**: forgive, remit, allow; **συνίημι**: understand.

οἶδα (ἰδ): know (perfect, with present sense, of obsolete εἴδω: see, know) (L. *video:* I see), aor. **εἶδον** used by ὁράω (eidetic, eidolon, idol).

φημί (φα), **ἔφην**: say (L. *fari, fans,* hence infant; E. prophecy, euphemism).

VERB:	εἰμί (ἐσ)	-εἶμι (ἰ)	-ἵημι (ἑ)		οἶδα (ἰδ)	φημί (φα)
SENSE:	I am	I go	I send	I sent	I know	I say
INDIC.:	present	present	present	aorist	perfect	present
Sing. 1.	εἰμί	εἶμι	ἵημι	ἧκα	οἶδα	φημί
2.	εἶ	εἶ	ἵης	ἧκας	οἶδας	φής
3.	ἐστί	εἶσι	ἵησι	ἧκε	οἶδε	φησί
Plur. 1.	ἐσμέν	ἵμεν	ἵεμεν	ἥκαμεν	οἴδαμεν	φαμέν
2.	ἐστέ	ἵτε	ἵετε	ἥκατε	οἴδατε	φατέ
3.	εἰσί	ἵασι	ἱᾶσι	ἧκαν	οἴδασι	φασί
	imperfect	imperfect	imperfect		pluperfect	imperfect
Sing. 1.	ἤμην	ᾖειν	ἵειν		ᾔδειν	ἔφην
2.	ἦς	ᾖεις	ἵεις		ᾔδεις	ἔφης
3.	ἦν	ᾖει	ἵει		ᾔδει	ἔφη
Plur. 1.	ἦμεν	ᾖμεν	ἵεμεν		ᾔδειμεν	ἔφαμεν
2.	ἦτε	ᾖτε	ἵετε		ᾔδειτε	ἔφατε
3.	ἦσαν	ᾖσαν	ἵεσαν		ᾔδεισαν	ἔφασαν
SUBJ.:	present	present	present	aorist	perfect	present
Sing. 1.	ὦ	ἵω	ἵω	ὧ	εἰδῶ	φῶ
2.	ᾖς	ἵῃς	ἵῃς	ἧς	εἰδῇς	φῇς
3.	ᾖ	ἵῃ	ἵῃ	ᾖ	εἰδῇ	φῇ
Plur. 1.	ὦμεν	ἵωμεν	ἵωμεν	ὧμεν	εἰδῶμεν	φῶμεν
2.	ἦτε	ἵητε	ἵητε	ἧτε	εἰδῆτε	φῆτε
3.	ὦσι	ἵωσι	ἵωσι	ὧσι	εἰδῶσι	φῶσι
IMPTV.:	present	present	present	aorist	perfect	present
Sing. 2.	ἴσθι	ἴθι	ἵει	ἕς	ἴσθι	φάθι
3.	ἔστω	ἴτω	ἱέτω	ἕτω	ἴστω	φάτω
Plur. 2.	ἔστε	ἴτε	ἵετε	ἕτε	ἴστε	φάτε
3.	ἔστωσαν	ἴτωσαν	ἱέτωσαν	ἕτωσαν	ἴστωσαν	φάτωσαν
INFIN.:	present	present	present	aorist	perfect	present
	εἶναι	ἱέναι	ἱέναι	εἶναι	εἰδέναι	φάναι

[cont'd]

PART.:	present	present	present	aorist	perfect	present
Nom. M.	ὤν	ἰών	ἱείς	εἷς	εἰδώς	φάς
F.	οὖσα	ἰοῦσα	ἱεῖσα	εἷσα	εἰδυῖα	φᾶσα
N.	ὄν	ἰόν	ἱέν	ἕν	εἰδός	φάν
Gen. M.	ὄντος	ἰόντος	ἱέντος	ἕντος	εἰδότος	φάντος
F.	οὔσης	ἰούσης	ἱείσης	εἴσης	εἰδυίας	φάσης
N.	ὄντος	ἰόντος	ἱέντος	ἕντος	εἰδότος	φάντος

NB: 1) These verbs are used almost entirely in the active voice, given here.

2) *Variant forms* are omitted here to avoid confusion. See Analyses, Lexica.

3) The verbs ἵημι and φημί are conjugated much like the verb τίθημι.

4) *To distinguish* these verbs, it is essential to keep the stems in mind.

5) The verb εἰμί (I am) is sometimes used in the optative mood (should-would) which has otherwise largely disappeared from use in the New Testament. The present optative is conjugated thus: *Sing.*: εἴην, εἴης, εἴη. *Plur.*: εἴημεν, εἴητε, εἴησαν.

V.   Exercises:

A.   RECOGNITION PRACTICE: Please *identify* and *translate* the following forms—

ἀφῆκα	ἵστην	δίδως	τίθησι	ἐδίδοσαν	ἵστη
ἀφεῖκα	ἔστην	διδῷς	τιθεῖσι	διδότωσαν	ἱστῇ
ἔδωκα	ἔβητε	θῇς	ὀμνύν	ἵστησι	ἐπίσταται
ἔδωκαν	βῆτε	θείς	ὤμνυν	ἱστᾶσι	ἐφίσταται
ἱστάναι	ἔστε	ἀφῇ	ἦσαν	εἰσι	ᾔει
ἑστάναι	ἴστε	ἔφη	ἦσαν	εἰσί	εἴη

B. *Read aloud, translate,* and *explain the underlined words* in the following:

Μαρία δὲ <u>εἰστήκει</u> πρὸς τῷ μνημείῳ ἔξω <u>κλαίουσα</u>. ὡς οὖν

<u>ἔκλαιεν</u> <u>παρέκυψεν</u> εἰς τὸ μνημεῖον, καὶ <u>θεωρεῖ</u> δύο ἀγγέλους ἐν
      <small>she peered</small>

λευκοῖς <u>καθεζομένους</u>, ἕνα πρὸς τῇ κεφαλῇ καὶ ἕνα πρὸς τοῖς

ποσίν, ὅπου <u>ἔκειτο</u> τὸ σῶμα τοῦ Ἰησοῦ. καὶ <u>λέγουσιν</u> αὐτῇ ἐκεῖνοι,

Γύναι, τί κλαίεις; λέγει αὐτοῖς ὅτι Ἦραν τὸν κύριόν μου, καὶ οὐκ
<small>Woman (voc.)</small>

<u>οἶδα</u> ποῦ <u>ἔθηκαν</u> αὐτόν. ταῦτα <u>εἰποῦσα</u> <u>ἐστράφη</u> εἰς τὰ ὀπίσω, καὶ

<u>θεωρεῖ</u> τὸν Ἰησοῦν <u>ἑστῶτα</u>, καὶ οὐκ <u>ᾔδει</u> ὅτι Ἰησοῦς <u>ἐστιν</u>. λέγει

αὐτῇ Ἰησοῦς, Γύναι, τί κλαίεις; τίνα ζητεῖς; ἐκείνη <u>δοκοῦσα</u> ὅτι ὁ

<u>κηπουρός</u> <u>ἐστιν</u> λέγει αὐτῷ, Κύριε, εἰ σὺ <u>ἐβάστασας</u> αὐτόν, <u>εἰπέ</u>
<small>gardener</small>

μοι ποῦ <u>ἔθηκας</u> αὐτόν, κἀγὼ αὐτὸν <u>ἀρῶ</u>. λέγει αὐτῇ Ἰησοῦς,

Μαριάμ. <u>στραφεῖσα</u> ἐκείνη λέγει αὐτῷ Ἑβραϊστί, Ῥαββουνι* (ὃ
                      <small>in Hebrew   My Teacher</small>

λέγεται Διδάσκαλε). λέγει αὐτῇ Ἰησοῦς, <u>Μή μου ἅπτου</u>, οὔπω γὰρ
                                    <small>hold</small>

<u>ἀναβέβηκα</u> πρὸς τὸν πατέρα· <u>πορεύου</u> δὲ πρὸς τοὺς ἀδελφούς μου

καὶ <u>εἶπε</u> αὐτοῖς, Ἀναβαίνω πρὸς τὸν πατέρα μου καὶ πατέρα ὑμῶν

καὶ θεόν μου καὶ θεὸν ὑμῶν. . . . <u>Οὔσης</u> οὖν ὀψίας τῇ ἡμέρᾳ ἐκείνῃ
                                   <small>evening</small>

τῇ μιᾷ σαββάτων . . . <u>ἦλθεν</u> ὁ Ἰησοῦς καὶ <u>ἔστη</u> εἰς τὸ μέσον καὶ
     <small>week</small>

λέγει αὐτοῖς, Εἰρήνη ὑμῖν . . . <u>Λάβετε</u> πνεῦμα ἅγιον· ἄν τινων

<u>ἀφῆτε</u> τὰς ἁμαρτίας <u>ἀφέωνται</u>** αὐτοῖς, ἄν τινων <u>κρατῆτε</u>

<u>κεκράτηνται</u>.

    *Transliterated (unaccented) Aramaic term.
    **Alternate New Testament form of ἀφεῖνται (ἀφίημι).

19 Final Matters of Moment

Nouns, Adjectives, Adverbs, Numerals

I. **Introduction:** In this chapter, we will examine the following—

A. Irregular nouns and adjectives.

B. Comparison of adjectives and adverbs.

C. Enumeration in New Testament Greek.

II. **Irregular nouns and adjectives:**

A. IRREGULAR NOUNS:

1. *Explanation:*
   a. These consist primarily of **loan words** from Hebrew, Aramaic, etc., including some common nouns, but mostly names of persons and places.
   b. The common nouns are **usually indeclinable;** the proper nouns are sometimes at least **partially declined,** sometimes indeclinable.
   c. **A helpful "rule of thumb"** for the proper nouns is this:
      1) Those which end in letters like those of Greek regular nouns, e.g.: α, ε, ι, ο, υ; ν, ρ, ς, are *usually declined*, at least in part.
      2) Those which end in some other letter are *usually indeclinable.*
   d. **Most are easily recognizable,** but some examples will be helpful.

2. *Examples:* (NB: loan words often appear without accent or breathing.)
   a. **Proper nouns** at least partially declined:

   Ἀνδρέας, ου, ᾳ, αν, ὁ: Andrew (cf. ἀνήρ)

   Βηθάνια, ας, ᾳ, αν, ἡ: Bethany

   Ἡρῴδης, ου, η, ην, ὁ: Herod

   Θωμᾶς, ᾶ, ᾷ, ᾶ, ὁ: Thomas

   Ἰάκωβος, ου, ῳ, ον, ὁ: James

   Ἰησοῦς, οῦ, οῦ, οῦν, ὁ: Jesus

Ἰωάννης, ου, η, ην, ὁ: John
Μαρία, ας, ᾳ, αν, ἡ: Mary
(cf. below)

Μωϋσῆς, έως, ῆ/εῖ, ῆν/έα, ὁ: Moses

Σίμων, ωνος, ωνι, ωνα, ὁ: Simon

b. **Common nouns** at least partially declined:

γέεννα, ης, η, αν, ἡ: hell (fire)

σάββατον, ου, ῳ, ον, τό: sabbath (in plural, often translated as "week(s)")

c. **Proper nouns** which are **indeclinable**:

Ἀβραάμ, ὁ: Abram/ Abraham
Γαββαθα:* Gabbatha
Γεθσημανί: Gethsemane
Γεννησαρέτ: Gennesaret(h)
Δαυίδ, ὁ: David
Ἐλισάβετ, ἡ: Elizabeth

Ἰερουσαλήμ/-οσόλυμα, ἡ/τά: Jerusalem
Ἰσραήλ, ὁ: Israel
Ἰωσήφ, ὁ: Joseph
Λευί/Λευίς/Λευεί, ὁ: Levi
Μαριάμ, ἡ: Mary (cf. above)
Ναζαρά/έθ/έτ, ἡ: Nazareth

d. **Common nouns** which are **indeclinable**:

αββα,* ὁ: father, "daddy" (abbot)
κορβᾶν: gift to God (corban)
μάννα, τό: manna (mannite, mannose)
πάσχα, τό: pasch, passover (paschal)

ραββί/ραββουνι:* teacher (rabbi)
σαβαωθ:* armies, hosts (sabaoth)
ταλιθα:* young girl

B. IRREGULAR ADJECTIVES:

1. *Explanation:* These comprise three main groups, which will be studied in *descending order of frequency and importance* in the New Testament.

2. *Variant stem adjectives:*

a. **Description:** Two very common first and second declension adjectives use *shortened stems* and *third declension endings* in the nominative and accusative masculine and neuter singular, namely:

μέγας, μεγάλη, μέγα: great, large (omega, megalith, megalopolis, megaton, megaphone)

πολύς, πολλή, πολύ: much, many (hoi polloi, polygamy, polyglot, polytheism, polymer, polygraph)

*NB: No accent or breathing.

b. **Declension** of **μέγας** and **πολύς**, with irregular forms underlined:

	Masc.	Fem.	Neut.		Masc.	Fem.	Neut.
		Sing.				Sing.	
N.	<u>μέγας</u>	μεγάλη	<u>μέγα</u>	N.	<u>πολύς</u>	πολλή	<u>πολύ</u>
G.	μεγάλου	μεγάλης	μεγάλου	G.	<u>πολλοῦ</u>	πολλῆς	πολλοῦ
D.	μεγάλῳ	μεγάλη	μεγάλῳ	D.	<u>πολλῷ</u>	πολλῇ	πολλῷ
A.	<u>μέγαν</u>	μεγάλην	<u>μέγα</u>	A.	<u>πολύν</u>	πολλήν	<u>πολύ</u>
		Plur.				Plur.	
N.	μεγάλοι	μεγάλαι	μεγάλα	N.	πολλοί	πολλαί	πολλά
G.	μεγάλων	μεγάλων	μεγάλων	G.	πολλῶν	πολλῶν	πολλῶν
D.	μεγάλοις	μεγάλαις	μεγάλοις	D.	πολλοῖς	πολλαῖς	πολλοῖς
A.	μεγάλους	μεγάλας	μεγάλα	A.	πολλούς	πολλάς	πολλά

3. *Defective adjectives:* Some (mostly compound) adjectives belong to the *second declension only,* having but *two terminations* or sets of endings, one for the masculine and feminine, the other for the neuter gender—

ἄδικος, ον: unjust (ἀ + δίκη)

ἀδύνατος, ον: impossible (ἀ + δύνατος)

ἄζυμος, ον: unleavened (ἀ + ζύμη)

αἰώνιος, ον: eternal (αἰών)

ἄνομος, ον: lawless (ἀ + νόμος)

ἄπιστος, ον: unbelieving (ἀ + πιστός)

ἔνοχος, ον: guilty (ἐν + ἔχω)

ἔρημος, ον: deserted (hermit, eremetical)

οὐράνιος, ον: heavenly (οὐρανός) (Uranus, uranium)

4. *Contract adjectives:*

a. **Description:**

1) These less common *first and second declension* adjectives are declined regularly *but with contractions* between a final ε of the stem and the first vowel of the endings.

2) Easily recognized by the *circumflex accent* over the ultima, which is normally a diphthong, they fall into two principal classes.

b. **Vocabulary** of contract adjectives, in *two classes,* referring to

1) *Precious materials:*

ἀργυροῦς, ᾶ, οῦν: silver

πορφυροῦς, ᾶ, οῦν: purple (porphyry)

χαλκοῦς, ῆ, οῦν: bronze (Chalcolithic)

χρυσοῦς, ῆ, οῦν: golden (Chrysostom)

2) *Numbers of times:*

ἁπλοῦς, ῆ, οῦν: single (haploid)

διπλοῦς, ῆ, οῦν: double (diploma)

τριπλοῦς, ῆ, οῦν: threefold (triple)

τετραπλοῦς, ῆ, οῦν: fourfold (tetraploid)

III. Comparison of adjectives and adverbs:

A. EXPLANATION:

1. Comparison refers to the degrees of a quality or characteristic indicated by an adjective or adverb, especially *in contrast* with another.

2. In NT Greek there are *regular and irregular* forms of comparison, as there are in English, e.g. great, greater, greatest; good, better, best.

B. REGULAR FORMS of comparison of adjectives:

1. *Description:* Following *regular rules* and used extensively in classical Greek, these two forms of comparison are less common in NT Greek.

2. *First form:*
a. The **comparative** and **superlative** add -τέρος and -τάτος respectively to the stem, especially of *strong vowel* and *sibilant* adjectives.
b. Both are **declined** like first and second declension adjectives, e.g.:
ἅγιος, α, ον (holy, p. 16); ἁγιώτερος, α, ον; ἁγιώτατος, η, ον
δίκαιος, α, ον (just, p. 33); δικαιότερος, α, ον; δικαιότατος, η, ον
ἀληθής, ές (true, p. 120); ἀληθέστερος, α, ον; ἀληθέστατος, η, ον

3. *Second form:*
a. The **comparative** and **superlative** add -ίων and -ιστος respectively to the stem, especially of *weak vowel* and *liquid* adjectives.
b. The comparative is **declined** like liquid adjectives (ἄφρων, ον, p. 104), the superlative like first and second declension adjectives, e.g.:
ταχύς, εῖα, ύ (swift, p. 123); ταχίων, ον; τάχιστος, η, ον.
σώφρων, ον (sane, temperate); σωφρίων, ον; σώφριστος, η, ον.

C. IRREGULAR FORMS of comparison of adjectives:

1. *Description:* Though less regular and traditional, these two forms are *more common in NT Greek* and therefore *more important* for our purpose.

2. *First form:*
a. The comparative and superlative **differ widely** from the positive, the same form sometimes being used for more than one adjective.

b. They are **declined** like the second form above: *-ίων, ον; -ιστος, η, ον.*

c. **Principal examples** are the following (*in contrasting pairs*):

POSITIVE:	COMPARATIVE:	SUPERLATIVE:
ἀγαθός: good, noble	*κρείσσων:* better	*κράτιστος:* best
κάκος: bad, wicked	*χείρων/ἥσσων:* worse	(*χείριστος:* worst)
μέγας: great, large	*μείζων:* greater	*μέγιστος:* greatest
μικρός: small, little	*ἐλάσσων:* smaller, less	*ἐλάχιστος:* smallest, least
πολύς: much, many	*πλείων/πλέων:* more	*πλεῖστος:* most
ὀλίγος: few, little	*ἐλάσσων:* fewer, less	*ἐλάχιστος:* fewest, least

3. *Second form:* Comparison is sometimes expressed *periphrastically*, by using the *comparative or superlative of adverbs* (cf. next page), e.g.: *μᾶλλον, μάλιστα* (more, rather; mostly, especially), *πλεῖον, πλεῖστον* (more, mostly), *περισσόν, περισσότερον* (exceedingly, more), etc.

D. FORMATION AND COMPARISON OF ADVERBS:

1. *Description:*

a. Adverbs in NT Greek are **formed and compared in various ways,** some of which we have already studied on page 35, summarized here:

1) Adverbs formed from first and second declension adjectives, nouns, and pronouns, e.g. *ἀξίως, σήμερον, οὕτως.*

2) Adverbs classified according to ending, e.g. *πῶς, πότε, ποῦ.*

3) Adverbs which defy classification, e.g. *ἄρα, ἄρτι, γέ, οὐκέτι,* to which can be added the adverbial particles on pages 26 and 27.

b. **Now** we need to examine the formation and comparison of adverbs, as they are derived from first, second, and especially third declension adjectives; some in a *regular*, others in an *irregular* fashion.

2. *Regular formation and comparison of adverbs:*

a. The **positive** uses the ending *ως*, derived from the genitive plural of the adjective *ων*, e.g.: *ἀληθῶς* (truly), *ἀξίως* (worthily), *εὐθέως* (immediately), *κακῶς* (badly), *καλῶς* (well), *ὁμοίως* (likewise), *περισσῶς* (exceedingly), *ταχέως* (swiftly, quickly).

b. The **comparative** adopts the neuter singular of the adjective comparative, e.g.: *ἔλασσον* (less), *πλεῖον* (more), *τάχιον* (more quickly).

c. The **superlative,** rarely used, employs the neuter plural of the superlative of the adjective, e.g. *τάχιστα:* as soon as possible.

3. *Irregular formation and comparison of adverbs:*
a. The **positive** may be formed in various ways, e.g.:
   1) Exactly like the adjective: εὐθύς (straightway, immediately).
   2) Like the neuter singular: πολύ (much, greatly), ταχύ (quickly).
   3) In other ways: μακράν/μακρόθεν (far off), μόνον (only), πολλάκις (often), πρῶτον (first), etc.
b. The **comparative and superlative** of these irregular adverbs, when used, are normally formed regularly, e.g. πρότερον (formerly, previously), τάχιον, τάχιστα (more, most quickly).

E. USAGE of comparison in NT Greek:

1. In the New Testament, the superlative is *rarely used* except in an "elative" sense (meaning "very" rather than "most"); instead, the comparative is often used for the superlative, e.g. μείζων δὲ τούτων ἡ ἀγάπη = but the <u>greatest</u> of these (is) love.
   (I Co. 13:13)

2. Even more often, the *positive* is used for either the comparative or the superlative, e.g. Διδάσκαλε, ποία ἐντολὴ <u>μεγάλη</u> ἐν τῷ νόμῳ; = Master, which is the <u>greatest</u> commandment in the law? (Mt. 22:36) αὕτη ἀπογραφὴ <u>πρώτη</u> . . . = this <u>first</u> (<u>former?</u>) census. . . . (Lk. 2:2)

3. As already seen to some extent, *comparison* may be expressed variously:
a. **By the genitive:** ὁ πατὴρ <u>μείζων μού</u> ἐστιν = the Father is <u>greater than</u> I. (Jn. 14:28)
b. **By the conjunction** ἤ (than, or) with a noun, an infinitive, or a clause: Ἰησοῦς <u>πλείονας</u> μαθητὰς ποιεῖ . . . <u>ἤ</u> Ἰωάννης . . . = Jesus is making . . . <u>more</u> disciples <u>than</u> John (is) . . . (Jn. 4:1)
c. **By the prepositions** παρά and ὑπέρ with the accusative: φρωνιμώτεροι <u>ὑπὲρ</u> τοὺς υἱοὺς τοῦ φωτός = wiser <u>than the children</u> of the light. (Lk. 16:8)

IV. Enumeration in NT Greek:

A. INTRODUCTION:

1. We must now study the *numerals* used in the Greek New Testament, and even some not used therein but important for completeness and other reasons.

2. Our study will comprise *cardinal, ordinal,* and *adverbial* enumeration, in decreasing order of importance in the New Testament and otherwise.

3. Numbers with English derivatives will be *underlined* for visibility.

B. THE CARDINAL NUMBERS, meaning *one, two, three* (1–4, 200, etc. declined)

1. εἷς (henotheism)	11. ἔνδεκα	200. διακόσιοι, αι, α
2. δύο (dyad, duet)	12. δώδεκα (Dodecanese)	500. πεντακόσιοι
3. τρεῖς (triad, trio)	20. εἴκοσι (ν)	600. ἑξακόσιοι
4. τέσσαρες (tessera)	30. τριάκοντα	1000. χίλιοι, αι, α
5. πέντες (Pentateuch)	40. τεσσαράκοντα	χιλιάς, άδος, ἡ (chiliad, chiliasm)
6. ἕξ (six, Hexateuch)	50. πεντήκοντα	5000. πεντακισχίλιοι
7. ἑπτα (Heptateuch)	60. ἑξήκοντα	10000. μύριοι, αι, α
8. ὀκτώ (octane, octopus)	70. ἑβδομήκοντα	δέκα χιλιάδες
9. ἐννέα (ennead)	80. ὀγδοήκοντα	12000. δώδεκα χιλιάδες
10. δέκα (decalogue)	90. ἐνενήκοντα	100000. ἑκατον χιλιάδες
	100. ἑκατόν (hecatomb)	1000000. μυριάδες μυριάδων (myriad)

C. THE ORDINAL NUMBERS, meaning *first, second, third* (all declined)

1. πρῶτος (proton)	6. ἕκτος	11. ἐνδέκατος
2. δεύτερος (-onomy)	7. ἕβδομος	12. δωδέκατος
3. τρίτος (trigon)	8. ὄγδοος	15. πεντεκαιδέκατος
4. τέταρτος	9. ἔνατος	20. εἰκοστός
5. πέμπτος	10. δέκατος	50. πεντεκοστός (Pentecost)

D. THE ADVERBIAL NUMBERS, meaning *once, twice, thrice* (undeclined)

1. ἅπαξ (hapax legomena)	4. τετράκις	20. εἰκοσάκις
2. δίς (disyllabic)	5. πεντάκις	50. πεντεκοντάκις
3. τρίς (trisyllabic)	7. ἑπτάκις	70. ἑβδομηκοντάκις

E. DECLENSION of δύο: two (dual, hendiadys), τρεῖς: three (trilogy, triceps). (Please review the declensions of εἷς and τέσσαρες on page 105.)

	Masc.-Fem.-Neut.	Masc.-Fem.	Neut.
Nom.	δύο	τρεῖς	τρία
Gen.	δύο	τριῶν	τριῶν
Dat.	δυσί	τρισί	τρισί
Acc.	δύο	τρεῖς	τρία

F. COUNTING AND GEMATRIA:

1. The Greeks did not have Arabic numerals (1, 2, 3) and seldom borrowed Roman numerals (I, II, III) but, like the Hebrews and Phoenicians, used the *letters of the alphabet* (including three extinct ones) for counting.

2. In Greek, then, as in Hebrew, *Gematria* is possible, whereby numbers and letters are interchanged, e.g. as in *the name 666* in Rev. 13 : 18. Further information on Gematria will be found under "Teaching Aids" at the back.

V. **Exercises:**

A. *Be able to decline* the very common adjectives: μέγας and πολύς.

B. *Be able to match* the following irregular comparisons of adjectives:

POSITIVE:	COMPARATIVE OR SUPERLATIVE:	(ADJECTIVE)	(DEGREE)
1. ἀγαθός	ἐλάσσων		
2. κακός	κράτιστος		
3. μέγας	πλείων		
4. μικρός	μέγιστος		
5. ὀλίγος	ἥσσων		
6. πολύς	ἐλάχιστος		

C. *Be able to count to ten* in cardinal numbers, *to three* in ordinal numbers.

D. *Be able to decline* the Greek numerals for *two* and *three*.

E. *Read aloud, translate,* and *explain the underlined expressions* below:

1. Καὶ σύ, Βηθλέεμ γῆ Ἰούδα, οὐδαμῶς ἐλαχίστη εἶ ἐν τοῖς
by no means

ἡγεμόσιν Ἰούδα· ἐκ σοῦ γὰρ ἐξελεύσεται ἡγούμενος, ὅστις
leaders   *a leader*

ποιμανεῖ τὸν λαόν μου τὸν Ἰσραήλ.
will shepherd

2. Οὐδεὶς δύναται δυσὶ κυρίοις δουλεύειν· ἢ γὰρ τὸν ἕνα μισήσει

καὶ τὸν ἕτερον ἀγαπήσει, ἢ ἑνὸς ἀνθέξεται καὶ τοῦ ἑτέρου
uphold

καταφρονήσει· οὐ δύνασθε θεῷ δουλεύειν καὶ μαμωνᾷ.
despise   *money*

3. Τί ὑμῖν δοκεῖ; ἐὰν γένηταί τινι ἀνθρώπῳ ἑκατὸν πρόβατα καὶ
be, belong   *sheep*

πλανηθῇ ἓν ἐξ αὐτῶν, οὐχὶ ἀφήσει τὰ ἐνενήκοντα ἐννέα ἐπὶ τὰ

ὄρη καὶ πορευθεὶς ζητεῖ τὸ πλανώμενον;

4. Τότε προσελθὼν ὁ Πέτρος εἶπεν αὐτῷ, Κύριε, ποσάκις

how many times

ἁμαρτήσει εἰς ἐμὲ ὁ ἀδελφός μου καὶ ἀφήσω αὐτῷ; ἕως

will sin

ἑπτάκις ; λέγει αὐτῷ ὁ Ἰησοῦς, Οὐ λέγω σοι ἕως ἑπτάκις ἀλλὰ

ἕως ἑβδομηκοντάκις ἑπτά.

5. Οἴδατε ὅτι οἱ δοκοῦντες ἄρχειν τῶν ἐθνῶν κατακυριεύουσιν

lord it over

αὐτῶν καὶ οἱ μεγάλοι αὐτῶν κατεξουσιάζουσιν αὐτῶν. οὐχ οὕτως

exercise authority

δέ ἐστιν ἐν ὑμῖν· ἀλλ᾽ ὃς ἂν θέλῃ μέγας γενέσθαι ἐν ὑμῖν, ἔσται

ὑμῶν διάκονος, καὶ ὃς ἂν θέλῃ ἐν ὑμῖν εἶναι πρῶτος, ἔσται

πάντων δοῦλος.

6. παρέδωκα γὰρ ὑμῖν ἐν πρώτοις, ὃ καὶ παρέλαβον, ὅτι

Χριστὸς ἀπέθανεν ὑπὲρ τῶν ἁμαρτιῶν ἡμῶν . . . καὶ ὅτι

ἐγήγερται τῇ ἡμέρᾳ τῇ τρίτῃ . . . καὶ ὅτι ὤφθη Κηφᾷ, εἶτα τοῖς

Cephas

δώδεκα· ἔπειτα ὤφθη ἐπάνω πεντακοσίοις ἀδελφοῖς ἐφάπαξ ἐξ

then   more than   at one time

ὧν οἱ πλείονες μένουσιν ἕως ἄρτι.

20 Final Review and Development

I. Introduction:

A. Like Paul in II Tim. 4:7, we have now "finished our course" and "merited the crown" of victory and achievement.

B. It remains for us, however, to review the preceding four chapters, in order to insure our understanding and learning of the material therein.

C. Final development or "finishing touches" will include the following:

   1. Some additional *vocabulary* which will be helpful for the future.

   2. A summary of *Semitic influences* on the Greek of the New Testament.

II. Review of the preceding four chapters:

A. CHAPTER 16: Third Declension Concluded—Sibilant, Vowel, and Diphthong Nouns, Adjectives, and Verbs.

   1. *Review* the declension and vocabulary of *sibilant nouns and adjectives.*

   2. *Review* the declension and vocabulary of *weak vowel nouns and adjectives.*

   3. *Review* the declension and vocabulary of *diphthong nouns.*

   4. *Review* the conjugation of the *sibilant verb:* εἰμί (ἐσ): I am.

   5. Test knowledge of the *additional vocabulary* of weak vowel and diphthong verbs.

B. CHAPTER 17: Strong Vowel Verbs, Part I—Contract Verbs.

   1. *Review* and clinch knowledge of the *guiding principles of contraction.*

   2. *Test* knowledge of the *principal parts* of ἀγαπάω, λαλέω, πληρόω.

3. *Review* the conjugation in the present system of the same verbs.

4. *Test* knowledge of the vocabulary of contract verbs in α, ε, ο.

C.   CHAPTER 18: Strong Vowel Verbs, Part II—Athematic Verbs.

1. *Review* the *guiding principles* of the conjugation of athematic verbs.

2. *Test* knowledge of the meaning and *principal parts* of δίδωμι, ἵστημι, τίθημι, as well as their *principal compounds*.

3. *Review* the conjugation in the *present* and *aorist* of these same verbs.

4. *Review* the meaning and *principal parts* of *deponent* athematic verbs.

5. *Review* the conjugation in the *aorist active* of -βαίνω and γινώσκω.

6. Clinch knowledge of the five kinds of aorists in New Testament Greek.

7. Clinch knowledge of *irregular athematic verbs* by:
a. Reviewing the **meaning, stem,** and **principal parts** of εἰμί, εἶμι, -ἵημι, οἶδα, φημί, and their compounds.
b. Reviewing their **conjugation** in the tenses given on pages 143–144.
c. Testing ability to **identify** and **distinguish** their forms by reviewing the exercise provided for this purpose on page 144.

D.   CHAPTER 19: Final Matters of Moment—Nouns, Adjectives, Adverbs, and Numerals in NT Greek.

1. *Review* the explanation and examples of *irregular (Semitic) nouns*.

2. *Review* the declension and vocabulary of *irregular adjectives*, namely: variant stem, defective, and contract adjectives.

3. *Review* the regular and especially *irregular comparison* of adjectives.

4. *Review* the regular and irregular *formation* and *comparison* of *adverbs*.

5. *Review* the *syntax or usage of comparison* in New Testament Greek.

6. *Test* knowledge of the *meaning* and, where given, *declension* especially of the *cardinal numbers* in New Testament Greek.

III. Development:

A. EXPLANATION:

1. On the remainder of this page, we will look at *additional vocabulary* which, though not essential, will be useful in reading the New Testament.

2. On the following pages, we will carefully examine—especially for use in reading the New Testament—the principal *Semitic influences* thereon.

B. ADDITIONAL VOCABULARY:

1. *Additional contract verbs* in α:

διψάω: be thirsty (dipsomaniac)

ἐάω: permit, allow, let go

κλάω: break (e.g. bread) (iconoclast)

κοιμάομαι: sleep (cemetery)

κοπιάω: work hard, grow weary

μεριμνάω: be anxious, worry

πεινάω: be hungry, hunger

τελευτάω: die, end (teleology)

τολμάω: dare, take upon oneself

χράομαι: use, need (catachresis, chrestomathy)

2. *Additional contract verbs* in ε:

ἀγνοέω: not know (agnostic)

ἀδικέω: am wrong, unjust (δική)

ἀναιρέω:* take up, away (heresy)

ἀσθενέω: am weak (neurasthenia)

γαμέω: marry (monogamy, etc.)

γρηγορέω: watch, guard (Gregory)

δέομαι: need, beseech (deontology)

διακονέω: serve, minister (deacon)

ἐλεέω: have mercy, give alms

ἐνεργέω: work, effect (energy)

ἐπικαλέω: call on, invoke (call)

εὐδοκέω: think well of (Eudoxia)

ἡγέομαι: lead, rule; think (hegemony)

καταργέω: abolish, cancel

κατηγορέω: accuse, prove (category)

κληρονομέω: inherit (by lot) (cleric)

νοέω: understand, think (noosphere)

οἰκοδομέω: build up, edify (οἶκος)

*This verb is somewhat irregular, being both contract and liquid, thus: ἀναιρέω (αἴρε, ἐλ), ἀνελῶ, ἀνεῖλα/ον, ἀνηρέθην.

ὁμολογέω: agree, profess, confess

προσκαλέομαι: call to myself, summon

πωλέω: sell (bibliopole, monopoly)

ὑστερέω: lack, am inferior to

φρονέω: think (phrenology, frenzy)

ὠφελέω: gain, profit, achieve, help

3. *Additional liquid verbs:*

αὐξάνω: cause to grow (L. *augere*, E. augment)

διαμαρτύρομαι: testify (martyr)

ἐντέλλομαι: order, command (ἐντολή)

κερδαίνω: gain, earn, make a profit

ξηραίνω: dry up (xerography, Xerox)

περιτέμνω: cut around, circumcise

IV. Semitic expressions in New Testament Greek:

A. INTRODUCTION:

1. Many of the variations of NT from classical Greek, once attributed to Semitic influence, have been found to be characteristic of Koine Greek.

2. However, there still remain instances of genuine Semitic influence, resulting from the Semitic background of New Testament speakers and writers.

3. It will be helpful, then, to summarize these instances, particularly to capture the Semitic flavor and sometimes the meaning of certain passages.

4. In a work such as this, we cannot examine this matter thoroughly but only summarize it, leaving fuller treatment for more advanced New Testament study.

B. TRANSLITERATED SEMITIC EXPRESSIONS:

1. *Explanation:* The New Testament contains a number of expressions which are transliterated from the original Hebrew or Aramaic languages.

2. *Semitic nouns:*

a. Many common and proper Semitic nouns are already listed on pages 146 and 147.

b. To these could be added more **personal names,** e.g. Βοανηργές (Sons of Thunder—James and John, Mk. 3:17) and **place names,** e.g. that of Γολγοθά (Calvary, Place of the Skull, Jn. 19:17).

3. *Semitic adverbs and interjections,* e.g. ἀμήν (amen, truly,

indeed), **οὐαί** (alas! woe! horrors!, Mt. 23), **ἀλληλουϊά** = Praise the Lord!, Praise Yah(weh)! (Rev. 19:1, 3)

4. *Semitic sentences,** e.g.:

Ηλι ηλι λεμα σαβαχθανι = My God, my God, why have you forsaken me? (Ps. 22:1, Mt. 27:46, Mk. 15:34, the latter worded: Ελωι ελωι . . .)

Μαρανα θα/Μαραν αθα = Our Lord, come!/Our Lord has come! (I Co. 16:22) reflected also in Rev. 22:20: ἔρχου, κύριε Ἰησοῦ = come, Lord Jesus!

Ταλιθα κουμ = Little girl, arise! (Mk. 5:41), with a possible parallel in Acts 9:40: Ταβιθά, ἀνάστηθι = Tabitha, arise!

C. SYNTACTICAL SEMITIC EXPRESSIONS:

1. *Explanation:* Even more frequent than transliterated Semitic expressions are those of *grammatical usage* derived from Hebrew or Aramaic influence. (Part of this section is adapted from Zerwick-Smith: *Biblical Greek*, Rome, Italy: Biblical Institute Press, 1977.)

2. *Nouns (and pronouns):* Semitic influence in the use of cases—

a. **The nominative:**

   1) "Hanging nominative": ὁ νικῶν . . . δώσω αὐτῷ ἐξουσίαν . . . He who is victorious . . . I will give him authority . . . (Rev. 2:26).

   2) Predicate nominative (or accusative) replaced by εἰς with a **noun**, e.g.: ἔσονται οἱ δύο εἰς σάρκα μίαν = they will be two into (in) one flesh (Mt. 19:5).

b. **The genitive:**

   1) "Hebrew genitive" instead of an adjective: ὁ ἄνθρωπος τῆς ἀνομίας = the man of sin (the sinful man). II Thess. 2:3

   2) "Son of" with the genitive to express *relationship* of some kind: ὁ υἱὸς τῆς ἀπωλείας = the son of destruction (the one bound for destruction). II Thess. 2:3

c. **The dative with** ἐν, influenced by Hebrew "b'" (*in, at, with,* etc.):

   1) Associative use: ἄνθρωπος ἐν πνεύματι ἀκαθάρτῳ = a man in (with) an unclean spirit. (Mk. 5:2; cf. also 5:25)

   2) Causal use ("because of"): δοκοῦσιν γὰρ ὅτι ἐν τῇ πολυλογίᾳ αὐτῶν εἰσακουσθήσονται = for they think that they will be heard in (because of) their many words (long prayers).
   Mt. 6:7

*Transliterated loan words often have no accents or breathing marks.

3. *Pronouns:* Semitic influence is seen in—
a. **Frequent use** of pronouns when not necessary for clarity or emphasis.
b. **Proleptic or anticipatory use:** Αὐτὸς γὰρ ὁ Ἡρῴδης . . . ἐκράτησεν τὸν Ἰωάννην = For he, Herod . . . (had) arrested John. (Mk. 6:17)
c. The use of ψυχή (soul) instead of the personal or reflexive pronouns: Περίλυπός ἐστιν ἡ ψυχή μου ἕως θανάτου = My soul is (I am) sorrowful (even) to death. (Mk. 14:34)

4. *Adjectives and adverbs:* Semitic influence helps explain the use of the positive instead of the comparative or superlative. Cf. page 151.

5. *Verbs:* Semitic influence is seen especially in the use of—
a. **Graphic and periphrastic participles,** as indicated on pages 88–89.
b. **The verb** ἐγένετο (It happened that . . .), especially in Luke, e.g. Ἐγένετο δὲ ἐν ταῖς ἡμέραις ἐκείναις ἐξῆλθεν δόγμα . . . It happened in those days (that) there went forth a decree . . . (Lk. 2:1)
c. **Infinitives with the prepositions** ἐν τῷ (while) and especially πρὸς τό (to, but, like the Hebrew *l'*, without necessarily expressing purpose), e.g. ὁ βλέπων γυναῖκα πρὸς τὸ ἐπιθυμῆσαι αὐτήν . . . he who looks at a woman to lust (lusting) after her . . . (Mt. 5:28)

6. *Clauses:* Semitic influence is most noticeable in the use of—
a. **Coordination instead of subordination,** especially through the varied uses of καί to mean: and, but, and yet, so that, when, who, that is, though, etc., e.g. ἐν τῷ κόσμῳ ἦν, καὶ ὁ κόσμος δι᾽ αὐτοῦ ἐγένετο, καὶ ὁ κόσμος αὐτὸν οὐκ ἔγνω = he was in the world, and (though) the world was made by him, and the world (or omit the "and") did not know him. (Jn. 1:10)
b. εἰ (if) **in oaths and direct questions:**
   1) In oaths, e.g. ἀμὴν λέγω ὑμῖν, εἰ δοθήσεται τῇ γενεᾷ ταύτῃ σημεῖον = Amen I say to you: (May God do so and so to me) if a sign will be given to this generation! (No sign . . . !)
   Mk. 8:12
   2) In direct questions, e.g.: Κύριε, εἰ πατάξομεν ἐν μαχαίρῃ; Lord, if (what if, shall) we strike with the sword? (Lk. 22:49)
c. **Various conjunctions** (ὅτι, ἵνα, ὅτε, ὥστε) to reflect or render the Aramaic particle "di," which has at least seven meanings, e.g. οὐ γάρ ἐστιν κρυπτὸν ἐὰν μὴ ἵνα φανερωθῇ = for there is nothing hidden except in order that it may (which will not) be revealed. (Mk. 4:22)

7. *Negation:* Semitic influence appears in the use of—

a. **Absolute negation for comparison:** Ὁ πιστεύων εἰς ἐμὲ οὐ πιστεύει εἰς ἐμὲ ἀλλὰ εἰς τὸν πέμψαντά με = He who believes in me does <u>not</u> (not so much) believe in me <u>but</u> (as) in him who sent me. (Jn. 12:44)

b. οὐ . . . πᾶς (Hebrew ". . . kol") for οὐδείς, e.g. οὐκ ἂν ἐσώθη πᾶσα σάρξ = <u>all</u> flesh would <u>not</u> (no flesh would) have been saved. (Mt. 24:22)

V. *Read aloud, translate,* and *explain the underlined words* in the following:

1. ἐ<u>γένετο</u> δὲ ἐν ταῖς ἡμέραις ἐκείναις ἐ<u>ξῆλθεν</u> δόγμα παρὰ
     dogma

Καίσαρος Αὐγούστου ἀπογρά<u>φεσθαι</u> πᾶσαν τὴν οἰκουμένην.
  Caesar Augustus be enrolled inhabited world

αὕτη ἀπογραφὴ <u>πρώτη</u> ἐ<u>γένετο</u> ἡ<u>γεμονεύοντος</u> τῆς Συρίας
   census of Syria

Κυρηνίου. καὶ ἐ<u>πορεύοντο</u> πάντες ἀπογρά<u>φεσθαι</u>, ἕκαστος εἰς
Quirinius be enrolled

τὴν ἑαυτοῦ <u>πόλιν</u>. Ἀ<u>νέβη</u> δὲ καὶ Ἰωσὴφ ἀπὸ τῆς Γαλιλαίας

ἐκ <u>πόλεως</u> Ναζαρὲθ εἰς τὴν Ἰουδαίαν εἰς <u>πόλιν</u> Δαυὶδ <u>ἥτις</u>
           Judea

καλεῖται Βηθλέεμ, διὰ τὸ εἶναι αὐτὸν ἐξ οἴκου καὶ πατριᾶς
                                                   family

Δαυίδ, ἀπογρά<u>ψασθαι</u> σὺν <u>Μαριὰμ</u> τῇ ἐμνηστευμένῃ αὐτῷ,
        be enrolled   engaged

οὔσῃ ἐγκύῳ. ἐ<u>γένετο</u> δὲ ἐν τῷ <u>εἶναι</u> αὐτοὺς ἐκεῖ ἐπλήσθησαν
   pregnant

αἱ ἡμέραι τοῦ τεκεῖν αὐτήν, καὶ ἔτεκεν τὸν υἱὸν αὐτῆς τὸν
           to give birth she bore

πρωτότοκον· καὶ ἐσπαργάνωσεν αὐτὸν καὶ ἀνέκλινεν αὐτὸν
 first born wrapped laid

ἐν φάτνῃ, δι<u>ότι</u> οὐκ ἦν αὐτοῖς τόπος ἐν τῷ καταλύματι.
 manger inn (caravansary)

2. Εἰ<u>σῆλθεν</u> οὖν πάλιν εἰς τὸ πραιτώριον ὁ Πιλᾶτος καὶ ἐ<u>φώνησεν</u>
                                  praetorium Pilate

τὸν Ἰησοῦν καὶ εἶ<u>πεν</u> αὐτῷ, Σὺ <u>εἶ</u> ὁ <u>βασιλεὺς</u> τῶν Ἰουδαίων; . . .
                                            of the Jews

ἀ<u>πεκρίθη</u> Ἰησοῦς, Ἡ βασιλεία ἡ ἐμὴ οὐκ <u>ἔστιν</u> ἐκ τοῦ κόσμου

τούτου . . . εἶ<u>πεν</u> οὖν αὐτῷ ὁ Πιλᾶτος, Οὐκοῦν <u>βασιλεὺς</u> <u>εἶ</u> σύ;
                                            So, then,

ἀ<u>πεκρίθη</u> ὁ Ἰησοῦς, Σὺ λέγεις ὅτι <u>βασιλεύς</u> <u>εἰμι</u>. ἐγὼ εἰς τοῦτο

γε<u>γέννημαι</u> καὶ εἰς τοῦτο ἐ<u>λήλυθα</u> εἰς τὸν κόσμον, ἵνα

μαρτυ<u>ρήσω</u> τῇ ἀληθείᾳ . . .

3. τοῦτο <u>φρονεῖτε</u> ἐν ὑμῖν ὃ καὶ ἐν Χριστῷ Ἰησοῦ, ὃς ἐν μορφῇ θεοῦ
                                                                                                  form (nature)

   <u>ὑπάρχων</u> οὐχ ἁρπαγμὸν <u>ἡγήσατο</u> τὸ εἶναι ἴσα θεῷ, ἀλλὰ ἑαυτὸν
          privilege   thought   equal

   ἐκένωσεν μορφὴν δούλου <u>λαβών</u>, ἐν ὁμοιώματι ἀνθρώπων
   emptied   form   likeness

   <u>γενόμενος</u>· καὶ σχήματι <u>εὑρεθεὶς</u> ὡς ἄνθρωπος <u>ἐταπείνωσεν</u>
                         in appearance

   ἑαυτὸν <u>γενόμενος</u> ὑπήκοος μέχρι θανάτου, θανάτου δὲ σταυροῦ.
                   obedient   cross

   διὸ καὶ ὁ θεὸς αὐτὸν ὑπερύψωσεν καὶ <u>ἐχαρίσατο</u> αὐτῷ τὸ ὄνομα
                              exalted

   τὸ <u>ὑπὲρ πᾶν ὄνομα</u>, ἵνα ἐν τῷ ὀνόματι Ἰησοῦ πᾶν γόνυ κάμψῃ
                                                              might bend

   ἐπουρανίων καὶ ἐπιγείων καὶ καταχθονίων, καὶ πᾶσα γλῶσσα
   those in heaven   on earth   under earth

   <u>ἐξομολογήσηται</u> ὅτι κύριος Ἰησοῦς Χριστὸς εἰς δόξαν θεοῦ
   might confess

   <u>πατρός</u>.

4. Εἰρήνη τοῖς ἀδελφοῖς καὶ ἀγάπη μετὰ <u>πίστεως</u> ἀπὸ θεοῦ

   <u>πατρὸς</u> καὶ κυρίου Ἰησοῦ Χριστοῦ. ἡ χάρις μετὰ πάντων τῶν

   <u>ἀγαπώντων</u> τὸν κύριον ἡμῶν <u>Ἰησοῦν</u> Χριστὸν ἐν ἀφθαρσίᾳ.
                                                                immortality

English Index of Subjects

K

Perfect System:
Scope or Content:
Perfect Active:
Indicative: 40–44, ff.
Infinitive: 66, ff.
Participle: 87, ff.
Pluperfect Act. Indicative: 40–44, ff.
Forms or Kinds of Perfect Systems:
1st Perfect: with System Sign, 40–44.
2nd Perfect: sans System Sign, 93, 140.
Perfect Middle System:
Scope or Content: 40–44, 66, 87, 93,
107, ff.
Perfect Middle and Passive.
Indicative, Infinitive, Participle.
Special: Mute and Liquid Verbs, 94, 107.
Perfect Tense: cf. Perf. Systems above.
Formation: 40–44, ff. as above.
Meaning and use: 40, 66, 87, ff.
Past Action continuing in Present: 39.
Act or State Complete, Perfect: 66, 87.
Periphrastic (Roundabout):
Forms: Mute/Liquid Perf. Mid. System,
94.
Usage: Participle and "to be" (Semitic):
90, 160.
Person:
In general: 42–43, ff.
First, Second, and Third Persons.
All Conjugations, Sing. and Plural.
Exceptions:
Imperative: Second and Third only,
63–64.
Infinitive and Participle: None, 68, 85.
Impersonal Verbs: 3rd Person only, 67.
Personal Pronoun:
1st and 2nd Persons: Proper Forms,
20–21.
3rd Person Nom.: Demonstrative Pro-
noun, 20.
Oblique Cases: Intensive Pronoun, 19.
Place, indicated by:
Cases, esp. with Prepositions, 13–14,
25–26.
Genitive: Place from which.
Dative: Place at which.
Accusative: Place to, toward which.
Adverbs, with special Endings: 35.
"-θεν": Place from which.

"-ου": Place at which, where.
"-ο": Place to or toward which.
Pluperfect Tense: (cf. Perfect System)
Form: Built on Perfect Active, 40–44;
93, 140.
Usage: only active in the New
Testament, 40.
Meaning: Action before a Past Time, 39.
Plural: cf. Number above.
Possession, expressed by:
Genitive or Dative of Possession:
13–14.
Pronominal Adj. of Possession: 21.
Postpositives: 26.
Adv. Particles or Conjunctions.
Never first in a Sentence or Clause.
Prayers, New Testament ("Urgent
Requests"): 65.
Generally couched in the Aorist Tense.
Positive: 2nd or 3rd Person Imperative.
Negative: 2nd Person Subjunctive.
Predicate Nom. after Intran. Verb: 12.
Predicative use of:
Adjectives: 17.
Participles: 89.
Prepositions:
Proper, with various cases: 25.
Improper, normally with Genitives:
25–26.
Present System, comprising (39, 43, ff.):
The Present Tense in all Moods and
Voices.
The Imperfect Indicative in all Voices.
Present Tense, meaning of in the
Moods:
Indicative: Single/Continued Present
Action.
Subj., Imp., Inf.: Continued Action.
Participle: Contemporaneous Action.
Price or Value, Genitive of: 13.
Primary: (cf. Endings)
Tenses: Present, Future, Perfect, 39.
Mood: Subjunctive (Primary Endings):
57–58.
Primitive:
Endings: 42, 138–139, 143, Appendix.
Verbs (Athematic, Mi-Verbs): 138–143.
Principal:
Mood: the Indicative, 38, 47, ff.

T

U

Greek Vocabulary and Index

A

ἀνοίγω (-οἰγ): open, restore, heal 96
ἄνομος, ον: lawless, criminal 148
ἀντί: over against, instead of 25, 68
ἄνω: above; ἄνωθεν: fr. above, again 35
ἄξιος, α, ον: worthy, proper, fitting 16
ἀξίως: worthily, suitably 35, 150
ἀπαγγέλλω (-άγγελ): tell, proclaim
   107, 116
ἀπάγω (-άγ): lead away/astray, arrest
   115
ἅπαξ: once, once for all 152
ἅπας, ασα, αν: all, whole, every 80
ἀπέρχομαι (-ἐρχ, ἐλθ): depart 115
ἀπέχω (-ἐχ, ἐχ, σχε): be distant 115
ἄπιστος, ον: unbelieving 148
ἁπλοῦς, οῦσα, οῦν: single 148
ἀπό: from, away from, by, of 25
ἀποδίδωμι (-δο): repay, reward 138
ἀποθνῄσκω (-θαν): die 114
ἀποκάλυψις, εως, ἡ: revelation 122
ἀποκρίνομαι (-κριν): answer 108, 116
ἀποκτείνω (-κτεν): kill 108
ἀπόλλυμι/λλύω (-ὀλ): destroy 141
ἀπολογέομαι (-λογε): defend self 115
ἀπολύω (-λυ): free, dismiss 45
ἀποστέλλω (-στελ): send out 106–108
ἀπόστολος, ου, ὁ: apostle 10
ἄρα: therefore, then, and so 35, 150
ἀργυροῦς, οῦσα, οῦν: silver (adj.) 148
ἀριθμός, οῦ, ὁ: number 32
ἁρπάζω (ἁρπαγ): grasp, rob 97
ἄρτι: now, just now 35, 150
ἄρτος, ου, ὁ: (loaf of) bread 32
ἀρχή, ῆς, ἡ: beginning, rule 11
ἀρχιερεύς, έως, ὁ: high priest 124
ἄρχω (ἀρχ): rule, (Mid.) begin 67, 96
ἄρχων, οντος, ὁ: ruler, leader 79
ἀσθενέω (-σθενε): be weak, ill 157
ἀσθενής, ές: weak, ill, helpless 121
ἀσπάζομαι (ἀσπαδ): greet 97
ἀστήρ, έρος, ὁ: star 103
αὐξάνω/αὔξω (αὐξ/ε): make grow 158
αὐτός, ή, ό: self, same 18
αὐτοῦ: here, there 35
ἄφεσις, εως, ἡ: forgiveness 122
ἀφίημι (-ἐ): forgive, allow 143
ἄφρων, ον: foolish, senseless 104
ἄχρι: up to, until 26

B

βαθύς, εῖα, ύ: deep, profound 123
-βαίνω (βα): go, advance 108, 142
βάλλω (βαλ): throw, cast, put 106–108
βαπτίζω (βαπτιδ): wash, baptize 97
βάπτισμα, ατος, τό: baptism 78, 97
βαρύς, εῖα, ύ: heavy, hard, serious 123
βασιλεία, ας, ἡ: kingdom, reign 11
βασιλεύς, έως, ὁ: king, ruler 124
βασιλεύω (βασιλευ): rule, reign 126
βαστάζω (βασταδ): carry, endure 97
Βηθάνια, ας, ἡ: Bethany 146
βῆμα, ατος, τό: tribunal, court 82
βιβλίον, ου, τό: book, scroll 32
βίβλος, ου, ἡ: book, record 10
βλασφημέω (βλασφημε): blaspheme
   134
βλέπω (βλεπ): see, look, consider 96
βοανηργές: Sons of Thunder 158
βούλομαι (βουλ/ε): want, wish, will 67,
   108
βοῦς, βοός, ὁ: ox 124
βρῶμα, ατος, τό: food 82

Γ

Γαββαθα: Gabbatha, Lithostratos 147
γαμέω (γαμε): marry, give in marriage
   157
γάρ: for, because 26
γαστήρ, τρός, ἡ: womb, stomach 103
γέ: indeed, even, truly 35, 150
γεέννα, ης, ἡ: gehenna, hell 147
Γεθσημανί: Gethsemane 147
γενεά, ᾶς, ἡ: generation, period 33
γεννάω (γεννα): beget, bear 134
Γεννησαρέτ: Gennesaret(h) 147
γένος, ους, τό: family, race, kind 120
γεύομαι (γευ): taste, experience 126
γῆ, γῆς, ἡ: earth, country, mankind 11
γίνομαι (γεν): become, be, happen 29,
   108, 160
γινώσκω (γνο): know 114, 142
γλυκύς, εῖα, ύ: sweet 123
γλῶσσα, ης, ἡ: tongue, language 11
γνωρίζω (γνωριδ): make known 97
γνῶσις, εως, ἡ: knowledge 97, 122
Γολγοθά: Golgotha, Calvary 158

γονεύς, έως, ὁ: parent 124
γόνυ, ατος, τό: knee 82
γράμμα, ατος, τό: letter 78
γραμματεύς, έως, ὁ: scribe 124
γραφή, ῆς, ἡ: writing, scripture 11
γράφω (γραφ): write, record 96
γρηγορέω (γρηγορε): watch 157
γυνή, αικός, ἡ: woman, wife 77

Δ

δαιμόνιον, ου, τό: demon, devil 10
Δαυιδ, ὁ: David 147
δέ: but, however, and 26
δεῖ (δε): it is necessary 67, 114
δείκνυμι/νύω (δεικ): show 126, 141
δέκα: ten 152
δέκα χιλιάδες, ων, αἱ: 10,000 152
δένδρον, ου, τό: tree 32
δέξιος, α, ον: right (arm, etc.) 33
δέομαι (δε): beg, pray, please! 157
δεύτερος, α, ον: 2nd, later 34, 151
δέχομαι (δεχ): receive, accept 96
δέω (δε): bind, compel 66, 134
διά: through, on account of 25
διακονέω (διακονε): serve 157
διακονία, ας, ἡ: service 33
διάκονος, ου, ὁ: servant, deacon 10
διακόσιοι, αι, α: two hundred 152
διαλέγομαι (-λεγ): discuss 115
διάλεκτος, ου, ἡ: language 10
διαλογίζομαι (-λογιδ): discuss 116
διαμαρτύρομαι (-μαρτυρ): testify 158
διατάσσω (-ταγ): arrange 116
διαφέρω (-φερ, κτλ.): differ 115
διδάσκαλος, ου, ὁ: teacher 32
διδάσκω (διδαχ): teach, instruct 96
διδαχή, ῆς, ἡ: teaching, instruction 33
δίδωμι (δο): give, grant, allow 137–140
διέρχομαι (-ἐρχ, ἐλθ): go through 115
δίκαιος, α, ον: just, holy, right 33, 149
δικαιοσύνη, ης, ἡ: justice, holiness 33
δικαιόω (δικαιο): justify, acquit 134
δικαίως: justly, uprightly 35
διό (διά+ὅ): for this reason, hence 27
διότι (διά+ὅτι): because, therefore 51
διπλοῦς, ῆ, οῦν: double 148
δίς: twice, more than once 152
διψάω (διψα): be thirsty 157

διώκω (διωκ): pursue, persecute 93, 95
δοκεῖ (δοκε): it seems good 66, 134
δοκέω (δοκε): think, suppose 66, 134
δοκιμάζω (δοκιμαδ): test, prove 97
δόξα, ης, ἡ: glory, honor, pride 11, 97
δοξάζω (δοξαδ): glorify, praise 97
δουλεύω (δουλευ): serve as a slave 126
δοῦλος, ου, ὁ: slave, servant 10
δράκων, οντος, ὁ: dragon, devil 82
δύναμαι (δυνα): be able, can 67, 141
δύναμις, εως, ἡ: power, miracle 122
δυνατός, ή, όν: powerful, possible, able, influential 33
δύο: two 152
δώδεκα: twelve, the twelve 152
δωδέκατος, η, ον: twelfth 152
δώδεκα χιλιάδες, ων, αἱ: 12,000 152
δωρεάν: freely, gratuitously 35
δῶρον, ου, τό: gift, offering 10

E

ἐάν: if, even if, though, when 54, 60
ἑαυτοῦ, ῆς, οῦ: of himself, etc. 22
ἐάω (ἐα): allow, permit, let go 157
ἑβδομήκοντα: seventy 152
ἑβδομηκοντάκις: seventy times 152
ἕβδομος, η, ον: seventh 152
ἐγγίζω (ἐγγιδ): draw near 109
ἐγγύς: near, on the verge of 26
ἐγείρω (ἐγερ): raise, rouse 108
ἐγκαταλείπω (-λιπ): abandon 116
ἐγώ, ἐμοῦ/μου: I, me 21
ἔθνος, ους, τό: nation, people 120
ἔθος, ους, τό: custom, practice 120
εἰ: if, whether, that 51, 52, 60, 160
εἴδω (ἰδ): see, know (obs. cf. ὁράω) 114, 143
εἰκοσάκις: twenty times 152
εἴκοσι: twenty 152
εἰκοστός, ή, όν: twentieth 152
εἰκών, όνος, ἡ: image, form 102
εἰμί (ἐσ): be, exist 29, 125, 143–144
-εἶμι (ἰ): go (w. compounds) 143–144
εἰρήνη, ης, ἡ: peace, harmony 11
εἰς: into, in, to, etc. 25, 54, 68, 159
εἷς, μία, ἕν: one, single 105, 152
εἰσάγω (-ἀγ): lead, bring into 115
εἴσειμι (-ἰ): go in, enter 143

εἰσέρχομαι (-ἐρχ, ἐλθ): enter 115
εἰσπορεύομαι (-πορευ): enter 126
ἐκ, ἐξ: out of, from, of, etc. 25
ἕκαστος, η, ον: each, every 21
ἑκατόν: one hundred 52
ἑκατὸν χιλιάδες: 100,000 152
ἐκβάλλω (-βαλ): drive out 116
ἐκεῖ: there, in that place 27
ἐκεῖθεν: from there, thence 35
ἐκεῖνος, η, ον: that; he, she, it 19
ἐκκλησία, ας, ἡ: church, assembly 11
ἐκκόπτω (-κοπ): cut off, remove 116
ἐκλέγομαι (-λεγ): choose 115
ἐκλεκτός, ή, όν: chosen, elect 33
ἐκπορεύομαι (-πορευ): go out 126
ἐκτείνω (-κτεν): extend, arrest 116
ἕκτος, η, ον: sixth 152
ἔλασσον: less (than) 151
ἐλάσσων, ον: smaller, fewer, less 150
ἐλάχιστος, η, ον: smallest, fewest,
    least 150
ἐλεέω (ἐλεε): have pity, give alms 151
Ἐλισάβετ, ἡ: Elizabeth 147
Ἕλλην, ηνος, ὁ: Greek, Gentile 102
ἐλπίζω (ἐλπιδ): hope (for, in) 109
ἐλπίς, ίδος, ἡ: hope 79
ἐμαυτοῦ, ῆς: of myself, my own 21
ἐμβαίνω (-βα): get into, embark 116
ἐμβλέπω (-βλεπ): look straight at 116
ἐμός, ή, όν: my, mine 21
ἔμπροσθεν: in front of, before 26
ἐν: in, within, among 25, 52, 54, 68, 160
ἔνατος, η, ον: ninth 152
ἐνδέκατος, η, ον: eleventh 152
ἐνδύω (-δυ): clothe; mid. wear 126
ἕνεκα: because of, for the sake of 26
ἐνενήκοντα: ninety 152
ἐνεργέω: work, be at work, effect 157
ἐννέα: nine 152
ἔνοχος, ον: liable, guilty 148
ἐντέλλομαι (-τελ): command, order 158
ἐντεῦθεν: from here, hence 35
ἐντολή, ῆς, ἡ: command, instruction 33
ἐν ᾧ: while 52
ἐνώπιον: in sight/presence of, before 26
ἕξ: six 152
ἐξάγω (-αγ): lead out, bring out 115
ἐξακόσιοι, αι, α: six hundred 152

ἔξειμι (-ι): go away, depart, leave 143
ἐξέρχομαι (-ἐρχ, ἐλθ): come out 115
ἔξεστι (ἐσ): it is proper, possible 67
ἑξήκοντα: sixty 152
ἐξουσία, ας, ἡ: authority, power 33, 46
ἔξω: outside, out of; outer, foreign
    26, 35
ἐπαγγέλλομαι (-ἀγγελ): promise 116
ἐπεί: since, when, as, otherwise 51, 52
ἐπειδή: since, because, when, after 51
ἐπερωτάω (-ἐρωτα): ask for, demand
    134
ἐπί: on, by, at, to, against, etc. 25
ἐπιβάλλω (-βαλ): lay on, throw on 116
ἐπιγινώσκω (-γνο): understand 115
ἐπικαλέω (-καλε): call (upon) 157
ἐπιλαμβάνομαι (-λαβ): seize 116
ἐπιμένω (-μεν): remain, persist 116
ἐπιπίπτω (-πετ, πτο): fall upon 115
ἐπίσταμαι (ἐπιστα): understand 141
ἐπιστολή, ῆς, ἡ: letter, epistle 33
ἐπιστρέφω (-στρεφ): turn back 116
ἐπιτάσσω (-ταγ): command, order 116
ἐπιτίθημι (-θε): put on, add 138
ἐπιτιμάω (-τιμα): order, rebuke 134
ἑπτά: seven 152
ἑπτάκις: seven times 152
ἐργάζομαι (ἐργαδ): work, do 97
ἔργον, ου, τό: work, deed, task 9, 10, 97
ἔρημος, ου, ἡ: uninhabited place 10
ἔρημος, ον: deserted, uninhabited 148
ἔρις, ιδος, ἡ: strife, rivalry 82
ἔρχομαι (ἐρχ, ἐλθ): come, go 114
ἐρωτάω (ἐρωτα): ask about, for 134
ἐσθίω/ἔσθω (ἐσθι, φαγ): eat 114
ἔσχατος, η, ον: last, lowest 16
ἔσω: inside; ἔσωθεν: fr. within 35
ἕτερος, α, ον: other, another 21
ἔτι: still, yet, further 27
ἑτοιμάζω (ἑτοιμαδ): prepare 97
ἔτος, ους, τό: year 120
ἐφίστημι (-στα): stand by 141
εὐαγγελίζω (-ἀγγελιδ): preach 97, 116
εὐαγγέλιον, ου, τό: good news 10, 97
Εὖγε: Well done! Splendid! Good! 6
εὐδοκέω (-δοκε): be pleased 157
εὐθύς, εῖα, ύ: straight, right 123
εὐθύς/εὐθέως: immediately 27, 150

εὐλογέω (-λογε): bless, praise 115, 134
εὑρίσκω (εὑρ, εὑρε): find 114
εὐχαριστέω (-χαριστε): thank 134
Εὐχαριστῶ (-χαριστε): Thanks! 23
ἔχω (ἐχ, ἑχ, ἐσχ, σχε): have, hold 114
ἕως: until, as far as 26, 52, 61, 68
ἕως ὅτου: until, while 61
ἕως οὗ: until, while 61

Z

ζάω (ζα): live, be alive 134
ζηλόω (ζηλο): be zealous, jealous 134
ζητέω (ζητε): seek, search, ask, try,
    consider 134
ζωή, ῆς, ἡ: (supernatural) life 11
ζῷον, ου, τό: living creature, animal 32

H

ἤ: or, either, than 26, 151
ἡγεμών, όνος, ὁ: ruler, governor 102
ἡγέομαι (ἡγε): lead, rule, think 157
ἤδη: now, already 27
ἥλιος, ου, ὁ: sun, the sun 32
ἡμεῖς, ῶν: we 21
ἡμέρα, ας, ἡ: day 11
ἡμέτερος, α, ον: our, ours 21
Ἡρώδης, ου, ὁ: Herod 146
ἥσσων, ον: worse, less 150

Θ

θάλασσα, ης, ἡ: sea, lake 33
θάνατος, ου, ὁ: death 10
θανατόω (θανατο): put to death 134
θαυμάζω (θαυμαδ): wonder, admire 97
θεάομαι (θεα): see, behold, visit 134
θέλημα, ατος, τό: will, desire 78
θέλω (θελ): will, wish, desire 67, 108,
    116
θεός, οῦ, ὁ, ἡ: god, goddess 10
θεραπεύω (θεραπευ): heal, cure 45
θεωρέω (θεωρε): see, watch 134
θηρίον, ου, τό: wild beast, animal 32
θρίξ, τριχός, ἡ: hair 77
θρόνος, ου, ὁ: throne 32
θυγάτηρ, τρός, ἡ: daughter 103
θύρα, ας, ἡ: door, gate, entrance 33
θυσία, ας, ἡ: sacrifice, offering 33

θύω (θυ): slaughter, sacrifice 126
Θωμᾶς, ᾶ, ὁ: Thomas 146

I

Ἰάκωβος, ου, ὁ: James 146
ἰάομαι (ἰα): heal, restore 134
ἴδιος, α, ον: one's own, private 21
ἱερεύς, έως, ὁ: priest 123
ἱερόν, οῦ, τό: temple, t. area 10
-ἵημι (ἑ): send 143–144
Ἰερουσαλήμ/οσόλυμα, ἡ/τά: Jerusalem
    147
Ἰησοῦς, οῦ, ὁ: Jesus 2, 146
ἱμάτιον, ου, τό: coat, cloak 32
ἵνα: that, so that, in order that 59–60
ἵνα μή: so that not, lest 59–60
Ἰσραήλ, ὁ: Israel 147
ἵστημι (στα): set, stand 137–140, 142
ἰσχύω (ἰσχυ): be strong, able 126
ἰχθύς, ύος, ὁ: fish 122
Ἰωάννης, ου, ὁ: John 147
Ἰωσήφ, ὁ: Joseph 147

K

καθαρίζω (καθαριδ): cleanse 109
καθαρός, ά, όν: clean, pure 33
καθέζομαι (-ἐδ): sit, remain 141
κάθημαι (-ἠσ): sit, live, stay 141
καθίζω (-ιδ): set, sit, stay 97
καθώς: as, just as, insofar as 35, 150
καί: and, but, even, etc. 26, 160
καινός, ή, όν: new, recent 16
καιρός, οῦ, ὁ: time, occasion 32
καίω (καυ): burn, light 126
κακός, ή, όν: bad, evil, wrong 16, 150
κακῶς: badly, wrongly 35, 151
καλέω (καλε): call, name 134
Καλημέρα: Good Morning/Day! 6
Καλησπέρα: Good Afternoon! 6
καλός, ή, όν: good, beautiful 16, 67
καλῶς: well, rightly 6, 15, 35, 150
Καλῶς: Good! Splendid! 6
κάμηλος, ου, ὁ, ἡ: camel 10
καρδία, ας, ἡ: heart, mind, will 11
καρπός, οῦ, ὁ: fruit, grain, result 31
κατά: down, against, according to 25
καταβαίνω (-βα): go down, descend 116

καταγγέλλω (-ἀγγελ): proclaim 116
κατακαίω (-καυ): burn down, up 126
κατάκειμαι (-κει): lie sick, sit 141
καταλαμβάνω (-λαβ): overtake 116
καταλείπω (-λιπ): leave, abandon 116
καταλύω (-λυ): tear down, lodge 126
καταργέω (-ἀργε): nullify, cancel 157
κατέχω (-ἐχ, κτλ.): hold, keep 115
κατηγορέω (κατηγορε): accuse 157
κατοικέω (-οικε): live, inhabit 134
κάτω: down, below, beneath 35
καυχάομαι (καυχα): boast, rejoice 134
κεῖμαι (κει): lie, be dead, be 141
κελεύω (κελευ): command, order 67,
   126
κερδαίνω (κερδα/ν): gain, win 158
κεφαλή, ῆς, ἡ: head, lord, chief 12
κήρυγμα, ατος, τό: message 78
κηρύσσω (κηρυγ): herald, preach 97
κλαίω (κλαυ): weep, cry 126
κλάω (κλα): break (bread) 157
κλείω (κλει): close, shut, lock 126
κληρονομέω (κληρονομε): inherit 157
κοιμάομαι (κοιμα): sleep, die 141, 157
κοινόω (κοινο): make common, defile
   134
κοινωνία, ας, ἡ: communion, community 33
κοπιάω (κοπια): work hard, tire 157
κορβᾶν: gift set apart for God 147
κόπτω (κοπ): cut, (Mid.) lament 97
κόσμος, ου, ὁ: world, universe,
   mankind 10
κράζω (κραγ): cry out 97
κρατέω (κρατε): seize, restrain 134
κράτιστος, η, ον: best, excellent 150
κράτος, ους, τό: strength, power 120
κρείσσων, ον: better, stronger 150
κρίμα, ατος, τό: judgment 78
κρίνω (κριν): judge, condemn 107, 108
κρίσις, εως, ἡ: judgment, justice 122
κρίτης, ου, ὁ: judge 33
κρυπτός, ή, όν: hidden, secret 33
κτλ. (καὶ τὰ λοιπά): etc. 17
κύριος, ου, ὁ: lord, master, sir 10
κωλύω (κωλυ): hinder, withhold 126

Λ

λαλέω (λαλε): speak, say 130, 132
λαμβάνω (λαβ): take, receive 109
λαός, οῦ, ὁ: people, nation, crowd 10
λατρεύω (λατρευ): serve, worship 126
λέγω (λεγ, ἐρ, ἐπ): say, speak 114
λείπω (λιπ): leave, lack 97
Λευί/Λευίς/Λευεί, ὁ: Levi 147
λευκός, ή, όν: white, shining 33
λέων, οντος, ὁ: lion 82
λίθος, ου, ὁ: stone 32
λογίζομαι (λογιδ): consider 97
λόγος, ου, ὁ: word, saying 9, 97
λοιπός, ή, όν: rest, remaining 17
λύω (λυ): loose, free, destroy 40

Μ

μαθητής, οῦ, ὁ: disciple, follower 12
μακάριος, α, ον: blessed, happy 33
μακράν: far, far off 151
μακρόθεν: far, from afar 151
μάλιστα: especially, mostly 150
μᾶλλον: more, rather 27, 150
μανθάνω (μαθ): learn 105
μάννα, τό: manna 147
Μαρία, ας/Μαριάμ, ἡ: Mary 147
μαρτυρέω (μαρτυρε): testify 134
μαρτυρία, ας, ἡ: testimony 33
μαρτύριον, ου, τό: evidence 32
μάρτυς, υρος, ὁ: witness, martyr 103
μέγας, μεγάλη, μέγα: great 147, 148,
   150
μέγιστος, η, ον: very great, greatest
   150
μεῖζον: more, all the more 151
μείζων, ον: more, greater 150
μέλλω (μελλ): be about to 67, 108
μέλος, ους, τό: limb, member 120
μέν: indeed, on the one hand . . . 18, 26
μένω (μεν): remain, dwell, last 108
μεριμνάω (μεριμνα): worry about 157
μερίς, ίδος, ἡ: part, portion, share 82
μέρος, ους, τό: part, piece, party 120
μέσος, η, ον: middle, in the middle 17
μετά: with, among; after, behind 25, 68
μεταβαίνω (-βα): leave, cross over 116
μετανοέω (-νοε): be converted 134

μετάνοια, ας, ἡ: change of heart 33
μέχρι: as far as, until 26
μή: not, lest (w. oblique moods) 48, 58
μηδείς, μηδεμία, μηδέν: no one,
   nothing 105
μῆν, μηνός, ὁ: month 102
μήτηρ, τρός, ἡ: mother 103
μικρός, ά, όν: small, little 17, 150
μιμνῄσκομαι (μνα): remember 114
μισέω (μισε): hate, disregard 134
μνημεῖον, ου, τό: memorial, tomb 32
μνημονεύω (μνημονευ): remember 126
μοιχεύω (μοιχευ): commit adultery 126
μονογενής, ές: only begotten 121
μόνον: only, alone 151
μόνος, η, ον: only, alone, sole 17
μυριάδες μυριάδων: one million 152
μύριοι, αι, α: ten thousand, myriad,
   countless thousands 152
μυστήριον, ου, τό: mystery, secret 10
Μωϋσῆς, έως, ὁ: Moses 147

N

Ναζαρά/έτ/έθ: Nazareth 147
ναός, οῦ, ὁ: temple, sanctuary 32
ναῦς, νεώς, ἡ: ship 124
νεκρός, ά, όν: dead, lifeless, useless 17
νέος, α, ον: new, fresh, young 17
νηστεύω (νηστευ): fast, abstain 126
νικάω (νικα): conquer, overcome 134
νοέω (νοε): think, discern 157
νομίζω (νομιδ): think, assume 97
νόμος, ου, ὁ: law, Torah 10
νοῦς, νοός, ὁ: mind, attitude 124
νῦν: now, at present, indeed 27
νύξ, νυκτός, ἡ: night 79

Ξ

ξηραίνω (ξηραν): dry up, wither 107,
   158
ξύλον, ου, τό: wood, tree, cross 32

O

ὁ, ἡ, τό: the; this; he, she, it 9, 27, 28
ὀγδομήκοντα: eighty 152
ὄγδοος, η, ον: eighth 152
ὁδός, οῦ, ἡ: road, way, journey 10

ὀδούς, ὀδόντος, ὁ: tooth 82
ὅθεν: from where, whence, hence 35
οἶδα (ἰδ): know, perceive 143–144
οἰκία, ας, ἡ: house, home, family 11
οἰκοδομέω (οἰκοδομε): build up 157
οἶκος, ου, ὁ: house, home, family 10
οἶνος, ου, ὁ: wine 32
οἷος, α, ον: such as, of what kind 34
ὀκτώ: eight 152
ὀλίγος, η, ον: few, little 17, 150
ὅλος, η, ον: whole, all, complete 17
ὄμνυμι/νύω (ὀμο): swear, vow 126, 141
ὅμοιος, α, ον: like, the same as 34
ὁμοιόω (ὁμοιο): liken; be like 134
ὁμοίως: likewise, similarly 35, 150
ὁμολογέω (ὁμολογε): confess 158
ὄνομα, ατος, τό: name, person, title 78
ὀπίσω: behind, after 26
ὅπου: where, whereas, while 35
ὅπως: so that, in order that 59–60
ὅπως μή: so that . . . not, lest 59–60
ὁράω (ὁρα, ὀπ, ἰδ): see 114, 134, 143
   (Ἴδε, Ἰδοὺ: Behold! 36, 73, ff.)
ὄρος, ους, τό: mountain, hill 120
ὅς, ἥ, ὅ: who, which, what 18, 49, 60
ὅσος, η, ον: as much/great/far as 34
ὅστις, ἥτις, ὅτι/ὅ τι: whoever, etc. 49,
   50, 52, 60, 104
ὅτε: when 35, 52, 61, 160
ὅτι: that, because 47, 50, 105, 160
ὅτου (ὅστις): when, until 61
οὐ/οὐκ/οὐχ: not 26, 48, 58, 161
οὗ: where, when, until 35, 60
οὐαί: Alas! Woe! Horrors! 158
οὐδέ (οὐ+δέ): neither, not even 27, 105
οὐδείς, οὐδεμία, οὐδέν: no one, nothing
   105
οὐκέτι (οὐκ+ἔτι): no longer 35, 150
οὖν: then, therefore, accordingly 26
οὐράνιος, ον: heavenly 148
οὐρανός, οῦ, ὁ: heaven, sky, "God" 10
οὖς, ὠτός, τό: ear, hearing 78
οὔτε (οὐ+τέ): neither, nor 27
οὗτος, αὕτη, τοῦτο: this; he, she, it 19
οὕτως: thus, so, in the same way 26, 35,
   150
ὀφείλω (ὀφελ): owe, ought; wrong 67,
   108
ὀφθαλμός, οῦ, ὁ: eye, sight 32

ὄχλος, ου, ὁ: crowd, (common) people
32

Π

πάθημα, ατος, τό: suffering, desire 82
παιδεύω (παιδευ): instruct, correct 126
παιδίον, ου, τό: child, infant 32
παῖς, παιδός, ὁ, ἡ: child, servant 82
παλαιός, ά, όν: old, former, ancient 34
πάλιν: again, back, furthermore 27
παντοκράτωρ, ορος, ὁ: almighty (God) 103
παρά: from, beside, near, with, etc. 25, 151
παραβολή, ῆς, ἡ: parable, proverb 12
παραγγέλλω (-ἀγγελ): command, order 116
παραγίνομαι (-γεν): arrive, appear 116
παράγω (-ἀγ): pass by, disappear 115
παραδίδωμι (-δο): hand on/over 138
παράδοσις, εως, ἡ: tradition 122
παρακαλέω (-καλε): urge, comfort 134
Παρακαλῶ: Please! 23
παράκλησις, εως, ἡ: encouragement 122
παραλαμβάνω (-λαβ): receive 116
πάρειμι (-εἰμί): be present 142
Πάρειμι (-εἰμί): Present! 6
παρέρχομαι (ἐρχ, ἐλθ): pass 115
παρέχω (-ἐχ, κτλ.): cause, do 115
παρθένος, ου, ὁ, ἡ: virgin 10
παρίστημι (-στα): show; come 138
παρουσία, ας, ἡ: presence, coming 33
πᾶς, πᾶσα, πᾶν: all, whole, every 80, 86
πάσχα, τό: pasch, passover 147
πάσχω (παθ, πενθ): suffer 114
πατήρ, πατρός, ὁ: father 103
παύομαι (παυ): stop, cease 126
πείθω (πειθ): persuade 93, 95
πεινάω (πεινα): be hungry 157
πέμπω (πεμπ): send, appoint 92, 95
πεντάκις: five times 152
πεντακισχίλιοι, αι, α: 5,000 152
πεντακόσιοι, αι, α: 500 152
πέντε: five 152
πεντεκαιδέκατος, η, ον: fifteenth 152

πεντηκοντάκις: fifty times 152
πεντηκοστός, ή, όν: fiftieth 152
πεντήκοντα: fifty 152
πέραν: across, beyond 26
περί: about, around, concerning 25
περιβάλλω (-βαλ): put on, dress 116
περιπατέω (-πατε): walk about 134
περισσεύω (περισσευ): be over 126
περισσόν/ῶς: exceedingly, more 150
περισσότερον/ως: all the more 150
περιτέμνω (-τεμ): circumcise 150
πίμπλημι (πλη, πλα): fill, fulfill 141
πίνω (πι, πο): drink 109
πίπτω (πετ, πτ, πτο): fall 114
πιστεύω (πιστευ): believe 45
πίστις, εως, ἡ: faith, trust, belief 122
πιστός, ή, όν: believing, faithful 34
πλανάω (πλανα): mislead; wander 134
πλατύς, εῖα, ύ: wide, flat 123
πλειστός, ή, όν: most (Adv. mostly) 150
πλείων/πλέων, ον: more, further 150
πλέω (πλε): sail, swim 124
πληγή, ῆς, ἡ: blow, wound 33
πλῆθος, ους, τό: multitude, crowd 120
πλήν: besides, except; however 26
πλήρης, ες: full, full-grown 121
πληρόω (πληρο): fill, fulfill 131, 133
πλοῖον, ου, τό: boat 32
πλοῦς, πλοός, ὁ: voyage, sailing 124
πλοῦτος, ου, ὁ: wealth, riches 32
πνεῦμα, ατος, τό: spirit, wind, breath 78
πόθεν: whence, from where? 35
ποιέω (ποιε): make, do, effect 134
ποιμήν, μένος, ὁ: shepherd, pastor 102
ποῖος, α, ον: of what sort, kind 34
πόλεμος, ου, ὁ: war, conflict 32
πόλις, εως, ἡ: city, town 122
πολλάκις: many times, often 151
πολύ: much, greatly 151
πολύς, πολλή, πολύ: much, many 147, 148, 150
πονηρός, ά, όν: evil, painful 34
πορεύομαι (πορευ): proceed, go 45
πορφυροῦς, ᾶ, οῦν: purple 148
πόσος, η, ον: how much/great/many? 34

πότε: when? at what time? 35, 48, 49, 150

ποτέ: once, at one time, sometime 35, 48, 49, 150

ποτήριον, ου, τό: cup, chalice 32

ποτίζω (ποτιδ): give to drink 97

ποῦ: where, at/to what place? 35, 48, 49, 150

πού: somewhere, someplace 35, 48, 49, 150

πούς, ποδός, ὁ: foot 79

πράσσω (πραγ): do, accomplish 97

πραΰς, εἰα, ύ: meek, gentle 123

πρεσβύτερος, ου, ὁ: elder 10

πρίν/πρὶν ἤ: before, until 68

πρό: before, ahead of, for 25, 68

προάγω (-ἀγ): go before/too far 115

προέρχομαι (-ἐρχ, ἐλθ): precede 115

πρός: for, near, to, against 25, 68

προσέρχομαι (-ἐρχ, ἐλθ): approach 115

προσεύχομαι (-εὐχ): pray, beg 97

προσέχω (-ἐχ, κτλ.): attend to 115

προσκαλέομαι (-καλε): summon 158

προσκυνέω (-κυνε): kneel, bow 134

προσλαμβάνομαι (-λαβ): welcome 116

προσφέρω (-φερ, κτλ.): offer 115

πρόσωπον, ου, τό: face, presence 32

πρότερον: formerly, originally 151

προφητεία, ας, ή: prophecy, word 33

προφητεύω (-φητευ): prophesy 126

προφήτης, ου, ὁ: prophet 12

πρῶτον: firstly, at first 151

πρῶτος, η, ον: first, former 34, 152

πυλών, ῶνος, ὁ: gate, porch 102

πῦρ, πυρός, τό: fire 103

πωλέω (πωλε): sell, market 158

πῶς: How?, in what way? 27, 35, 48, 49, 150

P

ῥαββί/ῥαββουνι: rabbi, teacher 147

ῥῆμα, ατος, τό: word, speech 78

ῥύομαι (ῥυ): save, deliver 126

Σ

Σαβαώθ: armies, hosts (God of) 147

σάββατον, ου, τό: sabbath, week 32, 147

σαλεύω (σαλευ): shake 126

σάλπιγξ, ιγγος, ή: trumpet 77

σάρξ, σαρκός, ή: flesh, nature 77

σεαυτοῦ, ῆς: of yourself, etc. 21

σημεῖον, ου, τό: sign, miracle 10

σήμερον: today, this day 35, 150

Σίμων, ωνος, ὁ: Simon 147

σκανδαλίζομαι (--ιδ): cause to sin 98

σκεῦος, ους, τό: vessel, (Pl.) goods 120

σκηνή, ῆς, ή: tent, tabernacle 12

σκότος, ους, τό: darkness; sin, evil 120

σός, σή, σόν: your, yours (sing.) 21

σοφία, ας, ή: wisdom, insight 12

σοφός, ή, όν: wise, learned, clever 17

σπείρω (σπερ): sow, broadcast 106, 108

σπέρμα, ατος, τό: seed, offspring 78

σταυρός, οῦ, ὁ: cross, gibbet 32

σταυρόω (σταυρο): crucify 134

στέφανος, ου, ὁ: crown, reward 32

στόμα, ατος, τό: mouth, stomach 78

στρατιώτης, ου, ὁ: soldier 33

στρέφω (στρεφ): turn, change 97

σύ, σοῦ/σου: you, of you, etc. 21

συγγενής, ές: related, Noun: relative 121

συλλαμβάνω (-λαβ): conceive 116

συμφέρω (-φερ, κτλ.): be useful 115

σύν: with, along with 25

συνάγω (-ἀγ): gather, assemble 115

συναγωγή, ῆς, ή: synagogue, assembly 12

συνέδριον, ου, τό: Sanhedrin 32

σύνειμι (-ἰ): gather, collect 143

συνέρχομαι (-ἐρχ, ἐλθ): gather 115

συνέχω (ἐχ, κτλ.): encircle, control 115

συνίημι (-ἑ): understand 143

σῴζω (σω): save, cure 98

σῶμα, ατος, τό: body, reality 78

σωτήρ, ῆρος, ὁ: savior, redeemer 98, 103, 126

σωτηρία, ας, ή: salvation 12

σώφρων, ον: sane, temperate 149

T

ταλιθα: young girl (Aramaic) 147

ταπεινόω (ταπεινο): level, humble 134

τάσσω (ταγ): arrange, order 97

ταὐτά (τὰ + αὐτά): the same things 19, 20

ταῦτα (οὗτος): these things 20

ταχέως/ταχύ: swiftly, quickly 150

ταχίον: more quickly 151

τάχιστα: as soon as possible 151

ταχύς, εῖα, ύ: swift, quick 123, 149

τέ: and, also, so, and so 26

τέκνον, ου, τό: child, offspring 32

τέλειος, α, ον: finished, perfect 34

τελειόω (τελειο): complete 134

τελευτάω (τελευτα): die, end 157

τελέω (τελε/σ): finish, complete 125

τέλος, ους, τό: end, conclusion 119

τελώνης, ου, ὁ: tax collector 33

τέσσαρες, α: four 105, 152

τέταρτος, η, ον: fourth 152

τετράκις: four times 152

τετραπλοῦς, ῆ, οῦν: fourfold 148

τηρέω (τηρε): keep, guard 134

τίθημι (θε): put, place 137–140

τιμάω (τιμα): honor, prize 134

τιμή, ῆς, ἡ: honor, price 12

τίς, τί: who, which, what? 5, 17, 48–50, 104

τις, τι: some/anyone/anything 5, 17, 48–50, 104

τοιοῦτος, η, ον: such, like 34

τολμάω (τολμα): dare, undertake 157

τόπος, ου, ὁ: place 10

τοσοῦτος, η, ον: so much/great/many 34

τότε: then, at that time 26, 34

τοῦ: in order to (w. Inf.) 68

τρεῖς, τρία: three 152

τριάκοντα: thirty 152

τριπλοῦς, ῆ, οῦν: triple, threefold 148

τρίς: thrice, three times 152

τρίτος, η, ον: third 34, 152

τυφλός, ή, όν: blind, unseeing 34

Υ

ὑγιής, ές: healthy, sound, whole 121

ὕδωρ, ὕδατος, τό: water 78

υἱός, οῦ, ὁ: son, offspring, heir 10, 126

ὑμέτερος, α, ον: your, yours (Pl.) 21

ὑπάγω (-αγ): go away, return home 115

ὑπακούω (-ακου): heed, obey 45

ὑπάρχω (-αρχ): be, have 115

ὑπέρ: on behalf of, above 25, 151

ὑπό: by (agency); under, below 25

ὑποκάτω: beneath, underneath 35

ὑποκριτής, ές: actor, hypocrite 33

ὑπομένω (-μεν): endure, persevere 116

ὑποτάσσω (-ταγ): subject, be under 116

ὑποστρέφω (-στρεφ): return home 116

ὑστερέω (ὑστερε): lack, be inferior 158

ὑψόω (ὑψο): lift up, exalt 134

Φ

φαίνω (φαν): shine, appear 106, 108

φανερόω (φανερο): reveal, show 134

φέρω (φερ, οἰ, ἐνεκ, ἐνεγκ): bear 114

φεύγω (φυγ): flee, shun 97

φημί (φα): say 143–144

φιλέω (φιλε): love (as a friend) 134

φίλος, ου, ὁ: friend 10

φοβέομαι (φοβε): fear, worship 134

φόβος, ου, ὁ: fear, reverence 32

φρονέω (φρονε): think, have in mind 158

φυλακή, ῆς, ἡ: guard, watch, prison 33

φυλάσσω (φυλακ): guard, protect 97

φύσις, εως, ἡ: nature, being 122

φωνή, ῆς, ἡ: sound, voice, cry 11

φῶς, φωτός, τό: light, fire 78, 87

Χ

Χαῖρε/ετε: Hello! Goodbye! 6

χαίρω (χαρ, χαρε): rejoice 6, 108

χαλκοῦς, ῆ, οῦν: bronze, brass 148

χαρίζομαι (χαριδ): give, grant 98

χάρις, ιτος, ἡ: favor, grace 79, 98

χάρισμα, ατος, τό: gift 78

χείρ, χειρός, ἡ: hand, power 103

χείριστος, η, ον: worst 150

χείρων, ον: worse, more severe 150

χιλιάς, άδος, ἡ: one thousand 152

χίλιοι, αι, α: thousand(s) 152

χιτών, ῶνος, ὁ: tunic, shirt 102

χράομαι (χρα): use, make use of 157

χρεία, ας, ἡ: need, lack 33

Χριστός, οῦ, ὁ: Christ, anointed 2 ff.

χρόνος, ου, ὁ: time, period 32

χρυσοῦς, ῆ, οῦν: gold, golden 148
χωρίς: without, apart from 26

Ψ

ψεῦδος, ους, τό: lie, falsehood 120
ψυχή, ῆς, ἡ: soul, self, person, (natural)
   life 12, 160

Ω

ὧδε: here, hence, thus 27
ὥρα, ας, ἡ: hour, time, moment 12
ὡς: as, as if, when, how, etc. 26, 35,
   51, 52
ὥσπερ: as, just as, like 51
ὥστε: so that, with the result that 68
ὠφελέω (ὤφελε): gain, help 158

Ἡ χάρις τοῦ κυρίου ἡμῶν Ἰησοῦ
Χριστοῦ μεθ᾽ ὑμῶν. ἡ ἀγάπη μου
μετὰ πάντων ὑμῶν ἐν Χριστῷ Ἰησοῦ.
(Ro. 16:20, I Co. 16:23–24)

Appendix: Teaching Aids

Introduction:

A. For the teacher using this NT Greek text, *Greek Without Grief*, in introducing his or her students to the language of the New Testament, as well as for the student attempting to teach himself or herself NT Greek without the aid of a formal teacher, these "TEACHING AIDS" are respectfully provided in the hope of rendering the enterprise even more successful and "griefless."

B. While most of the book itself is, I hope, self-explanatory, these TEACHING AIDS should be of some assistance, especially in two areas:

1. *In explaining matters* which would have required too much additional treatment in the text itself, e.g. how the regular verb endings have evolved from the primitive ones or how the system of "gematria" works in practice.

2. *In providing the references* for the New Testament quotations used as the exercises in this work, with the caution that the teacher and the self-teaching student should beware of simply looking up the quotation in an English New Testament in order to translate the Greek. Rather, let them use the references simply for the purpose of comparison and comprehension.

I. Explanation of Special Matters:

A. ENDINGS OF THE REGULAR VERB:

1. *Introduction:* Since the other endings seem clear enough in themselves or can easily be explained with an economy of time and space, we can confine ourselves in this explanation to the **Primary Endings of the Indicative** and the **Endings of the Subjunctive,** which is a Primary Mood.

2. *Primary Endings of the Indicative* (page 43):
  a. **Active Endings:**
    1) *First Person Singular:* μι is dropped and the variable vowel o is lengthened, by compensation, to ω.
    2) *Second Person Singular:* σι is reversed by "Metathesis" to ις and unites with the variable vowel ε to εις.
    3) *Third Person Singular:* τι is reversed by "Metathesis" to ιτ, then the τ is dropped because it cannot end a Greek word, and ι unites with ε to ει.
    4) *First and Second Person Plural* simply unite the variable vowels o and ε with the endings μεν and τε respectively.
    5) *Third Person Plural:* Of the ending νσι, ν is dropped before σ according to regular orthographic changes and the variable vowel o is lengthened to ου by compensation, resulting in ουσι.
  b. **Middle-Passive Endings:**
    1) *Second Person Singular:* Of the ending σαι, the σ is dropped between two vowels (the variable vowel ε and α of the ending) and the variable vowel ε contracts with αι to the resulting η.
    2) *All other forms* simply unite the variable vowel o or ε with the proper ending without any further changes.

3. *Endings of the Subjunctive* (page 58):
  a. **In General:** The *same changes* occur here as in the Indicative, the difference resulting from the *lengthening* of the variable vowel to ω/η.
  b. **In Particular:**
    1) *In the Active Forms:* μι is dropped in the first person singular, "Metathesis" occurs in the second and third person singular, and ν is dropped before σ in the third person plural.
    2) *In the Middle-Passive Forms:* σ is dropped between the two vowels in the second person singular, with resulting contraction of η and αι to η, all the other forms uniting ω/η with the endings.

B. THE PHENOMENON OF "GEMATRIA" (page 153):

  1. **Gematria,** according to some a Hebraicized form of γεωμετρία (geometry), according to others a corruption of γραμματεῖα (notebooks), is a form of (Jewish) interpretation, especially of Scripture, which uses numbers and letters interchangeably—largely because both Hebrew and Greek used the letters of their alphabets as numbers.

2. **Examples in the Old Testament** possibly include, among others, the 600,000 of Exodus 12:37 (which translates into "all the children of Israel") and "The Proverbs of <u>Solomon</u>, the son of <u>David</u>, king of <u>Israel</u>" in Proverbs 1:1, whose names (underlined) translate into 930, the approximate number of the proverbs in the entire book. (Gematria may occur also in Pr. 10:1 and 25:1.)

3. **The outstanding example in the New Testament** is that of "666" in Rev. 13:18, whose identification, unfortunately, still remains very problematic. The principal candidate seems to be Caesar Nero, whose name in Hebrew equals 666.

4. **Normally, the Greek Alphabet,** when used for enumeration or gematria, comprised three additional letters, which had dropped out of the language except for this usage, and which will be specially indicated below.

5. **The numerical equivalents** of the Greek Alphabet, then, are as follows:

1—α΄	(εἷς, μία, ἕν)	101—ρα΄	(ἑκατὸν καὶ εἷς, μία, ἕν)
2—β΄	(δύο)	200—σ΄	(διακόσιοι, αι, α)
3—γ΄	(τρεῖς, τρία)	300—τ΄	(τριακόσιοι, αι, α)
4—δ΄	(τέσσαρες, τέσσαρα)	400—υ΄	(τετρακόσιοι, αι, α)
		500—φ΄	(πεντακόσιοι, αι, α)
5—ε΄	(πέντε)	600—χ΄	(ἑξακόσιοι, αι, α)
6—ϛ΄	(ἕξ) A form of ϝ, the Digamma or Vau.*	700—ψ΄	(ἑπτακόσιοι, αι, α)
		800—ω΄	(ὀκτακόσιοι, αι, α)
		900—ϡ΄	(ἐνακόσιοι, αι, α) Sampi*
7—ζ΄	(ἑπτά)		
8—η΄	(ὀκτώ)	1000—,α	(χίλιοι, αι, α)
9—θ΄	(ἐννέα)	1001—,αα΄	(χίλιοι καὶ εἷς)
10—ι΄	(δέκα)	2000—,β	(δισχίλιοι, αι, α)
11—ια΄	(ἕνδεκα)	3000—,γ	(τρισχίλιοι, αι, α)
20—κ΄	(εἴκοσι)	4000—,δ	(τετρακισχίλιοι, αι, α)
30—λ΄	(τριάκοντα)	5000—,ε	(πεντακισχίλιοι, αι, α)
40—μ΄	(τεσσαράκοντα)	6000—,ϛ	(ἑξακισχίλιοι, αι, α) Vau*
50—ν΄	(πεντήκοντα)		
60—ξ΄	(ἑξήκοντα)	7000—,ζ	(ἑπτακισχίλιοι, αι, α)
70—ο΄	(ἑβδομήκοντα)	10000—,ι	(μύριοι, αι, α)
80—π΄	(ὀγδοήκοντα)	20000—,κ	(δισμύριοι, αι, α)
90—ϙ΄	(ἐνενήκοντα) Koppa*	100000—,ρ	(δεκακισμύριοι, αι, α)
100—ρ΄	(ἑκατόν)		

* Digamma (Vau) is pronounced like w; Koppa, like q; Sampi, like sp.

II. **New Testament Texts Used in Exercises:**

INTRODUCTION: For the convenience of the teacher or self-teaching student, all the quotations from the New Testament which are used as exercises are listed below according to *page number*, general *subject matter* for practice, and *order* of reference, which deliberately follows the order of appearance in the New Testament to avoid the inconvenience of having to turn pages back and forth.

A. *Page 7:* PRAYERS AND PRACTICE
   1. The Lord's Prayer: Mt. 6:9–13.
   2. Sign of the Cross and Doxology, adaptations of Matthew 28:19.

B. *Page 15:* FIRST TWO DECLENSIONS
   1. Mark 1:1.   3. John 1:1.
   2. Mark 1:3.   4. John 14:6.

C. *Pages 29–30:* PREPOSITIONS, PARTICLES
   Beginning of John's Gospel: 1:1–18.

D. *Pages 35–36:* REVIEW AND DEVELOPMENT
   John's Gospel continued: 1:19–34.

E. *Pages 53–55:* REG. VERB, INDICATIVE
   1. Mt. 7:24.
   2. Mt. 12:19.
   3. Mt. 17:18.
   4. Mt. 18:27.
   5. Mt. 19:2.
   6. Mt. 27:13.
   7. Mk. 4:41.
   8. Mk. 6:55.
   9. Lk. 2:29.
   10. Lk. 4:23.
   11. Lk. 7:11.
   12. Lk. 9:9.
   13. Lk. 12:3.
   14. Lk. 16:31.
   15. Lk. 17:6.
   16. Jn. 4:50.
   17. Jn. 5:18.
   18. Jn. 5:25.
   19. Jn. 5:46.
   20. Jn. 6:69.
   21. Jn. 7:48.
   22. Jn. 8:45–46.
   23. Jn. 9:35.
   24. Jn. 10:20–21.
   25. Jn. 15:15.

F. *Pages 61–62:* REG. VERB, SUBJUNCTIVE
   1. Mt. 14:22.
   2. Mt. 16:19.
   3. Mk. 4:11–12.
   4. Mk. 8:3.
   5. Mk. 10:11.
   6. Lk. 22:67–68.
   7. Jn. 4:48.
   8. Jn. 7:23.
   9. Jn. 12:47.
   10. Jn. 13:19.
   11. Ro. 10:14–15.
   12. I Jn. 3:8.

G. *Pages 69–70:* IMPERATIVE, INFINITIVE
   1. Mt. 1:19.
   2. Mt. 17:16.
   3. Mt. 24:6.
   4. Mk. 4:9.
   5. Lk. 4:23.
   6. Lk. 5:15.
   7. Lk. 8:50.
   8. Lk. 10:38.
   9. Lk. 13:16.
   10. Lk. 16:29.
   11. Lk. 23:8.
   12. Jn. 2:19.
   13. Jn. 10:37.
   14. Jn. 11:44.
   15. Jn. 19:10.
   16. Ac. 7:33.
   17. Ac. 13:25.
   18. Ac. 14:1.
   19. Ac. 15:7.
   20. Ac. 17:29.
   21. Ac. 25:22.
   22. Ro. 6:12.
   23. Eph. 6:1.
   24. Php. 1:29.

H. *Pages 73–74:* REVIEW OF THE VERB
John's Gospel continued:
1:35–51.

I. *Pages 82–83:* MUTE NOUNS AND ADJECTIVES
1. Mt. 28:29.   5. I Co. 11:27.
2. Jn. 3:5.
3. Jn. 6:53.   6. II Th. 2:16–17.
4. Ac. 17:24–26.   7. I Jn. 5:6.

J. *Pages 90–91:* THE PARTICIPLE
1. Lk. 1:45.   7. Jn. 8:31.
2. Lk. 8:2.   8. Ac. 1:11.
3. Lk. 9:57.   9. Ac. 2:5.
4. Lk. 16:18. 10. Ac. 4:4.
5. Lk. 19:33. 11. Ac. 4:14.
6. Jn. 6:64.   12. Ac. 4:32.

K. *Pages 98–100:* MUTE VERBS
1. Mt. 4:1.   11. Lk. 4:22.
2. Mt. 4:17. 12. Lk. 10:4.
3. Mt. 5:10–11. 13. Lk. 22:61.
4. Mt. 6:9.   14. Jn. 7:28.
5. Mt. 11:4–6. 15. Jn. 9:4.
6. Mt. 14:15. 16. Jn. 13:31.
7. Mt. 27:42. 17. Jn. 17:17, 19.
8. Mk. 9:37. 18. Ac. 25:25.
9. Lk. 2:17. 19. Ro. 4:3–4.
10. Lk. 3:4. 20. Phm. 21–23.

L. *Pages 109–110:* LIQUID STEMS
1. Mt. 11:29.   4. Mk. 11:29.
2. Mt. 13:19.   5. Mk. 14:63–64.
3. Mt. 21:39.   6. Mk. 15:24.

7. Lk. 9:36.   12. Ro. 13:8.
8. Lk. 12:49. 13. I Co. 15:41–43.
9. Jn. 3:17.
10. Jn. 14:28. 14. I Jn. 4:16.
11. Jn. 20:25.

M. *Pages 117–118:* REVIEW & DEVELOPMENT
Excerpts from Luke:
1:26–45, 56.

N. *Pages 127–128:* THE REMAINING STEMS
1. Mt. 5:14–15.   7. Ac. 22:30.
2. Mk. 10:14.   8. I Co. 12:12, 14.
3. Mk. 12:18.   9. II Co. 4:7.
4. Lk. 7:12. 10. I Pt. 2:9.
5. Lk. 7:13–14. 11. I Jn. 1:3.
6. Jn. 8:52–53. 12. I Jn. 2:18.
   13. I Jn. 3:17.
   14. I Jn. 3:18.

O. *Pages 135–136:* CONTRACT VERBS
1. Lk. 3:4–6.   3. Jn. 21:15–19.
2. Jn. 17:11–15.

P. *Page 145:* ATHEMATIC VERBS
Readings from John's Gospel,
Jn. 20:11–17, 19, 22–23.

Q. *Pages 153–154:* FINAL MATTERS
1. Mt. 2:6.   5. Mk. 10:42–44.
2. Mt. 6:24.
3. Mt. 18:12. 6. I Co. 15:3–6.
4. Mt. 18:21–22.

R. *Pages 161–162:* REVIEW & DEVELOPMENT
1. Lk. 2:1–7.   3. Phl. 2:5–11.
2. Jn. 18:33–37.   4. Eph. 6:23–24.

Index of New Testament References

INTRODUCTION: This is an index of all the New Testament references used as *examples* in this work, listed according to the *order* of the New Testament books, together with the *number* of the *page or pages* where each of these examples may be found herein.

C. **The Gospel According to Luke:**
1. Lk. 1:32 20
2. Lk. 1:34 51
3. Lk. 1:41 28
4. Lk. 1:63 81
5. Lk. 2:1 160
6. Lk. 2:2 151
7. Lk. 1:6 68
8. Lk. 2:7 51
9. Lk. 2:43 68
10. Lk. 2:44 69
11. Lk. 2:51 81
12. Lk. 3:6 81
13. Lk. 3:23 89
14. Lk. 11:3–4 65
15. Lk. 14:15 49
16. Lk. 14:27 52
17. Lk. 16:8 151
18. Lk. 22:16 61
19. Lk. 22:49 160
20. Lk. 23:6 48–49

D. **The Gospel According to John:**
1. Jn. 1:1 27, 28
2. Jn. 1:6 13
3. Jn. 1:10 160
4. Jn. 1:12 19, 67
5. Jn. 1:14 12
6. Jn. 1:17 28
7. Jn. 1:21 27
8. Jn. 1:29 28
9. Jn. 1:40 12
10. Jn. 1:47 18
11. Jn. 3:2 13
12. Jn. 3:3 50
13. Jn. 3:7 67
14. Jn. 3:16 53
15. Jn. 3:26 49
16. Jn. 4:1 151
17. Jn. 6:57 51
18. Jn. 6:67 48
19. Jn. 8:53 50
20. Jn. 8:58 68
21. Jn. 9:2 60
22. Jn. 10:11 27
23. Jn. 11:15 59
24. Jn. 11:16 60

25. Jn. 11:25 47
26. Jn. 11:40 48
27. Jn. 12:26 60
28. Jn. 12:44 161
29. Jn. 13:13 28
30. Jn. 13:26 48
31. Jn. 14:4 49
32. Jn. 14:27 14
33. Jn. 14:28 151
34. Jn. 15:12 60
35. Jn. 15:13 13
36. Jn. 15:15 81
37. Jn. 15:18 51
38. Jn. 15:19 52
39. Jn. 16:7 60
40. Jn. 16:27 47–48
41. Jn. 17:5 18
42. Jn. 18:11 58
43. Jn. 19:8 52
44. Jn. 19:17 158
45. Jn. 19:25 13
46. Jn. 20:13 48
47. Jn. 20:14 48
48. Jn. 20:17 64

E. **The Acts of the Apostles:**
1. Ac. 1:1 67
2. Ac. 2:38 13
3. Ac. 9:4 48
4. Ac. 9:7 13
5. Ac. 9:40 159
6. Ac. 10:21 18
7. Ac. 11:30 18
8. Ac. 12:2 13
9. Ac. 17:1 28
10. Ac. 20:18 81

F. **The Letters of Paul:**
1. Ro. 1:7 74
2. Ro. 8:9 28
3. I Co. 1:3 74
4. I Co. 3:16 28
5. I Co. 11:21 18
6. I Co. 13:13 151
7. I Co. 16:22 159
8. II Co. 1:2 74
9. II Co. 1:9 22

τὸν καλὸν ἀγῶνα ἠγώνισμαι, τὸν δρόμον τετέλεκα, τὴν πίστιν τετήρηκα· λοιπὸν ἀπόκειταί μοι ὁ τῆς δικαιοσύνης στέφανος, ὃν ἀποδώσει μοι ὁ κύριος ἐν ἐκείνῃ τῇ ἡμέρᾳ, ὁ δίκαιος κριτής, οὐ μόνον δὲ ἐμοὶ ἀλλὰ καὶ πᾶσι τοῖς ἠγαπηκόσι τὴν ἐπιφάνειαν αὐτοῦ. (II Tim. 4:7–8)